A BOOK ABOUT BELLS.

BELL OF ST. MURA.

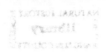

A Book . .
About . . .
Bells . . .

BY THE

REV. GEO. S. TYACK, B.A.,

Republished by Omnigraphics ● Penobscot Building ● Detroit ● 1991

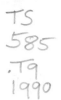

This is a facsimile reprint of the 1898 edition published in London by William Andrews and Company.

Library of Congress Cataloging-in-Publication Data

Tyack, Geo. S. (George Smith)
    A book about bells / by the Rev. Geo. S Tyack.
       p. cm.
    Reprint. Originally published: London : W. Andrews 1898.
    ISBN 1-55888-891-8 (lib. bdg. : alk. paper)
    1. Bells. I. Title
    [TS585.T9 1990]   89-2924
                                                          CIP

Printed in the United States of America

Preface.

BELLS are of interest to almost every one. Their voices to some tell only of daily duty, of trains to catch, of the return of the hours of toil, of the ceaseless flight of inexorable time; to others they speak of devotion, and are as the voice of a mother calling us to her knee for prayer; to others again the bells are means of healthful exercise and instruments of heart-stirring music. There is, however, an increasing number of people, who over and above the feeling of one or more of these interests in the voices of the bells, take an interest also in the bells themselves. To these the belfry has a story to tell, now full of the resources of art, now of the glamour of romance, now of the struggles of the Faith. Recent years have seen the publication of not a few books upon the subject, some dealing exhaustively with certain districts, others touching lightly a wider field. In the following pages the author has endeavoured to cover the whole of a subject admittedly large and varied, and to illustrate by the choice of the most striking examples all the many uses of the bells. How far he has succeeded in doing this in a popular way, others must, of course, determine; but the kindly manner in which the public has accepted at his hands some previous attempts of a somewhat similar kind, leads him to hope that this may prove not less worthy of a generous reception. It remains to be stated that Mr. William Andrews, of Hull, placed at the author's disposal his collection of books, notes, etc., relating to this subject; that Mr. J. Potter Briscoe, author of "Curiosities of the Belfry," kindly lent a number of illustrations which appear in this volume, and Mr. Robert Head, historian of Congleton, the one of "Ringing the Chains."

GEO. S TYACK.

CROWLE, DONCASTER,

 14th February, 1898.

Contents.

PAGE

CHAPTER I. INVENTION OF BELLS.— Early instruments of percussion—Early allusions to bells—Classical names for bells—Introduction of large bells—Church bells— Allusions in modern poetry.   1

CHAPTER II. BELL FOUNDING AND BELL FOUNDERS.— Primitive bells not cast—Monastic founders—Mediæval lay founders—Founders at York—Gloucester—London Loughborough — Itinerant founders—Bell-founder's window, York—Foundries in churchyards—Foreign bells in England—Foreign foundries—Scottish bells and founders—Irish founders—Various other founders—Bell metal—Alleged silver in bells—Bells made from cannon —Shape of bells—Tubular bells—Process of casting— The " Poor Sinner's Bell"—Tuning—Hanging of a Russian bell—Mode of hanging a bell—Chiming and ringing—The bell of S. Proculus.   12

CHAPTER III. DATES AND NAMES OF BELLS.—Ancient bells still in use—Claughton bell—Cold Ashby bell—Old Lincolnshire bells—York bells—Monastic bells still in use—Seventeenth century examples—Old Scottish bells Names of bells—Crowland Abbey bells—Principal of selection of names—Examples of names—Bells still known by name—Inscription of name upon the bell— Dedication of bells—The Roman rite—Modern English rite.   45

CHAPTER IV. THE DECORATION OF BELLS.— Artistic mouldings on bells—Initial crosses and stops—Makers' marks —Figures of saints—Royal heads—Heraldic decoration Inscriptions—Invocations of saints—Jesus and Trinity bells—Prayers for donors, parishioners, and others— Languages used for inscriptions—English inscriptions Insertion of dates and makers' names—Commemorations of donors—Makers' rhymed inscriptions—Boastful bells —Inscriptions allusive to change-ringing—Allusions to uses of bells—Records of parish authorities—Loyal inscriptions—Commemoration of public events—Of local events—Use of Scriptural quotations—A long inscription —Alphabetic inscriptions—Leonine verses—Doggerel verses—Curious errors—Bell-frame inscriptions.   ...   63

CHAPTER V. SOME NOTEWORTHY BELLS.—Large bells—A Burmese bell—Russian bells—Chinese bells—Japanese bells—Cologne—Olmutz—Erfurt—Bruges—French bells —English bells—Great Paul—Other London bells—S. Dunstan, Canterbury—Peter of York—Other York bells —Mighty Tom, Oxford—Other Oxford bells—Great Tom, Lincoln—Great Peter and Grandison, Exeter— Gloucester—Noteworthy secular bells—Big Ben, Westminster—Town Hall bells at Manchester—Leeds and elsewhere — Bow bells — Dorchester tenor bell — S. Andrew's, Plymouth — Wrexham — Scottish bells— Legend of Limerick bells—Shandon bells—Dublin bells —American bells—The peal at Zanzibar—Colonial bells.   97

CHAPTER VI. THE LOSS OF OLD BELLS. — Comparative scarcity of old bells —Loss by natural causes - Delicacy bells—Careless usage of bells—King Henry VIII. and church bells—Robbery of bells—Spoliation of Scottish belfries — Mutilated bells — Losses by fire — Change-ringing and the consequent re-casting of bells   122

CHAPTER VII. TOWERS AND CAMPANILES.—Introduction of belfries—Bells in trees—Detached towers in England —Central towers—Scottish belfries—Town steeples— Berwick bells—Effect of change-ringing on towers— Sanctus-bell gable.   131

CHAPTER VIII. BELL-RINGING AND BELL-RINGERS.—Clerical ringers—The "Scholars of Cheapside"—The "College Youths"—"Royal Cumberland Youths"—"Stedman's Principle"—Change-ringing—Ill-repute of ringers in the past—Ringers' jugs—Belfry rules—Examples in prose and verse—Ringers' epitaphs—Female ringers— Picture of ringers at Ecton—Modern ringers—Distinguished men as ringers—Bequests to ringers.   137

CHAPTER IX. THE CHURCH-GOING BELL. — The sacred trumpets of the Jews—Buddhist horns in Thibet— Summoning the faithful in primitive times—Greek substitutes for bells—Early monastic use of bells—Early use of hand bells—S. Francis Xavier—Canon law and bells—Sermon Bell—Early Sunday morning bells— Priest's Bell—Special ringing for the Eucharist— Survivals of ancient services—Instances in Scotland— Ringing out from church—The Catechism—Institution bell—The Moslem Muezzin.   159

CHAPTER X. BELLS AT CHRISTIAN FESTIVALS AND FASTS.— Advent ringing—S. Thomas' Day—Christmas peals— Childermas—The Circumcision, or New Year's Day— Epiphany peals—Candlemas—Shrove Tuesday and the " Pancake " Bell—Lenten usages—Disuse of the bells in Holy Week—Easter—Ascensiontide, Whitsuntide, and

Trinity—S. Andrew's Day—Festivals of the Blessed Virgin—S. George's Day—S. James' Day and the Armada —S. Hugh's Day and Queen Elizabeth's accession— Hallow-mass ringing—All Souls 170

CHAPTER XI. THE EPOCHS OF MAN'S LIFE MARKED BY THE BELLS.—Curious Spanish custom—Birthday peals— Baptism — Confirmation—Apprentice peals—Banns peals —Wedding bells—The morning after, and the Sunday after, marriage—Passing, or Soul Bell—Death Bell— "Tellers"—Invitation peal, or Company Bell—Funeral bells—Muffled peals—Month's mind and year's mind peals—Hand-bells rung for deaths and funerals— Execution Bell. 184

CHAPTER XII. THE BLESSINGS AND CURSINGS OF THE BELLS. —Belief in the power of bells against demons—Bells and the dying—Bells in storms—In pestilence—S. Anthony's emblem—Cursing by bell, book, and candle—Rise and character of the rite—A Cheshire instance—Quarterly general excommunication of sinners. 210

CHAPTER XIII. BELLS AS TIME-MARKERS.—The canonical hours—Invention of clocks—Strasburg clock—"Jacks o' the Clockhouse"—Curfew—Angelus—King's Cliff and its bells—Washerwoman's bell, Nottingham—Seed-sowing and harvest bells—Gleaning—"Gatherums" at Louth—'Prentice bells of Bow—Time at sea. 220

CHAPTER XIV. SECULAR USES OF CHURCH AND OTHER BELLS.—Harvest Home—The bells' greeting to distinguished people—Coronation peals—Royal Oak Day —Gowrie Conspiracy—Gunpowder Plot—Celebration of great victories—Plough Monday—May Day—Cock-fighting and horse races—Bells and politics—The Common bell—Stamford bull-running—Vestry bell—Some local secular usages—Market and fair bells—Market peals—Fire, and other alarm, peals—Lighthouse and buoy bells—Special usages at Stainton Dale and at Rosyth Castle—Ships' bells—La Lutine. 239

CHAPTER XV. SMALL BELLS, SECULAR AND SACRED.— Form of early small bells—The Jewish high-priest's bells—Bells on Christian vestments—Bells on lay garments—Jesters' bells—Morris dancers' bells—Bells on warlike arms and armour—The Greek sentry's bell— Bells on harness—Cattle bells—Bells as prizes for horse-races—Common uses of hand-bells—The domestic bell —Small bells in public worship—The Egyptian kemkem —Buddhist bells—The sanctus and consecration bells— Hand-bells in processions—"St. Peter's s" at Congleton—Burmese pagoda bells—Japan emple bells—Moslem "Bells of Paradise." .— .— 256

CONTENTS.

CHAPTER XVI. CARILLONS.—Derivation of the term—
Belgian carillons—Mechanism of the carillon—the
carillon à *Clavier*—Carillon recital by M. Denyn—
English chimes and carillons—Hand-bell peals—Bells
in military bands.   272

CHAPTER XVII. BELFRY RHYMES AND LEGENDS.—Satirical
verses — Bell "sayings"—"Ghost" peals — Demons,
fairies, and the bells—Miraculous bells—Stealing the
sanctus bell -The Sicilian Vespers—S. Bartholomew's
Day, 1572—The bell at Grosslaswitz—Conclusion.   ...   278

A Book about Bells.

CHAPTER I.

The Invention of Bells.

THERE can be little question that the earliest musical instruments were those of percussion. It is true that Holy Scripture, in naming Jubal as the "father" of those who play on such instruments, makes mention only of "the harp and the organ," or the music of strings and wind. Yet legend reports that Jubal caught the first suggestion of his art from the ring of his brother Tubal Cain's hammer on his anvil; and one cannot but realize the natural probability that such was indeed the case, when one considers how much more frequently the primitive man would hear a musical note struck out by a blow on some sonorous substance than in any other way The tones produced by Nature, or in the processes of the mechanical arts, are seldom definite and clear, except when caused by percussion. The second mention of music in those records, which claim our attention not only from their sanctity but from their antiquity, is the saying of Laban to Jacob (Genesis xxxi, 27): "I might have sent thee away with mirth, and with songs, with tabret, and with harp." Here the music of the strings is mingled with that produced by striking the tightened skin of the tabret, or tabor.

1

The song of praise with which Miriam and her maidens celebrated the triumphant exodus of the Israelites from Egypt, was accompanied exclusively by timbrels, instruments probably closely resembling the modern tambourine, in which the drum-like sound produced by the taps upon the skin is mingled with the jingling of small metal plates striking together, as the timbrel is swung or shaken in the air.

More striking illustrations of this fact are found if we turn to those oriental nations, which, with the conservatism apparently almost inseparable from the east, have retained through many ages the style of music and the musical instruments evolved in an early age of civilization.   One of the most elaborate instruments known to the Chinese is the *king*. invented by one of their emperors more than two thousand years before Christ.   It consists of sixteen flat stones suspended in two ranks within a frame, and so regulated in size as to give forth, when struck with a wooden mallet, a scale of notes.   Besides this they use drums of every kind and size, rows of copper plates, clappers of wood, wooden tubs struck with a hammer, and cymbals. A picture of a Japanese native orchestra, drawn from life, and engraved in Sieboid's work on Japan, shows us seven performers, who play respectively on a flute, a large drum shaped liked an hour-glass, two small drums, two bell-rattles, and a set of wooden clappers.   Here out of the seven instruments all but one are those of percussion. The other oriental nations exhibit usually a similar fondness for music of this kind, though wind and stringed instruments take a larger sh   in it.

This primitive and wid   read discovery of the tones

producible by blows on resonant substances being then granted, we readily see that something more or less resembling the modern bell in shape would almost certainly be a very early invention. We are not therefore surprised to find that almost all ancient authors have one or more allusions to the use of bells. Some of the passages are briefly referred to here as illustrating their early and almost universal employment, the special object of which in the several cases will be more fully considered in later chapters.

The book of Exodus gives us probably the earliest mention of bells, in its allusion to those golden ones which tinkled round the vestments of the Levitical high-priest. In the sacred volume we have also another reference to them in the words of the prophet Zechariah, who speaks of the harness of horses as adorned with them.

Turning to profane literature we find small bells, for similar purposes to these, spoken of by Euripides in his *Rhesus*, by Aristophanes in his *Frogs*, and in the fables of Phædrus. Plutarch alludes to them in his life of Brutus, and probably in the *Georgics* Virgil refers to them in speaking of the worship of Cybele. Ovid, too, and Tibullus, Martiall, Statius, Manilius, and Strabo, all have their witness to give on the matter.

The researches of antiquaries, also, have brought to light facts, which indisputably prove the early use of bells Bronze hand-bells were found by Layard in his excavations at Nimroud, and very ancient examples have been met with in various places in the far east ; while, turning to the far west, we have instances of copper bells found in ancient Peruvian tombs. In fact almost the only land which, in spite of acquiring in early times an advanced civilization,

made no use of bells, was Egypt ; and even the Egyptians
were accustomed to the not dissimilar tinklings of the
kemkem, or sistrum, which, in its use, was peculiarly
characteristic of the land of the Nile.

All the instances above quoted are those of small bells,
but the various names given to them in antiquity prove that,
if there were then no really large examples, they nevertheless
differed in size and in shape. The following classical and
sub-classical terms are used for bells.

Tintinnabulum is to some extent a general term, but its
sound, so suggestive of the tinkling of a little bell, shows us
its proper meaning, and in that sense it is used by Plautus
and by Suetonius. The corresponding Greek name was
Kodon, which is found in the dramatists above alluded to,
in Thucydides, and other writers.

Petasus originally meant a hat such as the Romans wore
when travelling, having a broad brim to protect the face
from the sun ; amongst the Greeks it was largely used by
hunters and shepherds, especially in Thessaly. From its
resemblance to this hat in shape a gong-like bell was so
called.

The district of Campania in Italy has given two names to
bells. *Campana* is applied to a bell sufficiently large for
hanging in a turret, and *Nola*, from the town of that name
in the same province, is a name given to little bells.

Lebetes were properly pots or cauldrons of copper, and the
word is used in Homer of hand-basins and of ornamental
bowls given as prizes in athletic contests. The word is
also applied, however, to bells or gongs by Heroditus, in
describing the funeral solemnities of the Spartans, and to
certain kettles of brass at the temple of Jupiter at Dodona

in Epirus, from the clashing and ring of which oracles were given by the priests.

Yet another term for a small bell was *Squilla*, which occurs in Italian writings. *Krotalon* or *Crotulum* strictly means a castanet or rattle, rather than a bell. *Signum*, which is equivalent to the word sign or token, and by classical usage is employed for a military standard, a watch-word, and in more general senses, is used in late writers of bells, as in the Excerptions of S. Egbert, 750 A.D. The Portuguese still call a bell *Sino*.

The word "Campana," spoken of above, is still the usual Italian word for a bell. The French and the Germans call it respectively *Cloche* and *Clocke*, words derived from a Teutonic root, which has also, as some suppose, given us "cloak," so called from the bell-like shape of the garment. The connection of these words with "clock" must be left to a subsequent occasion. Our English word comes to us from an Aryan root Bhal, through the Old English "bellan," to roar or bellow, or its cognate form "bella," signifying that which roars. "Bellow" and "bull" are both from the same source. From this it will be obvious that just as the first idea of the Romans on the subject was of a little instrument which tinkled (*tintinnabulum*), so the earliest knowledge which our forefathers had of it was of a swaying mass of metal that boomed and roared.

Thus we see that in far-off times bells of some sort, but mostly of a small size, and none very large, were known and used for various purposes all over the world. The metallic sound rang from Italy to China ; in busy cities and on lonely sheep-tracks, and in many quaint and curious ways and places which we hope hereafter to consider. To name the inventor of the bell is impossible; perhaps there was no inventor, but it grew into being and use from the combined ideas of many. Almost certainly there was no single inventor; the construction of something of the kind would occur so naturally to many a man who simply struck his staff by accident against a metal pan or bowl, that in almost every land the bell must have sprung independently into existence.

There is no trustworthy evidence of the use of really large bells before the dawn of Christianity, and they owe their existence to Christian influences. This being the case, we must not look for any traces of them in the first centuries of our era, during which time the faithful met frequently by stealth in groves and deserts, " in dens and caves of the earth," for fear of their persecutors. The credit of the invention has been given to Paulinus, bishop of that Nola, in Campania, which is previously mentioned. Paulinus flourished about 400 A.D., just after the public recognition of the Christian faith by the Emperor Constantine, and was a great patron of the arts. But his claim to this distinction is rendered very doubtful by the fact that, although in a letter to Severus the bishop describes very fully the decoration of his church, he makes no mention whatever of bells. A better title is made out for Pope Sabinianus, who succeeded S. Gregory in the papal chair in 604; in any case, from about that date notices of the use of bells which must have been more or less of the kind and size now seen in turrets, if not in towers, become increasingly frequent. The Venerable Bede tells us of one brought from Italy, about 680, by S. Benedict Biscop, and placed in his newly-built abbey at Wearmouth; and the same historian speaks of the sound of a bell as being well known at Whitby Abbey at the time of the death of S. Hilda, which was also in 680. By the year 750 church bells had become sufficiently common for Egbert, Archbishop of York (732-766), to order, in his *Excerptions*, that all priests should toll them at the appointed hours ; and if this was possible in the north, we may feel certain that it was even more so in the south, which, from its nearness to the Continent, was even from Cæsar's time more familiar with the products of European civilization than more remote districts of the island. Ingulphus, the chronicler of Croyland Abbey, mentions a peal of bells there about the year 960, and by his statement that England had then no peal to match it in tone, he distinctly implies that even by that time many churches had something more than a single bell.

For fully a thousand years, therefore, we may feel certain that Christendom, and England as part of it, has heard the far-reaching tones of the bells ring out, now gladly, now sadly, across broad acres of field and woodland, and over the busy hum of the bustling town. And in all that time there has been scarce an event of interest in the life of nations or of districts, not many even in the lives of private individuals, in which the tones of the bells have not mingled with the emotions that were aroused thereby. Nothing, perhaps, illustrates in a more striking way the place which bells have for ages filled in the lives of men, than the recollection of the position which they have assumed in literature, and especially in poetry. The true poet must surely be to a great extent the mouthpiece of his age ; he is the expression of those sentiments which fill the men of his time, and vainly strive for utterance in the hearts of uninspired mortals. And it is the poets above all to whom the bells tell the story of man's joys and sorrows, of his ambitions and disappointments.

To quote only a few of the most obvious instances, the following, taken at random, will suffice. The use of bells as tellers of the passing time finds especially frequent mention by the poets. Thus in a well-known passage in his " Night Thoughts," Young exclaims—

> "The bell strikes one. We take no note of time
> But from its loss."

In the " Lay of the Last Minstrel," Sir Walter Scott tell us—

> " When the convent met at the noontide bell
> The monk of S. Mary's Aisle was dead."

Campbell, alluding to the invention of the clock by the Germans, whom he addresses in one of his odes, expresses this wish on their behalf —

> " . . . The clock ye framed to tell,
> By its sound, the march of time,
> Let it clang oppression's knell
> O'er your clime !"

The sound of the Curfew, booming out from the gray church tower as the evening shadows are falling over the land, could not fail to wake an echo in the poet's breast. The Puritan Milton makes it an element in the calm surroundings of his " Il Penseroso "—

> " Oft on a plat of rising ground,
> I hear the far-off Curfew sound,
> Over some wide-watered shore,
> Swinging slow with sullen roar."

And the American Longfellow, amid the glare of Trans-atlantic newness, across which the mellowing shadows of

antiquity have not yet fallen, loves nevertheless to picture
an old-world eventide :—

> " Solemnly, mournfully,
>   Dealing its dole,
>   The Curfew bell
>   Is beginning to toll."

And yet again, the clang of the " Village Blacksmith's "
hammer speaks to him, as it has been suggested those
of Tubal Cain did to Jubal, of bell-music, and sounds

> " Like the sexton ringing the village bell,
>   When the evening sun is low."

Gray's opening line in the " Elegy "—" The curfew tolls the
knell of parting day "—is almost too well-known to quote ;
as also is the song of Tom Moore's Canadian *voyageurs*,
when they tell us—

> " Faintly as tolls the evening chime,
>   Our voices keep tune and our oars keep time ; "

and the same poet's apostrophe to " those evening bells."

Shakespere, who speaks of everything that men love
or fear, speaks of course of bells. In one place it is the
" remembered knolling a departed friend ; " in another
the little hand-bell of Lady Macbeth is to Duncan
" the knell to summon him to heaven or to hell ; " and later
in the same tragedy, Macbeth, driven at last to bay, cries—

> " Ring the alarum bell ! Blow, wind ! come, wrack !
>   At least we'll die with harness on our back."

It is Shakespere, too, who gives us the tenderest figure
for the mind deranged, as " Sweet bells jangled out of tune
and harsh," who speaks of the time-honoured association
" of bell and burial," and quotes the phrase, which to
English ears ever represents the village chimes, " Hark !
now I hear them,—ding, dong, bell."

To the gentle Cowper, and the thoughtful Wordsworth, the calm of a rural English Sunday, with the bells ringing out across the fields, appeals with special force, and the echoes of those chimes, meet us in their verse.   Thus Cowper in " The Task " :—

> " How sweet the music of those village bells,
>   Falling at intervals upon the ear,
>   In cadence sweet, now dying all away,
>   Now pealing loud again, and louder still,
>   Clear and sonorous as the gale comes on."

In a similar spirit he represents Alexander Selkirk on his desert island, as feeling his absolute loneliness to be emphasized by the fact that—

> " The sound of the church-going bell
>   These valleys and rocks never heard,
>   Never sighed at the sound of a knell,
>   Or smiled when a Sabbath appeared."

Wordsworth, in his " White Doe of Rylstone," tells of the time—

> " When the bells of Rylstone played
>   Their Sabbath music—*God us ayde*—
>   (That was the sound they seemed to speak)
>   Inscriptive legend, which, I ween,
>   May on those holy bells be seen."

To Coleridge's " Ancient Mariner " the bell speaks, too, of worship, when he exclaims :—

> " Hark the little vesper bell,
>   Which biddeth me to prayer."

Edgar Allan Poe has left us, among the best of his poems, one specially devoted to " The Bells," in which we hear them tinkle, or peal, boom, or clang according to their weight and purpose : and Schiller has told us in stirring lines the story of " The Founding of the Bell."   Throughout the masterpiece of Tennyson, the " In Memoriam," throb the chimes of Christmastide, " The merry, merry bells of Yule," and the bells' glad greeting of each New Year.   There is perhaps no finer lyric in the language, and certainly no fitter conclusion for this brief selection from the bell-music of the poets, than that section of the poem, which begins :—

" Ring out, wild bells, to the wild sky,
  The flying cloud, the frosty light ;
  The year is dying in the night ;
Ring out, wild bells, and let him die.

Ring out the old, ring in the new,
  Ring, happy bells, across the snow :
  The year is going, let him go ;
Ring out the false, ring in the true.

. . . .

Ring out old shapes of foul disease ;
  Ring out the narrowing lust of gold ;
  Ring out the thousand wars of old,
Ring in the thousand years of peace.

Ring in the valiant man and free,
  The larger heart, the kindlier hand ;
  Ring out the darkness of the land,
Ring in the Christ that is to be."

CHAPTER II.

𝕭𝖊𝖑𝖑 𝕱𝖔𝖚𝖓𝖉𝖊𝖗𝖘 𝖆𝖓𝖉 𝕭𝖊𝖑𝖑 𝕱𝖔𝖚𝖓𝖉𝖎𝖓𝖌.

THE earliest bells were probably not cast, but made of metal plates rivetted together. One, said to have belonged to S. Gall (A.D. 650), and still called by his name, is preserved at S. Gall in Switzerland; and another, traditionally associated with S. Patrick (about 465), is shown at Belfast. These are made of iron, and are only about six inches high. Another, which was in the possession of Mr. Llewellynn Jewitt, measures ten and a half inches in height, and other examples are preserved, both in England and Ireland. The bells of this kind are not round, but wedge-shaped, broad and square at the mouth, and rising to a ridge at the top. A very splendid specimen of the bells of this shape is that named after S. Mura, in the Londesborough collection. It is some twelve inches high, and made of bronze, to which plates of silver beautifully embossed have been attached. By an accident it was discovered that the bell itself, beneath this casing, is adorned with tracery of Runic scrolls in brass and gold. A large crystal is set in the centre of the outer case, and jewels were at one time placed at other points of it, all but one of which have now disappeared. This fine piece of work is ascribed to the seventh century.

The names of no very early bell-founders have come down to us, partly from the fact that it is a comparatively late custom for the makers to place their names upon their works. Probably the bell-founder's art, like others which were exercised chiefly for the furnishing or the adornment of the church, was originally practised almost exclusively by the ecclesiastics themselves. S. Dunstan, as famous for his labours in the advancement of ecclesiastical art as for his devotion and his fearless denunciation of sin in high places, was instrumental in hanging bells in several churches ; with regard to the cathedral at Canterbury, over which see and province he ruled from 954 to 968, it is recorded that he gave it not only bells, but also a series of rules for their correct use. Previously to this the saint had been Abbot of Glastonbury, and Bishop of Worcester and of London, all places which would provide ample scope for his artistic skill and energy in this, as well as in other directions ; and being the practised artificer that he was, it is highly probable that the founding of their bells would be at least superintended by him in person. A disciple of S. Dunstan's, S. Ethelwold, Abbot of Abingdon, and afterwards, from 963 to 984, Bishop of Winchester, followed his master in his love for the mechanical arts, and under his supervision bells were cast and hung in the restored abbey church at Abingdon. Another even more famous abbot was Thurkytul, or Turketul, of Croyland, who, about the year 930, cast the great bell of his abbey and named it after the patron saint, S. Guthlac ; and subsequently Egelric, a later abbot, added others, whose combined music was " the most exquisite harmony," according to the chronicler, Ingulphus.

As churches and monastic houses increased in number, naturally the art of bell-founding drifted into the hands of a professional class, and scattered records of some of its

members have come down to our time. In 1299, there was
at Lynn, in Norfolk, one Master John the Founder, and we
find records of two others of the same trade at this place
during the following century, namely Thomas Belleyetere
(or Bellfounder) in 1333, and Edmund Belleyetere twenty
years later. The chief centres of this art in England in
mediæval days were York, Gloucester, London and Nottingham ; and some of these places maintained their reputation
for a very long period. John of York was a great bell-
founder of about the middle of the fourteenth century,
whose works are to be found in several places in the
midland counties, as for example at Sproxton, in Leicestershire, where is a bell inscribed, "JHOHANNES DE YORKE
ME FECIT IN HONORE BEATA MARIE." The Fabric Rolls of
York Minster mention a bell-founder of the name of John
Hoton, in the year 1473. In the belfry of Christ Church,
King's Court, York, is a bell dated 1659, which was cast by
William Cureton, of Toft Green. At the same place Samuel
Smith, the father and the son, carried on the business of
bell-founding for many years. The father died in 1709 ;
and the son, who was Sheriff in 1723-4, followed him in
1731 ; both being buried at Holy Trinity Church, Mickle-
gate, York, where one of their bells hangs. Other examples
of their work are found at S. Martin's, S. Margaret's, S.
Crux, S. Cuthbert's, and S. Mary's, in the city of York, and
at numerous other places, as at Filey, where three bells bear
their mark, "S. S. Ebor," together with the dates 1675,
1682, and 1700. Another father and son who were alike
in name and business were the two bell-founders named
Edward Seller, whose place of business was in Jubbergate.
They cast a bell for the church of S. Denis in 1718, the

whole peal of eight for S. Martin-le-Grand in 1729, and a single one for S. Saviour's in 1730. Instances of their work, also, are found beyond the bounds of the city. The son, who was Sheriff in 1731-2, died in 1764. Curious to relate yet a third case meets us in York of this industry passing from father to son in the case of George and Robert Dalton. The foundry of this firm was in Stonegate, and bells therefrom are still hung in the steeples of S. Margaret's (one bell dated 1788), and of S. Olave's (six bells dated 1789). With the death of the younger Dalton, within the present century, the pursuit of the bell founder's art in the city of York ceased.

The originator of the industry at Gloucester seems to have been a man named Alexander, or Sandre, early in the fourteenth century, who combined with bell-founding the craft of potter. In 1346, mention is made in the Fabric Roll of Ely Cathedral of bells made by John of Gloucester, who probably succeeded Sandre in his business. The best known of the Gloucester founders, however, is Abraham Rudhall, who was established there in 1684. His descendants continued to follow the same art, and their works are found in many places, a fine peal of ten at Wrexham, for example, coming from their foundry in 1726. Half-a century later they issued a statement showing that, down to Lady Day, 1774, the Rudhall family had turned out 3,594 bells, including those at S. Dunstan's-in-the-East, S. Bride's, and S. Martin's-in-the-Fields, in London. This foundry afterwards passed into the hands of Messrs. Mears, who also carry on the work in London.

Of the founders in the Metropolis, one of the most conspicuous names is that of William Mot, who established the Whitechapel Bell Foundry in the sixteenth century. This passed at a later date into the hands of Messrs. Lester and Pack, who cast among other bells the great bell at Canterbury in 1762. The moulding in this case was entrusted to William Chapman, a nephew of the senior partner in the firm, which shortly after included him, and became Pack and Chapman. Under this name the Whitechapel Foundry turned out the six bells of S. Mary's, Bishophill Senior, at York, in 1770. Amongst those who witnessed the casting of the great bell at Canterbury, was a young man, who evinced so strong an interest in the work, that Chapman took notice of him, and offered to make a bell-founder of him if he would go to London. This was William Mears, and from this incident it came to pass that subsequently the foundry became the property of the Mears family. By them a fine ring of ten bells was hung in the great parish church at Yarmouth in 1807, and the "Beck-with Peal" in 1844, followed by "Great Peter," in 1845, in the minster at York. The style of the firm now is Mears and Stainbank. Other firms which flourished, or still flourish, in the Metropolis, include Christopher Hodson, the best known of whose works is "Great Tom" of Oxford, cast in 1681. Richard Phelps, who, in 1716, cast the predecessor of the modern great bell of St. Paul's, and Messrs. John Warner and Sons, who, to instance an example of their work, supplied two memorial bells to St. Maurice's, York, in 1883.

We touch, however, matters of a rather invidious nature in speaking of bell-founders of modern days, yet the fame of Great Paul of London, excuses our naming its makers, the firm of John Taylor and Company of Loughborough. John of

York, mentioned in an earlier page, is supposed to have introduced the industry into Leicestershire, and to have been eventually succeeded in business by the Newcombes, one of whose bells hung in the parish church of Loughborough until the whole peal was recast by a later successor, Thomas Eayres, of Kettering and St. Neots. The next to take up the work was Edward Arnold, who cast a peal for Quorndon, in 1773, and for Rothley in 1784; the bells of the former each bearing the legend, "Edward Arnold, of St. Neots, Huntingdonshire, cast us all six." One of Arnold's apprentices was Robert Taylor, the grandfather of the founder of "Great Paul." An offshoot from this firm was established by John Briant, another of Arnold's apprentices, at Hertford; and there bells were made for Prestwold, Ashby-de-la-Zouch, and other places, in the first quarter of this century; but the foundry did not survive its originator. The Taylors worked also at one time at Oxford, but on the death of William, one of the two brothers then composing the firm, in 1854, John, the other, closed the Oxford foundry, and gave his whole attention to the one at Loughborough, which had been established in 1840. Perhaps the special attention they have paid to the setting of carillons will also warrant the mention of the Messrs. Gillet and Bland, of Croydon.

It is probable that many of the earlier bell-founders had no fixed place for working, but travelled the country, rearing temporary foundries at various convenient centres, and casting there such bells as might be wanted throughout the neighbouring districts. Robert Merston and Symon de Hazfelde, whose bells are found in sundry places in south and mid Lincolnshire, may have been men of this class.

2

Miles Graye, who made two bells for Baldock church, Hertfordshire, in 1650 and 1655, carried on his work in this fashion, and in 1732, Henry Bayley advertised his readiness "to cast any ring or rings of bells in the town they belong." Daniel Hedderley, of Bawtry, also set up a foundry of this temporary sort at Winterton, in Lincolnshire.

A passing mention may also be given to William Oldfield, of Doncaster, who cast the "great bell" at Snaith, for "twenty nobles and twenty marks," in 1624, of Henry Knight of Reading, who recast six bells at Newbury, Berkshire, in 1680, making them a peal of eight, at the cost of £67. There was also a well-known foundry at Albourne in Wiltshire; the owner of which in the beginning of the eighteenth century was Robert Corr, and in the end of it James Wells.

In many cases it is certain that the bell-founder did not devote himself exclusively to that work, but combined with it some other more or less analogous trade. Ropeforde cast bells for Exeter Cathedral in 1284, and was also entrusted with the repairing of the organ and the horologe there; similarly Thomas Chyche, in 1500, supplied King's College, Cambridge, both with bells for its chapel and cooking-pots for its kitchen. Richard de Wimbish was a potter of London, who also cast bells, in the early fourteenth century, and the same trades were combined, as we have already seen, by Sandre of Gloucester. Sometimes, however, the second trade taken up was strangely incongruous with the other. For example we find one Roger Reve, who made both clothes and bells in the sixteenth century; and in the fourteenth century Daniel Founder, of London,

not only cast bells, but also sold wine. The surname
of the last-named artificer is an illustration of the growth of
these distinctive titles from the trades of our forefathers.
We meet with another artist in bell-metal called William
Founder, and others named Potter and Brazier, suggesting
the handicraft which usually employed them.

In the sixteenth century we find a notice of a priest, who,
like S. Dunstan and others before him, combined with an
earnest attention to his spiritual duties, a devotion to the
mechanical arts. This was William Corvehill, called,
according to the custom of the time in speaking of the
clergy, Sir William. The following record of him is
preserved in the register of the parish of Wenlock in Shropshire, kept by Thomas Botelar, the Vicar : " 1546, May 26,
buried out of tow tenements in Marfold Street, next S.
Owen's Well, Sir William Corvehill, priest of the Service of
our Lady in this church, &c. He was well skilled in
geometry, not by speculation, but by experience : could
make organs, clocks, and chimes ; in kerving in masonry,
and silk weaving and painting, and could make all instruments of music, and was a very patient and gud man, borne
in this borowe, and sometime monk in the monastery . . .
All this country had a great loss of Sir William, for he was
a good bell-founder and maker of frames."

Before leaving the bell-founders, reference may appropriately be made to two interesting relics, which exist at York.
The first is a memorial to some unknown master of the art,
who was probably buried at the Church of S. Denis. It
is an ancient cross, originally in that church but now in the
Hospitium, on the one side of which is a brazier, and on the
other an antique bell. The other takes the more elaborate

form of a stained window in the nave of the Minster, known as the "Bell-Founders' Window." Several of the processes of casting are represented ; among others the forming of the mould, the heating of the furnace, and the filling of the mould with molten metal, while bells are introduced in various places in the borders. This window was either given by Richard Tunnoc, or put up in memory of him. Tunnoc, who was bailiff of the city in 1320, and its representative in Parliament in 1327, is introduced in several places in the window, a scroll with the name inscribed being inserted for the purpose of identifying him. A legend now only partly decipherable, but commencing "Richard Tunnoc me fist" (fecit), runs along the bottom.

There is ample evidence that the migratory bell-founders, to whom allusion has already been made, not infrequently set up their temporary foundries in the garths of those churches for which they worked. Doubtless the conditions of the pathways, and even the highways, of the country in early times, made the transport of heavy masses of metal a matter of no little difficulty ; and the founders were therefore glad, not only to visit the places which might require new bells, but even there to work as near as possible to the towers, to which the bells were to be raised. The bells at Feering in Essex are said to have been cast by Miles Graye in a field adjoining the churchyard. During some excavations made in the churchyard at Scalford, in Leicestershire, traces of a furnace, together with a mass of bell-metal, were discovered, and similar remains were unearthed at Empingham, in Rutland, in 1876. In 1762 the great bell at Canterbury Cathedral was taken down and recast, when to avoid the expense of carriage the work was done in the Cathedral yard, as had also been the case at the recasting of Great Tom of Lincoln in 1610. The bells of Meaux Abbey were cast within the precincts. Occasionally a portion even of the church itself was made into a temporary foundry. Early in the fourteenth century the great bell of S. Alban's Abbey, called Amphibalus, was recast in the hall of the sacristy; and at Kirkby Malzeard, and at Haddenham, bells were cast within the sacred buildings.

In 1483 the importation of foreign bells into England was made illegal, a fact which would seem to imply that they were at that time being brought into the country in sufficient numbers to affect the home industry. Not many products of foreign foundries are, however, known in England at present. One is found at S. Crux, York, inscribed "Ic Ben Ghegoten Int Jaer Oons Heeren MCCCCCxxiij" (I was cast in the year of our Lord, 1523), the date of which is noteworthy as being only forty years after the issue of the prohibition. This bell is supposed to be the work of Van den Gheyn, one of the best-known of the old founders in the Low Countries. This family had works at Louvain, at Mechlin, and at Antwerp, at different periods, and a few other examples of their bells are to be found in England. The hall-bell at Peterhouse, Cambridge, a fine hand-bell belonging to the Corporation of Rye, and probably one at S. Giles's Hospital, Norwich, are specimens of the handicraft of Peter Van den Gheyn. At Culsalmond, in Scotland, is another bell by the same maker; and at Inverarity and Crail are two, both dated 1614, by a descendant of the same name. The representative of the firm in the eighteenth century was Matthias Van den Gheyn, whose daughter married Van Aerschodt: and two of her sons, Andre Louis J. Van Aerschodt and Severin Van Aerschodt, afterwards succeeded to the business at Louvain. A ring of bells made by them was hung only a few years since in the church at Lower Beeding, Sussex.

A famous foreign bell-foundry of bygone times was that of the Waghevens at Louvain. For far over a century this family maintained a high reputation; Henri, one of the greatest of them dying in 1483, and Jacop being still at work in 1590. Bromeswell, Suffolk, has a bell by Cornelis Wagheven, dated 1530; and two or three other English bells are ascribed to the same family. Deventer was another centre of this art, Gerrit Schimmel of that town being the maker of a bell now at Frindsbury, Kent, which is dated 1670. At the same place also about the same time wrought Henrick Ter Horst. The foundry at Middelburg, conducted by Jan Burgerhuys in the early seventeenth century, and after him by his descendants Michael and Jan the younger, appears to have no representative among English bells. And the same is true of the foundries at Rotterdam, of which there were several, such as those of Cornelis Ouderogge, Peter Ostens, Claudius Fremy, and Gerhard Koster, all working in the seventeenth century. Further north in Europe we find in the same century Gert Meyer casting bells at Stockholm, and also Gerhard Horner, a specimen of whose work is at Lavenheath, in Suffolk.

Foreign bells were more frequently imported into Scotland than into the southern Kingdom. Examples of the bells of most, if not all, of the makers just named still exist, or were at one time found, in that country, and also others by such Low Country founders as Peter Jansen, Andreas Ehem, Adam Danckwart and Jacop Ser. But Scotland was not without bell-founders of her own, Patrick Kilgour, of Old Aberdeen, laboured at this craft in the seventeenth century, and on his admission to the Burgess Roll of the city was specially restricted " only . . . to make or mend watches or cast bells as he may have occasion." His successors were Albert Gely, who probably died or retired about 1713, and John Mowat, who became a Burgess of the Gild of Hammermen in 1719, and died in 1771. Andrew Lawson, at one time an apprentice of Mowat's, carried on the business until 1783; and nothing is at present known of this foundry after that date. John Blaickie and Sons, however, cast bells at Aberdeen early in the present century, and still do so. A foundry at Montrose, originally belonging to David Barclay, and afterwards to J. Dickson, is about contemporaneous with the last named in birth, but it no longer exists. The older Scottish bells of native workmanship, are usually cast according to the model most popular in the Netherlands, one point of which is their thinness, in proportion to their size, as compared with English bells.*

Ireland has also had her masters in the art of bell-founding, of whom it must suffice to name Tobias Covey as one of the ancients, Thomas Hodges and James Sheridan, in the middle of this century, and John Murphy of the moderns.

The above paragraphs, do not by any means pretend to give an exhaustive list even of those bell-founders, ancient and modern, whose works are to be found in British belfries;

* For his information concerning Scottish bells, and for many interesting notes on oreign bells, the author is indebted to a recent contribution to bell-lore, namely " The Church and other Bells of Kincardineshire," by F. C. Eeles, (London : Elliott Stock, 1897.) This is, he believes, the first attempt to do for a Scottish county what has been so well done for English ones, and as such, as well as for its intrinsic excellence, it will be welcomed by all lovers of such literature.

such a catalogue, if accompanied with details of their work, would form a large and interesting volume by itself. No reference has been made to John of Stafford, in all probability mayor of Leicester in 1366 and in 1370, who cast bells for various places in Leicestershire; to the Norrises, who throughout the whole of the seventeenth century carried on the work of bell-founding at Stamford; nor to the Bilbies, who from 1700 to 1815 had a foundry at Chewstoke, in Somersetshire. The names most prominent in connection with the art in England have, however, had a place; and others will be noticed incidentally in later pages.

It is time to turn from men to methods, and to speak of the processes followed in the founding of a bell. And first we must give our attention to the materials employed, and to the shape and proportions most approved among experienced bell-founders.

Old French bells were often made of iron, while brass was more commonly employed in Italy and in England, the latter country probably obtaining her earliest examples, and her first lessons in the art of making them, from the former. The bells found by Layard at Nineveh were of bronze, and hand-bells are still made of every kind of sonorous metal, including gold and silver, according to the fancy of the maker or the buyer. Glass has also been employed for bells of a fair size, and one such still hangs at Borrowdale Grange; the tones of such bells are sweet but not far-reaching, and the brittleness of the material is greatly against its use. A foundry at Bochum, in Westphalia, has recently turned out bells of steel, but the experiment can only be called fairly successful at best. Lawrence Kirk, Scotland, has a bell of this metal, cast in 1895 by Vickers of Sheffield, who has cast steel peals for S. Clement's, Hastings, and other places. Wood does not strike one as a hopeful material for the manufacture of bells; yet in a chest at S. Mary Magdalen, Ripon, and also at the parish church of Lenton, wooden bells may be seen. It has been suggested that these may have been imitation bells only, meant to serve as guides to the maker of the bell-frame, or for some such purpose; they may however have been actually used during Holy week, according to a custom of which we must speak hereafter.

Bell metal, as now understood, consists of a compound of copper and tin. The proportions vary to some extent, but a common standard is three parts copper to one tin in small bells, and four parts copper to one tin in large ones. If the amount of tin be increased the bell becomes more brittle; while if the copper be in excess the brilliancy of its tone is damaged. Occasionally small quantities of other metals are also added; thus the proportions recommended in Paris for clock bells are copper 71 parts, tin 26, zinc 2, and iron 1. A document, still extant, which records the receipts and disbursements in connection with the casting of a new bell for Bridgewater in the thirteenth century, illustrates the composition of the metal used at that time. We learn that there were bought 896 pounds of copper, 40 pounds of brass, and 320 pounds of tin; moreover gifts of "pots, platters, basons, lavers, kettles, brass mortars, and mill pots" amounted altogether to 180 pounds, apparently of brass; and the old bell, which was melted down, weighed 425 pounds. If we take the brass, amounting in all to 220 pounds, as being composed of 9 parts copper to 4 parts zinc, according to the usual average, and also leave out of the account the old bell, as probably consisting of much the

same compound of metals as the new one was intended to
do, we get these quantities: 1049 pounds of copper, 320
pounds of tin, and 68 pounds of zinc, which is singularly
near the proportions of the French bell-metal quoted above,
except for the absence of iron.   It is a popular superstition
throughout the length and breadth of the country, that a
bell of specially sweet tone owes its excellence to the
presence of a quantity of silver in its composition.   Of the
Lavenham bells, for instance, concerning which the " Magna
Britannia " reports that " the tenor hath such an admirable
note, as England has none to compare to it," a local tradition
tells that at the casting some rich wool-staplers and others
gave great quantities of silver, and even some gold, to throw
into the furnace.   A similar story is told of Great Tom of
Lincoln, at the casting of which, in 1610, silver tankards,
spoons, and other like articles, are said to have been devoted
to the melting-pot.   When this bell was re-cast, however, in
1831, the following was found to be the composition of the
metal: 700 pounds of copper, 299 pounds of tin, and one
pound only of silver.   Other assays of old bell-metal yield
similar results, and conclusively prove that silver, if used at
all, was in almost inappreciable quantities.   It is, in fact,
alleged by experts that the employment of that metal would
have precisely the contrary effect upon the tone of the bell
to that which tradition assigns to it, silver being in its nature
too closely allied to lead to permit of its use in this case.
It has been suggested that the legend arose from a practice
among the workmen engaged in the casting. of asking the
bystanders for silver coins to throw into the molten metal,
on the plea that thus the composition would be improved ;
such coins being, as a matter of fact, put to a use more

calculated to loosen the workmen's tongues, than to mellow the tone of the bell. How far this is a libel on bell-founders, ancient and modern, the present writer does not pretend to determine.

The almost contradictory qualities needed in an ideal composition of bell-metal are thus summed up by Mr. Benjamin Lomax in his little work on "Bells and Bell-ringers":—"The typical bell should be flexible enough to bend, elastic enough to resume its original shape after the strongest vibration, tough enough to stand heavy blows without splitting, and hard enough to retain a form once taken." Experiments have been made in many directions; for instance, the alloy known as German silver, which consists of 100 parts of copper to 60 of zinc, and 40 of nickel, has been used for the casting of a large bell in Cathay; but practical experience has proved the superiority for this purpose of the compound above described. Bell-metal is very similar to what was known as gun-metal before the invention of ordnance first of cast iron, and then, as we have it to-day, of steel; and we have several instances of the metal being cast first in the one form and then in the other. Peter, the great Tsar, is said to have converted church bells into cannon, and the great bell of Rouen was put to a similar purpose in 1793. Several instances can be quoted on the other side. The bells of Liversedge, in Yorkshire, were made from guns captured by Lord William Bentinck at Genoa in 1814; in 1893, six bells, cast from copper cannon captured by the Russian forces in their last campaign in the Caucasus, were sent to Petrovsk to be hung in the churches of the Orthodox Faith in Daghestan; and in 1887 a great bell named Gloriosa, formed from the metal of no less than twenty-two French guns taken in the Franco-German War, was raised with much ceremony to its place in Cologne Cathedral.

Care is taken by the best modern founders to procure the purest possible metals for the construction of bells, experience having proved that, cumbersome as they may appear to the uninitiated, their tone requires as delicate consideration as that of a violin. Rougher methods at one time, however, prevailed. A writer in Knight's "Penny Magazine," for March, 1842, describing the method of casting bells, says, "The tin is usually brought to the foundry in blocks from the mining districts, and the copper is old ship-sheathing and other fragments."

Not less important to the voice of the bell than its material is its shape. Mediæval bells were, for the most part, longer and narrower than those of more modern make. At Mitford, in Northumberland, is preserved a bell of great, but unknown age, whose height is equal to the width, and whose sides, instead of forming the graceful curves now usually seen, are very nearly in straight lines, giving to the bell almost the shape of a cone with a rounded apex. An inscription on a plate affixed to the stock informs us that this quaint old bell hung in the belfry until 1862, when two new ones were given to the church by Admiral Robert Mitford, of Mitford. Chinese bells are frequently even greater in height than width. On the other hand a much flatter form, approaching the gong in outline, is very common in hand-bells, and has been used for those of larger proportions. In practise it is found that if the bell be too flat the vibrations expel the air from within with an almost explosive force, and the sound is loud and harsh.

If, however, the opposite error be committed, and the height be too great in proportion to the diameter, the air reverberates too much within the bell itself, and the sound does not travel satisfactorily. Some of the famous bells of Russia depart a good deal from the laws of proportion which are commonly observed in England. The well-known "Great Bell of Moscow" is practically as high as it is broad, measuring twenty feet in height, and only a quarter of a foot more in diameter; and a second monster bell in the same city stands twenty-one feet high and is eighteen in diameter. One of the most celebrated of European bells is the one at Erfurt, which is eight and a half feet in diameter, but ten and a quarter in height. All these will be referred to again more particularly when we come to speak of noted bells. A curious variation from the usually accepted form of the bell once existed in the church of S. Andrea, Mantua. Guido Ganzaga, who was abbot there in 1431, and became provost of the Cathedral in 1444, used the metal of an ancient bell, presented to the church in the year 1000, to make a newer and larger one. The peculiarity in the construction of this was that the design was a skeleton bell, eight long openings, like lancet windows, being left in its sides. It was adorned with much moulding in bands above and below the windows; and a number of full length figures and medallions enriched the spaces between them, the subjects selected including persons rather incongruously associated, such as Atlas, Hercules, Pallas, and Adam. On being rung the bell unfortunately cracked; and having been taken down from the tower, it was preserved in the church or its precincts until 1812, when after some repairs it was swung up into its old place once more, and rung in honour of Napoleon's birthday. The tone did not, however, prove satisfactory, and the bell was again taken down, and a few years later was sold and broken up. Another bell with windows, and dated 1593, is in the chapel of Our Lady "del Canossa" at Mantua.

In deciding the just proportions for a large bell, it is usual to take the thickness of the metal at the sound bow, that is the part where the clapper strikes, as the unit. This is sometimes called the brim, and the measurements are reckoned in brims. The commonly accepted proportions are as follows:—the diameter of the bell at the mouth should be from thirteen to fifteen of these units; the height, measured externally from the lip to the shoulder, twelve; and the diameter at the shoulder rather more than half that at the mouth. In thickness also the different portions of a bell vary; the sides at the top being two-thirds of the unit, or thickness at the bottom. These dimensions, from which bells of different sizes and from different foundries vary in small details, have been arrived at, not so much by scientific theorizing, as by long experience.

Curious shapes are sometimes seen in single bells that have been more or less roughly cast. In Scotland, for example, we find at Fettercairn, a bell cast by Dickson, of Montrose, in 1821, the crown of which is hemispherical; this, combined with its unusually short waist, reduces it almost to the shape of a basin. In the town steeple at Drumlithe is another with a projecting lip and no structural sound-bow; it is quite a modern bell in its present form, having been recast in 1868.

Mention ought, perhaps, also to be made of the modern invention known as the tubular bells. These are the

TUBULAR BELLS

work of Messrs. Harrington, Latham, and Company, of Coventry, and have been inserted in the belfries of several churches. Their tone is said to be sweet, though naturally not as powerful as that of an ordinary peal. But since these tubes, in spite of their name, are rather substitutes for bells, than actual bells in the accepted sense of the word, they call for no more than passing notice here.

Let us in imagination follow the process adopted in the casting of a church bell. In this the first important work is the construction of the core, by which term is meant a hollow cone of brick constructed on a cast-iron plate as a foundation, and in diameter somewhat smaller than the interior of the bell. Over this is plastered a specially-prepared mixture of clay, intended to bring up the core to the exact size and shape of this interior. The old method of gaining this end was by the use of a wooden "crook;" this was something like a huge pair of compasses standing open, and balanced on the top of a long stake running through the centre of the core, the two legs of the compasses being shaped to the exact curves of the inside and the outside of the bell respectively. The more workmanlike instrument now usually employed consists of a light iron frame, into which can be fixed metal templates, called the "sweep," cut to the precise form of each bell. The action in each case, however, is practically the same. While the clay on the core is still soft, the crook or sweep revolves upon its pivot in the middle of it, and by shaving and smoothing the clay, moulds it according to the model decided upon for the interior of the bell. This clay mould is then baked dry and hard by means of a fire lighted within the brick core. The old bell-founders then proceeded to build up upon this the

" thickness," by which name they called a second layer of clay of exactly the thickness, shape, and size of the proposed bell. The core was first dusted over with dry tan, to prevent the two layers of clay adhering; and then this thickness was built up of a friable composition, which was shaped, just as the core had previously been, by the use of the second arm of the crook, into the correct figure of the outside of the bell. The thickness was then also dusted over with tan, and upon this was constructed the " cope," an outer casing of clay several inches thick. The whole having been thoroughly dried by means of fire, the cope was carefully raised by the help of a crane, and the thickness was all destroyed ; the cope was then lowered into its former position, every care being taken to make it concentric with the core ; and the mould was ready. When means had been taken to prevent either core or cope from being moved even a hair's breadth by the influx of the molten metal, preparations were made for filling the space between the two from the glowing furnace hard by. Much time and trouble are saved by the more modern plan of abolishing the " thickness " altogether, for which purpose a cast-iron cope-case is used. This is placed mouth upwards and lined with clay, which is shaped exactly to the external form and dimensions of the bell by means of the outside template of the sweep. When this has been thoroughly dried it is lowered over the core. Whichever method is used one or two details have to be attended to before the baking of the cope. The first and most important is the moulding of the " canons," or hooks, for fastening the bell to the wooden stock, which forms the axis on which it revolves in the belfry. A clapper ring, or loop from which to suspend the clapper, has also to be moulded. In many modern bells, however, the canons are dispensed with, and the bell is bolted directly on to its stock, and the clapper ring is also made separately and bolted in. One great advantage of this plan is, that when the repeated blows of the clapper have worn the sound-bow at one spot, the bell can be turned round and bolted in a new position, and the clapper suitably adjusted, so that the blows may fall upon a fresh place. The perpetual beating of the clapper on one point of the sound-bow during many years, has been known to form a furrow in the metal which has eventually resulted in cracking the bell.

The clapper, which is technically divided into the "ball" or hammer, and the "flight," or shaft, is fastened into the crown of the bell by an iron staple; anciently, however, thongs of white leather, made from horse-hide, were used. These were known as bawdrills or bawtries, and since the frequent swinging of the clapper comparatively soon wore them through, the purchase of new ones is an item not seldom found in churchwardens' accounts. The following entries occur in the accounts of S. Michael's Church, Spurriergate, York :—

		s.	d.
" 1520. Item paid for a Baldrege to the second bell - - - - - -		vj	
1540. Item paid ffore helpyng of ij bawtrys off the bells - - - - -		vij	."

These thongs are also mentioned, under the name of "baudricks," in the accounts of the churchwardens of Newbury, Berkshire.

Most ancient bells bore some motto, and many some

3

sacred emblem or device, to which modern makers add the date, and the trade mark or name of the firm. There must, therefore, be impressed upon the cope any such lettering or device.

When all these details have been arranged, and the cope has been placed over the core with the greatest precision possible, to prevent one side of the bell being thicker than the other, the actual casting is begun. To facilitate this the invariable plan at one time was to erect the core in a pit, below the level of the furnace mouth, from which channels were cut to convey the metal; and this method is still common. Sometimes, however, where cope cases are employed, the course followed in ordinary castings is employed, the metal being brought to the mould (which in this case is not sunk) in a ladel by a travelling crane.

In ancient days, while the art of bell-casting was still retained in the hands of ecclesiastics, the blessing of heaven was invoked at the very outset of the work. "The brethren of the monastery," so Southey tells us in "The Doctor," "stood round the furnace, ranged in processional order, sang the 150th Psalm, and then, after certain prayers, blessed the molten metal, and called upon the Lord to infuse into it His grace, and overshadow it with His power, for the honour of the saint to whom the bell was to be dedicated, and whose name it was to bear."

In putting the metal into the furnace a very ample quantity is always provided, and as tin is more quickly melted and more volatile than copper, it is not thrown in until the latter is in a molten state. For filling the mould of Great Paul, which weighs something under seventeen tons, twenty tons of metal were allowed. A certain amount of waste must be reckoned upon, and moreover it is difficult, if not impossible, to calculate beforehand to a nicety the weight of a really large bell. In order to resist the pressure of such a flood of molten metal, it will be evident that the cope-case must be of great strength. The one made for the bell just referred to was capable of bearing a pressure of two hundred tons. When the casting takes place in a pit this strength is gained by filling up the pit with loam, so that the mould is embedded in solid earth.

A pathetic story, connected with the casting of a bell, is told concerning the "Poor Sinner's Bell" at Breslau. Some five hundred years ago a founder was employed in constructing a bell to hang in the south tower of the church of S. Mary Magdalene in that town. The mould had been duly made and the metal was nearly ready for tapping, when the master was called away for a short time; and, in leaving a boy in charge, gave him strict injunctions not to interfere with the furnace. Scarcely had he turned his back, however, when the lad, boy-like, began to finger the catch which kept the metal in, and presently to his horror the youngster saw the crimson stream of glowing metal come leaping from the furnace, and flowing in full tide to the pit where lay the mould. In terror at what he had done, he rushed from the foundry shouting wildly for his master; and the latter on entering, seeing, as he thought, his labour all thrown away, and his work absolutely ruined, struck the lad a blow, which passion rendered so severe that he fell lifeless at his feet. In due time the metal cooled, the cope was drawn off, and the bell was lifted from the core; when the amazed artificer beheld it smooth and perfect in finish, and found it, on testing, clear and sweet in tone. Overcome with remorse for the fatal consequence of his momentary rage, the master gave himself up to the authorities, accusing himself of the murder of his servant. The law took its course, and its full penalty was exacted ; and the first man on whose behalf the bell rung out, calling the faithful to pray for his parting soul, was the skilful maker of the bell itself. S. Mary's bell was the name given to it at its dedication, but from that day forward even to our own times the Breslau folk have called it the bell of the " Poor Sinner."

Formerly the furnace was heated entirely with wood fires, the form employed being that known as a reverberatory furnace, in which the flame and heat are made to pass over the metal, instead of being applied beneath. It is maintained by some that fires of this kind ensure greater purity in the metal than can be gained by the more modern use of coal.

Slowly the monster mass flows from this furnace into the mould. In casting the great bell of Montreal Cathedral, at Messrs. Mears' Foundry in London, in 1847, the mould was twelve minutes in filling ; the tons of metal required for the casting of Great Paul of London were over eight hours in melting, but were not as many minutes in running into the gigantic cope. Then follows a time of keen anxiety for the founder, especially if the work be one of unusual size and importance. In the case of the last-named bell six days were allowed to elapse before the metal was supposed to have set sufficiently solidly to allow of its being touched. At last, however, it is dug out from the pit, or the metal cope is raised from it, and the master is able to judge of the success of at least the outside of his work. But the bell has still to be hoisted up from the core, and when swung upon a temporary frame, to undergo the ordeal of testing its tone.

Next to the making of the bell itself, the size and weight of its clapper, or tongue, call for consideration. Too heavy a clapper will destroy the fineness of the tone, and perhaps even crack the bell ; while one that is too light fails to bring out the fulness and richness of the voice with which the bell should be endowed.

Both bell and clapper having been duly cast, and the latter secured in its place within the former, preparations are made for putting its sound to the proof; and, if the bell is to form one of a ring, it must be tuned so as to accord with the others. It but seldom happens that a bell, and still less frequently a ring of bells, is cast exactly true in pitch. If such be the case, the ring has the high distinction of being a " virgin peal."

If the note struck out be too flat, a portion of the edge of the bell is cut away, thus reducing the diameter; if it be too sharp, the thickness of the sound-bow is reduced. The former process is far more liable to damage a bell than the latter, and therefore in tuning a peal it is customary to take the bell which gives the flattest note as a basis, and to tune to that. The old method of reducing the thickness was exceedingly rough ; "the reduction is made," so says the article quoted above from the " Penny Magazine," " by chipping away the metal with a sharp-pointed hammer." A chisel of hard steel was an instrument the use of which was less dangerous to the bell, but both these are now superseded in good foundries by the employment of a specially-constructed machine, consisting of a kind of lathe. The bell is securely fastened to the face-plate, and the

requisite amount of metal can be cut away from any portion
of the interior, without dangerous violence, and with the
greatest accuracy.

The tuning of bells is not, however, so simple a matter
as the above paragraph might at first sight seem to imply.
If a bell struck out one note simply, it would not be
difficult to correct and alter it to the pitch required; but
such is not the case. A bell in perfect tune sounds a
perfect chord. There is the note struck out directly by the
clapper from the sound bow; this booms out most
prominently, and if the pitch of the bell be spoken of, it is
this tone to which reference is made. But as the vibrations
of the stroke set the whole mass of metal throbbing, the
following notes are also sounded; at one eighth of the
height of the bell from the brim a third above the
fundamental note is given; at three-quarters of the height, a
fifth; and at the shoulder the chord is completed by the
octave. Besides these there is also developed from them a
"hum note," as it is called, consisting of the octave below
the fundamental, An absolutely perfect bell would have
all these five notes absolutely in tune with each other; but
probably no such bell exists. The tenor at Lavenham,
already spoken of, which has been called "the matchless
tenor," has the fundamental and the octave above in
perfect tune. The fundamental has absorbed almost the
exclusive interest of tuners in England in most cases; but
its prominence in peal and change-ringing, although it
renders it the most important note, does not justify the
ignoring of the others.

The bell having been to   l and tuned, nothing remains
but to convey it to its desti   on, and to place it within the

belfry; and this is often accompanied with no little rejoicing and some formality.

The solemn reception and hanging of a new church bell is accompanied in Russia with a good deal of religious ceremony. The following account is given by an eye-witness :—*

"In the body of the church before the royal gates (answering to the western chancel screen), stood a low naloy (movable prayer-desk), on which were two candle-sticks with burning tapers, and a large pewter sort of tureen containing holy water, or rather water that was destined to be blessed. There was a good deal of going backwards and forwards among the readers and sextons, and evident preparation. At last the High Priest—who, in by no means so handsome canonicals as I had expected on this occasion, issued from the royal gates, followed by three other priests and a deacon, and placing himself before the naloy, with his back to the greater part of the congregation, and his face towards the gates—began a molében, and blessed the water by plunging the cross in it three times, each time holding the same, on taking it out of the water, over another smaller vessel, which the deacon held, and allowing the drops to fall from the cross into it : with these drops the bell was afterwards sprinkled. The congregation now approached the naloy, and each, as he kissed the cross, which the High Priest held, was sprinkled by him with water from the first vessel. . . . A procession was immediately afterwards formed, consisting of the clergy and readers, churchwardens and sextons, each with something

* "Sketches of the Rites and Customs of th Greco-Russian Church," by II. C. Romanoff. Rivingstons, 1868.

in his hand. Two readers went before with the church banners; two sextons followed with horrid, dull, wax-dropped lanterns containing tapers, as candles in the usual tall candlesticks would be liable to be blown out. . . . At the foot (of the church steps), with a quantity of linen wound round it to prevent its rubbing when it entered the belfry, lay the bell, a mystery of cordage and pulleys twisted about it; and when I looked at the immense mass, I felt nervously doubtful as to whether the means prepared were strong enough to raise it. My companions experienced the same dread, and we moved to the left, lest the 10,950 lbs. should fall on our heads. The High Priest read a few prayers on reaching the bell, not a word of which was audible, and then proceeded to sprinkle it in the manner I have described, walking round it as he did so. The choir, with the remaining priests, sang psalms and irmos, but the sound was completely drowned by the hum of voices and the shouts of the workmen to each other, as they arranged the cordage; a dozen or so of men were in the belfry, and *five hundred* in the street below, ready to pull at the cords; and when the service, which did not occupy more than five minutes, and which was by no means striking in any respect, was concluded, a great noise ensued, which ended in the signal to begin pulling being given, and in a few seconds the huge mass began to move. . . . When it began to ascend the shouts ceased, and the crowd made the sign of the cross devoutly, while the melodious singing of the choir, now agreeably audible, accompanied the bell on its rapid progress to its place of final destination." The bell here spoken of was one made for the church at Votkinsk by the bell-foundry at Slobodsky.

The ceremony observed in the west for the dedication and naming of a bell will be described in the next chapter, when the use of names for bells comes under consideration.

Even those, to whom an elaborate ceremonial makes the least appeal, must admit that this solemn way of placing within the church so important an article of its furniture, is to be preferred to the scenes of revelry, sometimes degenerating even into debauchery, which at one time frequently marked the occasion in England. White, in his "Antiquities of Selborne," tells us how the new bells were inaugurated there in 1735. "The old bells, three in number, loud and out of tune," were recast into a ring of four, to which Sir Simon (or Simeon) Stuart, a Hampshire baronet, added a fifth, in memory of his daughter Mary. "The day of the arrival of the tuneable peal was observed," says the chronicler, "as an high festival by the village, and rendered more joyous by an order from the donor that the treble bell should be fixed bottom upward in the ground and filled with punch, of which all present were permitted to partake." This is by no means a solitary instance of such a usage, and it needs little imagination to judge how such a practice, however well intended by the jovial but irreverent donor, would usually end. A more pleasant picture of the reception of a new peal of bells in an English rural parish is supplied by a record preserved by a late vicar of Blyth, near Retford. In 1842 the belfry of the splendid old monastic church in this Nottinghamshire village had a new and melodious ring cast for it, in place of the somewhat tuneless bells which had long served the church's needs. The whole village turned out to meet them with every sign of welcome ; a brass band proceeded the waggon, in which were the bells garlanded with flowers and evergreens ; and an ornamental arch was erected over the gateway leading into the churchyard.

Before leaving the question of the making of church bells, it will be convenient to speak of the manner of hanging them, and of fitting them for their work. The bell, once safely landed in the bell-chamber of the tower, is securely fastened to its stock, a solid wooden block, in length about equal to the diameter of the bell. From the lower ends of the stock project metal "gudgeons," or pivots, which, when the bell is raised into its place, fall into "brasses," or iron sockets in the massive wooden frame within which the whole ring of bells is suspended. Fastened to one end of the stock is a wooden wheel, in radius equal, more or less, to the diameter of the bell, the spokes of which are at one point doubled. At this point the rope is firmly secured, a deep groove in the rim of the wheel keeping it in its proper place. At the opposite end of the stock is the stay, a bar of stout, sound wood projecting upwards almost as far as the bell hangs below.

When a bell is chimed, it is gently swung to and fro, so that the side strikes regularly against the clapper, which hangs almost motionless within it. When, however, the bell is rung, it is made to revolve upon its gudgeons until it lies mouth upwards ; in which position the stay, now at the bottom, catches against the slide, a wooden bar fastened below the bell at one side of the frame, thus preventing the bell from actually turning over. The next pull of the rope, sends the whole mass spinning back again, until the stay strikes the slide again, the stopping of the bell on each side sending the clapper

on to the sound bow with a clang, while the position of the
bell allows the full power of the sound to float away from
the belfry through the louvres.   The slide is so fixed as
to turn on a pivot at one end, while the other moves a
few inches forward and backward when struck by the stay ;
in this way the bell performs something more than complete
revolution at every stroke.

The task of hauling such weighty matters as church bells
up to their lofty situation is not, as may be supposed, without
its anxiety to all concerned.   A belfry story from Italy
illustrates the danger involved in undertaking such a work
incautiously.   A volume published in 1691, called
" Observations on a Journey to Naples," tells how a new
bell was made for the Benedictine Monastery at Bemonia,
and in due time was blessed and dedicated in the name of
S. Proculus.   The sexton, who also bore that saint's name,
was unfortunately standing immediately beneath his
sonorous namesake, as it was being slowly swung to
its place.   Suddenly, without warning, some part of the
tackling gave way, and Proculus the bell fell to earth
once more, cracking itself and killing Proculus the
sexton.   The brothers of the community showed a somewhat disgraceful levity on the occasion, for the following
epigram was passed from one to the other in the
monastery :—

> " Si procul a Proculo Proculi campana fuisset,
> Jam procul a Proculo Proculus ipse fuisset."

To translate this literally so as to preserve the pun and the
epigram is, of course, impossible ; the following will convey
to those " not learned in the Latin tongue " some idea
of the point :—

> " If from father Proculus
> Our father's bell had farther been,
> Now farther from our father's breast
> Were father Proculus, I ween."

The sexton, probably some lay brother of the community, has no right, it must be admitted, to the honorary title of "father," but even if the exigencies of the translation of a pun count for nothing, we may surely pay a little extra posthumous respect to one whose tragic death was treated so flippantly.

CHAPTER III.

Dates and Names of Bells.

IT is impossible to say which bell in Europe, or even in England, can claim the distinction of having been in use for the greatest number of years, the custom of marking upon them the date of their founding not having become general until about the fifteenth century. It is certain, however, that in many cases where the bell bears a comparatively modern date, the metal of which it is composed represents one of much greater antiquity, many ancient bells having, for one reason or another, been recast in later times.

A bell at Fontenville, near Bayeux, in France, was reputed to be the oldest dated bell in Europe. It bears the date 1202, and was in use until the year 1858, when it fell and was cracked. Thus it swung in its steeple for over six-and-a-half centuries. At Freiborg, in the Black Forest, is a veteran which, although a little younger than the French bell, can boast that it is still serviceable. It is dated 1258.

The village of Claughton, in Lancashire, has the distinction of possessing the oldest dated bell known to exist in England. In a double bell-cot over the west end of the church hang two bells, one quite modern, and its fellow just over six hundred years old. On the shoulder of the latter is an inscription, forming a circle round it, which runs as follows:—

ANNO. DNI. M. CC. NONOG. AI

that is, " In the year of the Lord 1296." Two peculiarities

will be noted in the expression of the date; one is the curious fact that Roman numerals are mixed up with an abbreviation of the word nonaginta (ninety), and the other is the inversion of the v in the sign for six. The latter eccentricity is far from unique among the inscriptions on bells, as we may have further occasion to note hereafter. The Claughton bell measures slightly over sixteen inches in height, and twenty-one in diameter at the mouth, and sounds the note E flat.

Only a little later in date is the tenor bell, there being three in all, at Cold Ashby, in Northamptonshire. It bears the inscription—

MARIA. VOCOR. ANO. DNI. M. CCC. XVII.

preceding which is an initial cross, and following it the impressions of a seal, of a silver penny of the reign of King Edward I., and the maker's mark. The last consists of the figure of a bell with a fleur-de-lys on each side, an inscription surrounding it setting forth that it is the seal of William de Flint.

Lincolnshire provides us with eleven fifteenth century bells, which have been described by a competent authority* as "the most interesting group yet recorded in England." They consist of the second and third bells at South Somercotes, the first and third at Somerby, by Brigg, the second at Toynton S. Peter, a bell at Hainton, two at Somersby, and others at Hammeringham, Beesby, and Gunby S. Peter. The "family likeness" which connects all these together is the use of finely designed Gothic lettering in the inscriptions, together with initial crosses and ornamental stops of

---

* " English Bells and Bell Lore," by the late Thomas North, F.S.A., edited by the Rev. William Beresford. Leek, 1888.

INSCRIPTION ON THE OLD BELL AT CLAUGHTON.

exceptional beauty.   The letters are elaborated, like the
initials in an illuminated manuscript, by interweaving with
them all manner of figures and foliage : thus the "I" contains
the effigy of S. George in the act of piercing the dragon,
"O" surrounds the head of a bishop vested in an antique
mitre, and lions, trefoils, conventional foliage, and other
devices adorn the other letters.   The South Somercotes
bells are the most complete of the series in their decoration ;
the letters are all of this splendid type, the stops are large
and graceful, the trade mark of the maker is scratched on
each, and each bears a date, namely, 1423.   The bells at
Toynton S. Peter, at Hainton, and at Somersby have most
of the same characteristics, but are undated.   Those at
Somerby were cast in 1431.   They bear a double inscription ;
the first setting forth that each was made at the order of
Thomas Cumberworth, the second that the one bell is
dedicated in honour of S. Mary, and the other of the Blessed
Trinity.   The stops of these inscriptions are smaller than
those found at South Somercotes, and the inscriptions,
perhaps in consequence of their length, are in smaller and
simpler characters, the initial letters only being of the type
above noticed.   The bells at the remaining places, Hammeringham, Beesby, and Gunby S. Peter, are probably somewhat
later in date.   The smaller letters alone are here employed,
fragments of the larger ones, which must have been broken
up during the interval, appearing as stops between the words.

The tenor bell at Westminster Abbey was originally cast
in 1430 ; but, as is duly set forth upon it, it has been twice
since then recast.   Its legend runs, "Remember John
Whitmell, Isabel his wife, and William Rus, who first gave
this bell, 1430.   New cast in July, 1599, and in April, 1738.

Richard Phelps, T. Lester, fecit." It would go hardly with Masters Phelps and Lester were their bell-founding no better than their Latinity.

Of the seven bells, including a small Sanctus bell, hanging in the steeple of S. John's, York, one at least is an early fifteenth century example. Its inscription is much worn, but the date 1408, in Roman numerals, is legible. Other bells in this belfry are apparently ancient, but their dates do not appear upon them. Three of them came from the church of S. Nicholas, without Walmgate Bar, which was destroyed by fire during the seige of the city by the Parliamentarian army under Lord Fairfax in 1644. That commander is said to have shown a solicitude, unusual among his comrades, for the preservation of public buildings in the places which he was called upon to attack ; a fact to which the citizens of York have to be thankful that the damage done by the cannonade and the soldiery was not greater.

Other bells there are throughout the country, whose age, though not proclaimed upon their sides, can be approximately decided by circumstantial evidence.

At Goring, Oxfordshire ; Berechurch, Essex ; Burham, Kent ; Great Bradley, Suffolk ; and Slapton, Northampton-shire, are bells cast by a maker named in the preceding chapter, Richard de Wimbish. This founder, whose name also appears as Wimbis and " VV ambis," is, with every show of reason, identified with a man of that name who cast bells for Holy Trinity Church, Aldgate, in 1312. At S. Mary, Bishophill Junior, York, is a small bell with an inscription in Lombardic characters, which is supposed to have been cast by some local founder between 1390 and 1410. In

the same church is another, the sixth, which is ascribed to
John Hoton, who was a bell-founder of York in the end
of the fifteenth century.   From the similarity of the letters
and stamps used, it has been suggested that bells at
S. Nicholas' Cathedral, Newcastle, and at Heighington, in
Durham, are from the same source.

The bells of John of Stafford, and of John of York also,
though undated, are ascribed by antiquaries to the latter
half of the fourteenth century, or the early years of the
fifteenth.

The Reformation found the church in England rich in
bells, as in every other requisite for divine worship.   The
inventories of church goods compiled during the reign of
Edward VI., prove that three bells at the least were the rule
even in small parish churches.   Two are sometimes found,
but scarcely anywhere was there one only.   On the other
hand, few parishes, except those of more than ordinary
importance, had more than four bells.   Many of these have
disappeared from causes which will hereafter be considered,
and many more have been recast in subsequent times.   The
bells of the monastic houses, which probably possessed
larger and heavier peals in most instances than the simple
parish churches, were, no doubt, in many cases, seized upon
by the laymen, to whom the abbey lands were assigned ; in
some instances, however, they were sold or given to a
neighbouring church.   The tenor bell at Ormskirk is
alleged to have been the third bell of Burscough Priory ;
tradition indeed has it that the whole peal was originally
removed from the priory to that church, but that all except
this tenor were afterwards again transferred to Croston.
However that may be, all have been recast since then.   The

4

Ormskirk bell bears the inscription, " I. S. DE BURSCOUGH, ARMIG ET E UXOR ME FECERUNT IN HONOREM TRINITATIS. R.B. 1576." I. S. is probably for James Scarisbrick, and R.B. is intended to identify the founder. The same initials are found on a bell at Warburton, in Cheshire, the metal of which may possibly have come from the Praemonstratensian Priory of S. Werburgh there ; the inscription, which is only partly legible, runs, " R.B. . . . ANO DNI. MDLXXV."

When we come down to the seventeenth century, examples of dated bells are not so rare, though even at that period they are not so common as to lack interest. Two bells, now used for secular purposes, and dating from the end of the sixteenth century and the beginning of the following one, are noteworthy chiefly on account of their history. One hangs in the gateway tower of Lincoln's Inn. This was part of the plunder of the city of S. Sebastian, near Cadiz, which was stormed by the English under Essex in June, 1596. That date, which marks its capture, not its casting, is now seen upon the bell. The other bell, so tradition asserts, once hung in a Continental convent, but passed by purchase into the possession of Messrs. Dickens, at Tonge, in Lancashire, and was placed in their factory. It bears the legend, " MA. RO. MDCXIV. RA."

The little bell, known as the priest's bell, at Newbury, Berkshire, was recast at a time when probably such an event was exceedingly rare in England, namely, in 1652. It would be interesting to know if any other church was able to provide itself with a new bell in those dark times of Puritan ascendancy. The good folk of Newbury, however, were enthusiastic in defence of their ancient parish church ; it was only six years before, in 1646, that they redeemed their bells from the hands of the Parliamentary soldiery, together with the lead from the church roof, and the weathercock from the tower.

Among eighteenth century bells, mention may be made of one in Westminster Abbey, cast by Rudhall in 1743; of a peal of eight with a priest's bell at S. Mary's, Leigh, Lancashire, dated variously from 1740 to 1775; of ten out of the thirteen in Halifax parish church, which were cast in 1787, the remaining three dating only from 1814; but further it is needless to particularize, bells of that century being common enough in all parts of the kingdom.

Some of our finest churches and cathedrals have quite modern peals; the cathedral at Worcester, for instance, includes its bells among the details of its recent restoration, and the bells of S. Paul's were only dedicated on All Saints' Day, 1878.

The sister kingdom of Scotland has suffered far more severely than England in the matter of bells. The Reformation in that country being a thorough religious revolution, resulted in a more widespread destruction of church property than even the Church in England suffered; and consequently really ancient bells are rare. In the county of Kincardine, for instance—the only Scottish county whose bells have yet been systematically catalogued —there are but seventy-five public bells, sacred and secular, known; and of these one only is in any sense ancient. The contrast between the condition of things north and south of the Border, is, perhaps, even more strikingly illustrated by the absolute absence of rings of bells through-out that entire county. S. James' Episcopal Church, at Stonehaven, and the Town Steeple there, have each two bells; while at S. Cyrus there are, besides one bell in use, two clock bells that are not used at all. The other bells of the county are all found separately.

The one representative of mediæval workmanship among the Kincardineshire bells is not earlier in date than the end of the fifteenth, or the commencement of the sixteenth century. It is now preserved at the Sessions House, at Strachan, but formerly hung in a small belfry at the west end of S. Mary's Church. It has no inscription.

Turning to other parts of the country, mention should be made of the "Minister's bell" at S. Giles', Elgin, the work of Thomas of Dunbar in 1402. The cathedral at Kirkwall had several ancient bells; one, the first, still exists, the others, which dated originally from 1528, have been recast.

Towards the end of the sixteenth century, however, Scotland began to some small extent to arouse herself from that absolute deadness to all ecclesiastical art into which the Reformation had thrown her. Bells were again imported from the Low Countries, and a few native artificers are heard of. Robert Hog, of Stirling, cast bells for Glencairn in 1611, and foundries were at work soon after at Edinburgh and Aberdeen. A carillon of twenty-three bells was hung at S. Giles', Edinburgh, in 1698.

Within quite recent years many fine rings of bells have been cast, chiefly by English foundries, for Scottish churches, especially for the Episcopal Church of Scotland. S. Mary's Cathedral, Edinburgh, has a peal of ten bells, and octaves are by no means rare in large and important churches.

It has already been remarked that mediæval bells were

seldom impressed with the dates of their casting, or with
the names of their makers.   Yet the names of the bells
themselves were usually inscribed upon them ; in these
names they were dedicated, and by them they were
commonly called.   In the accounts of the churchwardens
for the parish of North Walsham, for the year 1583, a charge
is entered for "new casting the Gabrell," that is, S.
Gabriel's bell.   The Cathedral Rolls at Norwich, under the
date 1403, speak of new clappers provided for "Lakenham"
and for "Stokton."   A somewhat later phrase in notices of
bells is illustrated by the name of the Bell Harry Tower,
at Canterbury, so called from a bell which swung within it.
A similar expression occurs in the churchwardens' accounts
at S. Margaret's, Lynn, for 1673, where " Bell Margaret "
and " Bell Thomas " are referred to.

The earliest ring of bells, of which we know anything, in
England, was hung in Crowland Abbey, and each of the
seven composing it had its name.   Pega, Bega, Tatwin,
Turketyl, Betelin, Bartholomew, and Guthlac, their several
titles, were chosen for various local reasons ; thus, S. Guthlac
was the hermit whose residence within the isle of Crowland
had first sanctified the spot ; S. Bartholomew was a saint for
whom S. Guthlac ever evinced a special devotion, and it was
on his festival that the hermit first entered upon the isle ;
S. Pega was the sister of S. Guthlac, and lived a life of prayer
and self-discipline in Northamptonshire ; and Tatwin was the
guide who brought the saint through the fens to the spot
which he chose for his hermitage ; while Turketyl was Abbot
of Crowland about 930, and, as remarked in a former
chapter, cast some of the earlier bells there.   The dedication
in the names of S. Bega, or S. Bees, and Betelin is not so

readily explained. A fire at the abbey, then only a wooden structure, destroyed these bells in the year 1091.

The above instance illustrates the usual principle on which the names of bells were selected. The tenor bell, the heaviest of the peal, bore the name of the patron saint of the church, or the religious foundation ; the dedications of chapels within the building, or of gilds connected with it, suggested the titles for the others. Some benefactor of the church is sometimes also commemorated in this way, as in the case of Abbot Turketyl quoted above, and in that of Bishop Grandison, of Exeter (1327-1369), the ancient bells of that cathedral being named respectively Walter, Bockerel, Chauncel, Germacyn, Jesus, Mary, Peter, Trinity, and Grandison. The cathedral is dedicated in honour of S. Peter.

At Oseney was a peal of bells, in the thirteenth century, whose names in two cases were apparently meant to be merely descriptive of their tones ; they were called Haute-clare, Doucement, Austyn, Marie, Gabriel, and John.

Two names which frequently occur are those of the Blessed Virgin and S. Gabriel the Archangel. The first will strike everyone as being quite natural ; it would be strange if, in selecting a number of saints' names to confer upon a similar number of bells, the first of saints was forgotten. With equal appropriateness the name of the Angel of the Annunciation was generally given to the bell which was rung at the Angelus. Occasionally bells, like some churches, had a double dedication ; an inscription on the fourth bell at Killingholm, in Lincolnshire, proclaims it "the bell of the Holy Trinity and of All Saints."

Five bells at Pisa, dated 1664, named from mysteries of the faith instead of after persons, are called L'Assompta,

De Crucefisso, La Giustizia, La Pasquarreccia, and Del Pozzo. With taste which is more than questionable, but is none the less characteristic of its age, the eight bells at Ashover, in Derbyshire, cast in 1714, bear the names of the Queen and of the leading military triumphs and heroes of her reign; they are Blenheim, Barcelona, Ramilies, Menin, Turin, Eugene, Marlborough, and Queen Anne. Equally secular, but under the circumstances more reasonable, is the name of the large bell of S. Nicholas Cathedral, Newcastle, which was given in 1833 by Major Anderson, and from that fact is popularly known as the " Major."

A ring of bells sometimes received one common name, possibly in addition to the special title of each member of it. The well-known story of King Henry VIII. wagering a peal of bells against £100 at a game of dice with Sir Miles Partridge, is told by Stow in connection with four bells, which bore the name of " Jesus' bells," and which hung in a cloister in the ward of Farrington Without. The same name was given to a ring of bells at old S. Paul's, from the fact that it was used especially in connection with the services in the Jesus' Chapel; Lincoln had its "Lady Bells," which hung in Our Lady's Tower. In these instances, and in several others which might be quoted, the churches in question possessed two rings of bells, which were distinguished by the use of these general names.

Most of these names are entirely forgotten in England now, or have, at any rate, dropped out of use. In some few cases a name is still employed, usually in a somewhat familiar way; which probably is not so much a sign of irreverence, as of the traditional affection of the citizens for the bell whose tones have been familiar to them daily from the time of their earliest recollections. Thus we have still "Great Tom" of Lincoln, and in the same city, "Old Kate," of St. Mark's Church; "Mighty Tom" of Oxford, and "Black Tom of Sothill," at Dewsbury. Similarly the tenor at S. Nicholas, Aberdeen, was familiarly called "Old Lawrie," from its dedication in the name of S. Lawrence. The remembrance of this is still kept alive by a bell at Cults, in Kincardineshire, which was cast by Blaikie & Sons, Aberdeen, from a piece of the old bell, in 1883; it is inscribed, "I am a chip of Old Lawrie."

One of the most famous of Continental bells is Carolus, at Antwerp Cathedral, called after its donor, Charles V.; the good folk of that city hold the bell in such estimation that it is only sounded two or three times a year. The ancient alarm bell, or tocsin, of Antwerp, cast so long ago as 1316, bears the suggestive name of Horrida. In the fifteenth century the great bell of Paris was named Jacqueline, and that at Rouen, in the sixteenth, was Amboise, or more properly George d'Amboise, so called after its maker, who died of joy, tradition says, on first hearing its tone. The famous Russian bells are distinguished by titles suggestive of their size; the broken monster at Moscow being called the Tsar Kolokol, or King of Bells, and its almost equally gigantic neighbour, Bolshoi, or the Big.

The name of a bell was generally impressed upon it formerly. Sometimes the name only, or the name coupled with some title of the saint referred to, occurs; as in three bells dedicated to the Blessed Virgin at Brattleby, Lincolnshire, and at Farrington Gurney, and Holcombe, Somersetshire, which are inscribed respectively, "Maria," "Virgo Maria" and "Stella Maria Maris." A somewhat fuller form is a brief declaration, such as that on a bell at South Somercotes, Lincolnshire, "Vocor Maria;" or one at Northborough, Northamptonshire, "Ista Campana Facta est in Honore Sta. Andree." Of this kind was the legend on Mighty Tom of Oxford, before its recasting in 1612 :—

"IN THOMAE LAUDE RESONO BIM BOM SINE FRAUDE,"

which one may perhaps venture to translate—

"For Thomas' sake,
I cry Bim Bom, and no mistake."

A very similar inscription, though hardly so quaint, is on a bell of the same dedication at Marston S. Lawrence, Northamptonshire :—

"PRO THOME LAUDE RESONABO MODO SINE FRAUDE."

At Market Stainton, Lincolnshire, is a bell dedicated in the name of S. Mary, which simply has the initial M repeated seven times. The tenor bell at Fawsley, Northampton-shire, named after S. John Baptist, has the apt quotation :—

"JOHANNES EST NOMEN EJUS."

Brief forms of invocation are also frequently found. On bells dedicated to the Blessed Virgin, the "Ave Maria," or some part of it, is common. At Willington, in Bedford-shire, is a bell called after S. Christopher, with the inscription :—

"O MARTIR XROFORE PRO NOBIS SEMPER ORATE."

Many other instances might be given of the use of the formula, "ora pro nobis," or its equivalent.

The treatment of the names of bells would be incomplete were there no mention of the ceremony by which from very ancient times the name of each has been conferred upon it, and which has for that reason often been styled the baptism of the bell.

As under the Jewish ritual everything dedicated to the service of God was solemnly set aside for its holy purpose, so in the Christian church, from the earliest ages, every piece of church furniture was specially blessed before being used. That such was the case with bells is evident from the fact that forms for the benediction of them are to be seen in the Gregorian Sacramentary (about 590). One of the Capitulars of Charlemagne, issued in 789, declares that " bells are not to be baptized ;" but this has been supposed to refer either to bells other than those of the church, which were perhaps blessed with a view to making superstitious use of them; or to some details in the ceremonial as then employed, which seemed to resemble an actual baptism rather than a solemn benediction. In 961, we find a record of the consecration of the great bell of the Lateran Church at Rome by Pope John XIII., and the conferring on it of the name John. This is said to have been at that time the largest bell cast in Christendom. Southey mentions the blessing in his own time of a peal of bells in France, by the Bishop of Chalons, and speaks of the sermon preached by that prelate on the occasion.

Chauncy, writing in 1700 of the parish church of Baldock, mentions the fact that its six bells (there are now eight) had been duly blessed with the full pre-Reformation ceremony, which he goes on to describe, as follows :—

"The bell itself was placed at the lower end of the church hanging upon two gudgeons covered with rich velvet of a violet colour. . . . The pillars and walls of the church were curiously adorned with sheets of silk and pictures; an altar was erected near the bell very neatly set forth; a white satin robe was laid upon it, in order to cover the bell so soon as it was baptized; and a great fair garland of choice flowers stood by it to be placed on it. There was also a Roman ritual, a censer, and a vessel of holy water. . . ." The bishop "sang the first psalm, which was continued by the music, and when all the psalms were ended, he blessed the holy water, that it might afterwards sanctify the bell. This benediction was very long, but when it was finished the bishop and priests dipped sponges in it, with which they rubbed the bell within and without, from the crown to the skirts thereof, repeating in the meanwhile divers prayers full of heavenly blessings, to purify, sanctify, and consecrate the bell . . . The bell being thus washed, they dried it with clean napkins, and the bishop taking the vial of holy oil, he anointed the cross of metal fixed on the crown of the bell, in order to make the devil flee at the sound of it . . . Then he made seven other crosses with the oil on the outside, and four more on the inside of the bell."

The next portion of the ceremony is one over which writers on bells have more than once endeavoured to make merry, namely, the questioning of the "sponsers" for the bell; but it is obvious that those who thus ridicule the custom have not informed themselves of the nature of the interrogatories, which our author shows to be of an exceedingly practical kind. He continues as follows: "he (the bishop) then proceeded and asked whether the founder was paid and satisfied for the metal and workmanship of the bell? They answered, Yes. Then he demanded whether they believed all that the Catholic, Apostolic, Roman Church believes concerning the holiness and virtues of bells. The answer was, Yes. Lastly, he demanded of them what name they desired should be put upon the bell." Were the ceremony of dedicating a bell intended actually to copy the sacrament of Holy Baptism, it is at this point that the parallel would be most obvious, but the details as set forth in the account which we are following are far otherwise. The name having been communicated to the bishop, we are told, "then the bishop took two great silk ribbons, which had been fastened to the gudgeons, and gave each of them one in their hands, and pronounced, with a loud intelligible voice, the words of consecration . . . ' Let this sign be consecrated and sanctified in the name of the Father, Son, and Holy Ghost. Amen!' Then turning himself to the people he said, 'The name of this bell is Mary.' After that he took the censer and censed it round about on the outside, then put the censer under the bell, full of sacred fumes, repeating all the time prayers and invocations." During the ceremony many psalms were sung, and finally a Gospel was read, the passage appointed being the story of SS. Mary and Martha of Bethany (S. Luke x. 38), wherein we are reminded that the voice of Christ calls us at times to forsake earthly cares in order to sit at His feet and learn of higher things.

Such is the ceremony observed two hundred years ago, and in its leading features still used in the Roman Catholic Church. It is a solemn and stately act of benediction, which could hardly fail to impress anyone who realized the intimate part which the bells must hereafter take in the joys and sorrows, the work and worship, the life and death, of those who hear them.   Of course there are many to whom the details of the rite, the use of consecrated oil and water and incense, is offensive ; but even these must admit that there is no such attempt here to parody the sacrament of regeneration as is used, generally without protest, in the naming of a new-built ship.

A simpler ceremonial obtains in the English Church, and one which probably varies considerably in different dioceses. The following brief account of the dedication of the new bells of S. Paul's Cathedral in November, 1878, will sufficiently indicate its general character.

At the conclusion of Evensong a procession was formed, consisting of the choir, the cathedral clergy, and the bishop, which made its way by means of the Geometrical Staircase into the ringing chamber.   Here several psalms were sung, commencing with *De profundis* and concluding with *Laudate Dominum* (Ps. cl.), after which followed a number of versicles and responses.   The bishop then said several special collects ; the first prayed that the bells might be "blessed to the spiritual well-being" of the people ; the next, recalling the silver trumpets made by divine command for summoning the assemblies of the Israelites, asked that those who heard the bells might "joyfully obey the call to meet together in God's Holy Church ;" other collects were supplications on behalf of those who might hear, but through sickness or other cause be unable to obey, this call, and for the ringers that they might be "filled with reverence and godly fear."   After the singing of an appropriate hymn, the collect for S. Paul's Day was said, and the blessing given by the bishop, who, after a short pause, gave the word to the ringers to sound the bells. The ringing of a short peal completed the simple, but impressive ceremony.

CHAPTER IV.

The Decoration of Bells.

SEVERAL allusions have already been made incidentally
to the marks and inscriptions found decorating the
exterior of most bells; the subject is, however, of sufficient
interest to call for a chapter to itself.

In decoration, properly so called, ancient bells were as a
rule much richer than modern ones, at any rate in England.
It is no uncommon thing to find bands of gracefully designed
moulding running round the shoulder, waist, or sound-bow
of a bell. Sometimes they consist of conventional foliage
or rows of fleur-de-lys; grotesques, or figures borrowed from
classical mythology, meet us in other cases; while yet others
have simple scrolls. In many instances the founder had his
favourite and characteristic form of moulding, by which his
bells could be identified. At Kinneff, in Kincardineshire,
is a bell by Peter Ostens, of Rotterdam, dated 1679; it has
a moulded band above and below the inscription, the first
being a series of Cupids or cherubs with bells, seated amid
the convolutions of a scroll, and the second a band of ivy, or
other leaves of a similar character. A bell by the same
maker was cast in 1664, for Banchory Ternan, in the same
county; in this case the lower moulding is again seen, but
the upper one is simpler and narrower, consisting only of
foliage. These two again are met with on a bell at Skene,
in Aberdeenshire; but in this case they are divided by a

narrow plain moulding only, the inscription being above them both, and a line of fleur-de-lys forming a new upper band.

Oldfield, who was casting bells in the seventeenth century, used a simple but elegant border of foliage; and Purdue, of Bristol, employed one that was somewhat similar, but fuller, suggesting a conventional vine with bunches of grapes. One of the most curious forms of ornament found on bells is on the fourth bell at S. Mary's, Oxford. This was cast by Newcombe, of Leicester, in 1612, and has two lines of music around it, the ancient square-headed notes being used. At the commencement of the melody are the words, "Keepe tyme in anye case," and at its end, "Then let us singe it againe."

Closely related to these ornamental borders is the use of characteristic initial crosses and stops. As a rule each inscription on a bell begins with the sacred sign, and some kind of ornament is inserted after every word. Some of these crosses are very beautiful. Thomas Newcombe, who was named above, used an elaborate cross, entwined with foliage. The earlier and more splendid members of that family of eleven remarkable Lincolnshire bells, to which reference was made in the last chapter, bear a very fine initial cross; on the later ones we find a smaller and simpler example. John of York used a cross that is noteworthy for its dignity, rather than its elaboration. The curious cross known as the fylfot is found on a good many bells, as, for instance, within the initial G of the word "Gloria," on a bell at Bonsall, in Derbyshire, and in connection with the initials of R. Heathcote, a bell-founder.

The ornamental stops are full of variety. These some-

BELLFOUNDERS' MARKS.

times take the form of small crosses, sometimes of fleur-de-lys; and not seldom small sections of the ornamental band are used. On the Kinneff bell, above spoken of, a couchant ox and several heraldic roses are employed as stops. These last are characteristic marks of the Dutch maker of that bell, and are found on others of his works in Scotland. Floral designs are of frequent occurrence, as on the bells of John of York.

It has been already remarked that the names of the makers are not often to be seen upon ancient bells in many cases, however, the stamp, or trade mark, of the founder was placed upon them. This often consists of a shield or a circle, charged with some device and the owner's initials. Heathcote's mark, a shield with straight sides bearing the letters R.H. above a fylfot, has already been referred to. The same initials are also found, as at Baslow, in Derbyshire, surmounted by a royal crown. John Draper, who cast bells at Thetford, Norfolk, from 1601 to 1646, used a die in shape like an inverted shield, on which was a bell between the letters J.D. Ellis Knight, of Reading, used a hand holding a halbert between three bells, and the initials E.K. Occasionally the full name of the founder appears in his mark. A copy of the seal of Sandre, of Gloucester, was found in the Thames it is a vesica with the name round the edge, and in the centre a small bell, and a vessel something like a modern coffee-pot. The first bell at Cold Ashby, one of the oldest dated bells in England, as we have seen, has a circular stamp, in the middle of which is a bell between two fleur-de-lys, while around it runs the name of William of Flint. Robert Merston also put his full name on his stamp, around the figure of an

5

embattled castle surmounted by a crescent; an emblem which suggests Crusading associations. The stamp of William Founder, as seen on the seventh bell of Magdalen College, Oxford, and elsewhere, is a circle within which his name circumscribes the figures of a couple of birds perched upon a branch. Thomas Bartlet, whose mark is on the first bell of S. Nicholas, Rochester, used three bells surmounted by a crown, his name surrounding the whole.

Sometimes, on the contrary, neither name nor initials appear. Thus William and Robert Corr used merely a shield charged with a chevron between three bells. Others marked their work with quaintly conceived monograms, or merely scratched upon it a simple private mark. In not a few instances the owners of the initials found on bell-marks are not now known.

Other ornamental stamps are also occasionally found on bells. The effigy, as well as the name, of the saint, after whom the bell is called, is sometimes placed upon it. This is more frequently the case with examples in use abroad, than with those now existing in England, yet we are not without instances of the custom. On the second bell of S. Andrew's Church, Welham, Leicestershire, is a boldly conceived figure of the patron saint bound upon a cross of the type traditionally assigned to him. At Stanion, North-amptonshire, Thurcaston, Leicestershire, and elsewhere the effigies of the Blessed Virgin and the Holy Child are found; and at Bapchild, Kent, the bells bear the figures of our Blessed Lord and S. John Baptist. Angels are seen in several instances, probably on bells originally intended for ringing the Angelus, though dedications to Archangels other than S. Gabriel are not uncommon; there is a S. Michael's

bell at Cossington, Leicestershire, and another at Taddington, Derbyshire, and a S. Raphael's bell at Wymington,
Bedfordshire. The apocalyptic symbols for the four
Evangelists appear on a bell at Impington, Cambridgeshire.
The stop in the inscription of a bell at Shipton, Hampshire,
which is dedicated in the name of S. John, consists of a
full-faced bust, intended probably for that of our Lord,
round which are the three traditional names of the Magi,
Balthasar, Caspar, and Melchior. On the waist of the sixth
bell at S. Martin's, Salisbury (dated 1628), is the figure of a
bishop, mitred, holding in the left hand his crozier, while
the right is raised in the act of blessing. This is probably
intended for the patron saint of the church. In S. Magnus
Cathedral, Orkney, are three bells, each of which has on a
medallion a figure bearing a sword, with beneath it the name
"Sanctus Magnus."

Another order of marks found on old bells consists of
Royal Heads. These are assigned to a few royal personages
only, all of whom lived between the end of the thirteenth
century, and the early years of the fifteenth. The following
are supposed to be represented in various instances,
Edward I. and his consort Queen Eleanor, Edward III. and
his Queen Philippa, Henry VI., Margaret of Anjou, and
their unfortunate son, Prince Edward. Loyal emblems
are more frequently seen on bells. In many cases in all
parts of the country are the royal arms, as used in England
from the time of Henry IV. to that of Elizabeth, or more
strictly from about 1405 to 1603. This was quarterly
modern France (three fleur-de-lys) and England (three lions
passant gardant). The shield is sometimes, but not always,
crowned. The four bells of S. Botolph's, Cambridge, have

this stamp.   The tenor bell at Ormskirk has, as stops, the
royal badges of the rose, the portcullis, and the fleur-de-lys,
alternately.   North Newton, Wiltshire, has a bell dated
1606, and Steeple Ashton, in the same county, one of 1607,
each of which has the rose and crown, and the initials J. R.
(Jacobus Rex).

The shields of the donors of bells, of the corporate body
in whose church they hang, or of the great landed proprietor
on whose estate the church is situated, are also sometimes
employed as decorations.   At Headington, Oxfordshire, the
fourth bell (dated 1624) bears the name and arms of Thomas
Whorwood, Esq., lord of the manor, by whom probably it
was given.   The tenor bell at Heytesbury, Wiltshire, has
two shields, that of the family of Knollys, and that (probably)
of Fowells.   The bells at Orkney Cathedral, in addition to the
figure of the patron saint, have the arms of Bishop Maxwell,
who ruled that ancient See from 1525 to 1541.   An inscription informs us that they were "made by Master Robbert
Maxvell, Bis-chop of Orkney, the yeer of God MDXXVIII,
the year of the reign of King James the V."   A bell at S.
Ternan's, Arbuthnott, Kincardineshire, has the arms of the
Arbuthnott family.   The present bell was recast in 1890,
but the decoration and inscriptions of an ancient predecessor
were reproduced upon it.   "Great Paul" of London, has
the arms of the chapter of S. Paul's Cathedral.

Probably the most popularly interesting form of bell-
decoration is supplied by the inscriptions, the number and
variety of which are almost endless.   The earliest of these
were declarations of the name in which the bell was
dedicated, and what a wealth of ingenuity is displayed in
varying this is well illustrated by a single set of such

inscriptions, collected in a recent book on the subject.* In a list there given of inscriptions on bells named in honour of the Blessed Virgin, we have no less than seventy different forms, all found in England, though the catalogue makes no pretension to be exhaustive. Amongst the simplest is the seven-fold repetition of the initial M, on the first bell at Market Stainton, Lincolnshire, and cases, such as were quoted in the last chapter, where the name " Maria," or the brief invocation " Ave Maria," forms the whole of the legend. One of the longest formulae is at Conington, Cambridge-shire ; " Assumpta : est : Maria : in : Celvm : Gavdent : Angeli : Lavdantes : Benedicvnt : Dominum." A complete litany of the Virgin could be compiled from these old bells. She is hailed as " Virgo virginum " (Somerleyton, Norfolk) ; " Mater Dei " (Milton Clevedon, Somerset) ; " Celi Regina " (Weasenham S. Peter, Norfolk); " Concipiens Christum Virgo " (Sedbergh, Yorkshire) ; " Virgo Pia " (Kempsey, Gloucester); " Stella Maria Maris " (Billesdon, Leicester); " Virgo Coronata " (Theddlethorpe S. Helen, Lincolnshire); and under yet other titles. Naturally such a profusion of titles is not found in the case of other saints. The usual form is either the simple name, as " Sancta Catherina " (Bristol Cathedral), and " Sc'e Michael " (Stowe, Lincoln-shire) ; or a mere declaratory phrase, as " Campana Sancti Johannis Baptiste " (Priddy, Somerset), and " Hujus campanae nomen est Jesu speciale " (Swyncombe, near Henley) ; or again, that briefest of invocations involved in a vocative only, as " O Sancta Ihoannes " (Downton, Wilt-shire), and " O Sancta Andrea " (Colne, Wiltshire); or, finally

* North's " English Bells and Bell Lore," edited by Rev. Wm. Beresford, already referred to.

and most commonly, the "ora pro nobis." Connected with
this invocation we meet the names of an immense number
of saints ; as for instance, S. Anne (S. Edward's, Cambridge),
S. Andrew, and S. Margaret (S. Botolph's, Cambridge), S.
Gabriel (Upminster, Essex), S. Peter (Aveley, Essex), S.
George (Sudeley Castle, Gloucester), S. Nicholas (Shipton,
Hampshire), S. Lawrence, (Week, Hampshire), S. Oswald
(Luddington, Lincolnshire), S. John (Aston Rowant,
Oxfordshire), S. Dunstan (Bury, Sussex), S. Thomas
(Norton Bavant, Wiltshire), S. Michael (Holt, Wiltshire),
S. Osmund (Great Cheverell, Wiltshire), S. Luke (Wink-
field, Wiltshire) ; and many more, for the catalogue might
be almost indefinitely extended. Next to the Blessed
Virgin, the favourite saints in England, in the dedication of
bells, seem to have been S. Peter, S. Margaret, and S.
Catherine.

It may be interesting briefly to note the names of some
other saints found in English bell inscriptions. Among
worthies whose works are recorded in the New Testament,
we have, in addition to those above given, Saints Matthew,
Thaddeus, Paul, Clement, Cornelius, and the Holy
Innocents. Of English saints, again excluding those
already named, we find Saints Cuthbert, Edward, Edmund,
Petroc, Richard, Wilfred, and Etheldreda. Others are
Saints Agatha, Ambrose, Anthony, Appolonia, Barbara,
Benedict, Christopher, Denis, Faith, Giles, Gregory, Helen,
Leo, Nicholas, Vincent, Augustine, and All Saints.

Many bells have inscriptions proving their dedication in
the Holy Name. At several places in Devonshire are
found the words "Est Michi Collatum, I.H.S. istud Nomen
Amatum ;" such are Sidmouth, Teignmouth, Churston

Ferrers, Clyst S. George, and Whetstone. At Leighton
Bromswold, Huntingdonshire, and at Dunton and Froles-
worth, in Leicestershire, is the prayer, "I.H.S. Nazarenus
Rex Judaeorum Fili Dei Miserere Mei." Frequently the
superscription of the Cross is alone used, as on the Bishop's
Bell of Salisbury Cathedral, where it stands in full, "Jesus
Nazarenus Rex Iudeorum." Invocations of the Holy
Spirit are not so common, but there are not wanting
instances. "Great Tom," of Lincoln, recast in 1835, has an
inscription beginning "Spiritus Sanctus a Patre et Filio
Procedens Suaviter Sonans ad Salutem." Dedicatory
inscriptions to the Holy Trinity are found in many places.
The fifth bell of a former peal at Bakewell, Derbyshire, was
inscribed, "Trinitate sacra fiat haec campana beata;" and
the same occurs on the tenth at Christ Church, Oxford
(dated 1589). At Ogbourne S. George, Wiltshire, is a bell
with the legend, "Trinitatem adoremus."

The inscriptions which take the form of invocations are
sometimes petitions of a more definite character than any
given above. The safety of the bell itself is occasionally a
matter of solicitude. "Augustine tuam Campanam protege
sanam," is the prayer of the fifth bell at Trent, Somersetshire; "Serva Campanam Sancta Maria Sanam," that of
one at Dyrham, Gloucestershire; while the second at
Winthorpe, Lincolnshire, has "Antonius Monet vt Campana
Bene Sonet," which, though scarcely a prayer, may fairly be
classed with the former ones. To the same effect, but in
more general terms, is the petition of the two bells at
Oxford and at Bakewell, quoted in the last paragraph.

Supplication is sometimes offered through the inscriptions
for the donors of the bells. A rather full form of this meets

us at Albourne, Wiltshire, the eighth bell bearing the words,
"Intonat: de. celis: vox: campana: Michaelis: Deus:
propicius: esto; a'i'abus (animabus): Ricardi: Godard:
quondam: de: Uphan. Elizabeth: et: Elizabeth: uxorum:
eius: ac: a'i'abus: o'i'm (omnorum): liberorum: et:
parentum: suorum qui: hanc: campanam: fieri: fecerunt:
anno: Dni: MCCCCCXVI." At Bolton-in-Craven, Yorkshire,
are two bells inscribed, the first, "Sc'e Ioh'is ora pro a'i'abus
Ioh'is Pudsey Militis et Marie consorte sue" (Sancte
Johannis ora pro animabus Johannis Pudsey militis, et
Mariae, consortae suae): and the second, "S'ce Paule ora
pro a'i'abus Henrici Pudsey et Margarete consorte sue."

Again the bells sometimes pray for those who hear their
voices, as at Grittleton, Wiltshire, where the fifth bell is
inscribed, "Protege pura via quos convoco virgo Maria."

The inscriptions on old bells are usually in Latin. One
or two in Dutch have already been quoted; and one with a
legend in Norman French hangs in Bitterley Church,
Shropshire; it offers a prayer for the soul of Alice Turye.
A few only of our ancient examples have English words.
Two with inscriptions of the kind that we have been considering are at Alderford, Norfolk, and Gunby S. Nicholas,
Lincolnshire, respectively. The former bears the words, "I
am mad in name of Sen Ion Baptist"; and the latter, "In
ye nam of ye Trynyte Nicholas Bel men cal me."

Towards the end of the sixteenth century English inscriptions become more common, though Latin is by no means
abandoned, and their sentiments are of a more general
character, and take the form of admonitions rather than
of prayers.

We find a bell at Winterbourne Dantsey, in Wiltshire,

inscribed " God be our guyd. I. W 1583." The initials
probably stand for John Wallis, a founder at Salisbury. The
same words occur also in connection with the date 1600,
and the initials R. B. (perhaps Richard Bowler), at Shipton,
Hampshire.   Other examples that may be quoted are
" Praise God.   1595," at Fotheringhay, Northamptonshire ;
"Geve God the glory," found, with the date 1600, at
Kimpton, Hampshire, and, with the date 1606, at S. John's,
Winchester: " Praysed be thy name O Lord, 1580, at S.
Peter the Less, Chichester ; "Cum, cum and Prey Anno
Domini 1599," at Bowden Magna, Leicestershire ;   and
"Jhesus be our speed 1589," at Wakerley, Northamptonshire.
Of Latin inscriptions of the time, Thornton Curtis, Lincoln-
shire, gives us a good instance, " O Deus absque pare fac
nos Tibi dulce Sonare, 1592."

At this period names of makers and donors, and the dates
of making, are of common occurrence ; and often the
religious aspiration disappears entirely, to make way for a
bald statement concerning the bell itself.   The second bell
at S. Benet's, Cambridge, has simply the figures " 1588 " ;
and scarcely less terse is the announcement on a bell at
Benniworth, Lincolnshire, " Anno Domini 1577." S. Peter's
bell, at Cambridge, tells us a little more in the sentence,
" Ricardus Bowler me fecit, 1602 ", which S. Sepulchre's,
in the same town, matches with " Robard Gurney made me,
1663." An earlier instance is supplied by Findon, Sussex,
where, however, at any rate, the sacred monogram reminds
one that the bell is still a part of the furniture of the church ;
its first bell has the words, "I Col Belfunder mad me,
1576, I. H S."

The commemoration of benefactors on the bells of this

and subsequent centuries is often very curious. The reverend and humble spirit in which the faithful of old time gave their offerings to God's Church is well illustrated by an old bell at Botolphs, Sussex, whose legend runs, "Of your charitie prai for the soulles of John Slutter, John Hunt, and William Slutter." An inoffensive formula is the one which merely records without comment the donor's name. At Dalby-on-the-Wolds, Leicestershire, is a case in point, where the inscription on the third bell reads "Andrevv Nouel, Esquier Ano. D. 1584." A bell, about contemporaneous with the last named, and hanging in the chapel of Sudeley Castle, has, in addition to an invocation of S. George, the statement, "The Ladie Doratie Chandos, Widdowe, made this." At Stapleton, and at Westerleigh, are bells inscribed respectively, "The gift of John Bubb. A. Rudhall, 1694," and "The gift of John Astry, Esq., 1702."

Several bells are not, however, content to honour their donors in this modest fashion, but enter into vulgar details concerning the exact amount of the monetary offering made. In Hampshire, are two instances of this. At Bentley the first bell announces that—

> "John Eyer gave twenty pound
> To meck mee a losty sound. 1703."

Binstead was not so fortunate ; it can only record that—

> "Doctor Nicholas gave five pound
> To help cast this peal tuneable and sound."

The tenth bell at Bath Abbey thus declares its origin,—

> "All you of Bathe that hear me sound
> Thank Lady Hopton's hundred pound."

There are cases where no one donor could be lauded in this way, yet the numerous helpers are not forgotten. The treble of a peal cast for Milton Lislebourne, Wiltshire, by Robert Wells, of Aldbourne, in 1789, has this inscription—

> " My chearfull note aloft shall raise,
> To sound my benefactors praise."

Bugbrooke, Northamptonshire, varies this—

> " Kind benefactors unto me
> My note shall sound your piety."

And yet another version is seen at Buxted—

> " At proper times my voice I'll raise,
> And sound to my subscribers' praise."

The inscription on a bell at S. Giles's Northampton, sounds rather like an after-dinner toast, . " Long life and prosperity to our worthy subscribers." If these excellent benefactors must needs be alluded to, the manner displayed by a bell at Leominster is in far better taste—

> " Kind heaven increase their bounteous store,
> And bless their souls for evermore."

Dollington, too, while mentioning the source whence the needful funds were drawn, puts the subscribers into their right place in its declaration---

> " I, by subscription that was raised,
> Re-casted was to celebrate God's praise."

Calne, on the other hand, while depriving the subscribers of their praise, gives it not to God, but to him who collected their donations,—

> " Robert Forman collected the money for castinge this bell
> Of well-disposed people as I doe you tell."

Many of these doggerel rhymes commemorate the makers of the bells. One at Eydon, Northamptonshire, on a bell dated 1603, informs us—

> " Be yt knowne to all that doth me see
> That Newcombe of Leicester made me."

Thomas Hedderley, a relative probably of Daniel Hedderley, who was casting bells at Bawtry about 1720, is mentioned on a bell of 1752, at Westborough, Lincolnshire, in the words—

"Tho. Hedderley made us all,
Good luck attend us all."

A founder named Henry Pleasant, who wrought early in the eighteenth century, is punningly alluded to in a bell inscription at Towcester—

"When four this steeple long did hold
They were the emblems of a scold,
No music ;
But we shall see
What Pleasant music six will be."

On one of Rudhall's bells the founder is not happy in merely praising himself, he takes the opportunity of disparaging a predecessor in the art at the same time ; this is at Badgworth, in Gloucestershire, where a bell is inscribed :—

"Badgworth ringers they were mad
Because Rigbie made me bad ;
But Abel Rudhall you may see
Hath made me better than Rigbie."

The church bells, thus taught to praise their subscribers and their founders, rather than God, His angels and His saints, only follow the natural course of earthly depravity in praising themselves. The treble bell is found to be specially self-assertive. At All Saints', Northampton, it declares

"I mean it to be understood
That though I'm little yet I'm good.

A bell at Coventry, dated 1774, has this inscription—

"Though I am but light and small
I will be heard above you all."

Varieties of this couplet are found at South Witham, Lincolnshire, and at Broadchalk, Wiltshire.

"When we doe ring I sweetly sing,"

is the legend on a bell of 1723 at Brington, Northamptonshire. The second bell at Broadchalk, not to be silenced
by the self-satisfied motto of the treble, avows

> " I in this place am second bell,
> Ile shurly doe my parte as well."

At several places, among others at Grantham (on a bell of
1775), and at Knaresborough (on one of 1777), we find
the words—

> " If you have a judicious ear
> You'll own my voice is sweet and clear."

The usual Latin formula used for a bell motto of this
boastful kind is

> " Me melior vere non est campana sub ere."
> Better than I, there is no bell beneath the sky.

This is on a bell at Portlemouth, Devonshire, at Vale
Church, Guernsey, and at East Dean, near Eastbourne. At
another Guernsey church, namely, S. Pierre du Bois it
appears as

> " Me melior vere non est campana q'm me."

Not often do the bells depreciate their own importance, yet
one or two instances exist. At Bakewell is a bell dated
1798 which bears the moral dictum,—

> " Mankind, like us, too oft are found
> Possessed of nought but empty sound ; "

and this appears, with slight variation, at Kirton-in-Holland,
Lincolnshire.

Another set of inscriptions came in apparently with the
introduction of change ringing, and alludes to the order of
the bells in the peal. The ring of six bells at S. Mary's,
Ticehurst, furnishes a good illustration of this ; the legends
running as follows :—

FIRST, or TREBLE BELL.	" I am she that leads the van, Then follow me now if you can."
SECOND BELL.	" Then I speak next, I can you tell, So give me rope and ring me well."
THIRD BELL.	" Now I am third, as I suppose, Mark well now time and fourth close."
FOURTH BELL.	" As I am fourth, I will explain, If you'll keep time you'll credit gain."
FIFTH BELL.	" Now I am fifth, as I suppose, Then ring me well, and tenor close."
SIXTH, or TENOR BELL	" This is to show for ages yet to come, That by subscription we were cast and hung, And Edward Lulham is his name, That was the actor of the same."

The church of S. Mary the Virgin, Thame, Oxfordshire, provides us with a briefer set—

> TREBLE.—" I as treble begin."
> 2.—" I as second ring."
> 3.—" I as third will ring."
> 4.—" I as fourth in my places."
> 5.—" I as fift will sound."
> TENOR.—" Richard Keene cast me, 1664."

Bakewell possesses a ring of eight bells, some of which have inscriptions of this nature ; those only are here quoted :—

TREBLE.—" When I begin our merry din
    This band I lead, from discord free,
  And for the fame of human name
    May every leader copy me."

  5.—" Through grandsires and triples with pleasure men range,
    Till death calls the Bob, and brings on the last change."

  7.—" Would men like me join and agree,
    They'd live in tuneful harmony."

  8.—" Possessed of deep and sonorous tone
    This belfry king sits on his throne :
  And when the merry bells go round,
    Adds to, and mellows every sound.

> So in a just and well-poised state
> Where all degrees possess just weight,
> One greater power, one greater tone,
> Is ceded to improve our own."

One wide-spread result of the introduction of change-ringing into England was the multiplication of the bells ; and in order to do this in many cases the three or four heavy bells of ancient make were melted down, and recast into a larger number of smaller ones. To this subject we shall have occasion to return hereafter ; it is mentioned here because not a few epigraphs on bells refer to it. At Laneast, Cornwall, a bell of 1742 tells us : " F. V. Goodall all we did contrive to cast three in five." At Bentley, Hampshire, we find :—

> " Thomas Eyer and John Winslade did contrive
> To cast from four bells this peal of five,"

and at Northfield, Worcester, again :—

> " Thomas Kettle and William Jarvis did contrive
> To make us six that was but five."

The number of bells in the peal was commemorated at S. Patrick's Cathedral, Dublin, where one of them, before the hanging of the new peal, was inscribed

> " Henry Paris made me with good sound
> To be fift in eight when all ringe round."

A very natural subject for bell-legends is the reason of their ringing, and to this many of them allude. Most of the ancient instances of this are included in the following Monkish rhyme :—

> " En ego campana, nunquam denuncio vana,
> Lando Deum verum, plebem voco, congrego clerum,
> Defunctos plango, vivos voco, fulmina frango,
> Vox mea, vox vitae, voco vos ad sacra venite.

Sanctos collaudo, tonitrua fugo, funera claudo,
Funera plango, fulgura frango, Sabbatha pango,
Excito lentos, dissipo ventos, pace cruentos."

The last two of these lines have been thus translated :—

> ' Men's death I tell
> By doleful knell."

> " Lightning and thunder
> I break asunder."

> " On Sabbath all
> To church I call."

> " The sleepy head
> I raise from bed."

> ' The winds so fierce
> I doe disperse."

> " Men's cruel rage
> I doe asswage."

Fragments of these lines, variously arranged, are found all over Europe. The Minster bell at Schaffhausen has the inscription—

> " Defunctos plango, vivos voco, fulmina frango,"

which we may translate

> " For the dead I moan make,
> The living I call, the lightning's power break."

At Geneva was formerly a bell inscribed with a variant of two of the above lines—

> " Laudo Deum verum, defunctos ploro, congrego clerum,
> Vox mea cunctorum fit terror Daemonorum."

> " The true God I adore, the clergy I summon, the dead I deplore ;
> My voice is a terror to spirits of error."

The tenor bell at Wilsford, Wiltshire, has

> " Sabbata pango, Funera plango."
> " Sabbath's coming I tell, and toll the death knell."

At Darley Dale, in Derbyshire, another fragment appears, namely,

"Sacra Clango, Gaudia Plango, Funera Plango."

The old "Mittags" of Strasbourg Cathedral bore the legend

"Vox ego sum vitae
Voco vos, orate, venite."
"The voice of Life am I,
I call, pray ye, draw nigh."

Many will remember, in this connection, the prologue of Longfellow's "Golden Legend." The scene is the summit of the tower of Strasbourg Cathedral, round which in storm and thunder wheels a host of evil spirits, vainly endeavouring to drag the great cross from its lofty seat; and the hoarse shouts of the demons mingle with the chant rising from the choir below, and with the voices of the pealing bells, which boom forth words taken from this antique series of belfry epigraphs; which run as follows, a rough translation being here added :—

Laudo Deum verum,	I laud the true God,
Plebem voco,	I summon the people,
Congrego clerum ;	The clergy I gather ;
Defunctos ploro,	The dead I deplore,
Pestem fugo,	The plague put to flight,
Festa decoro ;	The festivals honour ;
Funera plango,	For fun'rals I toll,
Fulgora frango,	The lightning I shatter,
Sabbata pango ;	And mark Sabbath's coming ;
Excito lentos,	The sleeping I rouse,
Dissipo ventos,	The hurricanes scatter,
Paco cruentos.	And tame evil passions.

The inscriptions upon several English bells seem to be intended as free translations, or imitations, of these Latin lines. The tenor bell at S. Peter's, Nottingham, for example, has this verse,—

"I toll the funeral knell,
I hail the festal day,

6

> The fleeting hour I tell,
> I summon all to pray."

The sixth bell at Colne, recast in 1848, is inscribed—

> " I call the living, mourn the dead,
> I tell when days and years are fled,
> For grief and joy, for prayer and praise,
> To heaven my tuneful voice I raise."

In other cases the employment of the bells to summon the people for certain specific services, or to mark some special occurrence, has suggested the motto for them to bear. Among these particular uses, to all of which full notice will be given hereafter, the passing bell, and that so nearly related to it, the funeral bell, are perhaps the most impressive, and consequently receive most frequent mention. The simple warning, "Remember death," is found on several Lincolnshire bells, as at Cleethorpes (1701), Candlesby (1704), Wadingham (1713), and Addlethorpe (1770); while Croft, in the same county, has one (dated 1716) equally brief and expressive, "Prepare to Die." Again, Fotherby (1608) Lincolnshire, and Whissendine (1609), in Rutland, have the quaint rhyme—

> " My roaring sound doth warning give
> That men cannot heare allwaies live."

An old bell at Bakewell had the words—

> " All men who hear my mournful sound
> Repent before you lye in ground."

An almost grotesque variant of this is found on some seventeenth century bells, among others on one of 1658, at Addington—

> " When you hear this mournful sound
> Prepare yourselves for underground."

The following lines are met with in a great many places in different counties :—

> " I to the church the living call
> And to the grave do summon all."

They are on the fifth bell at Foulden, Norfolk, and on the tenors at Bremhill, Heddington, Rowde, and Edington, Wiltshire, at Quedgeley, Gloucestershire, at Cotterstock and other places in Northamptonshire, and at numerous other churches. A more striking form of it is employed at Bentley, in Hampshire,—

> " Unto the Church I do you call,
> Death to the grave will summons all ;"

while at Chilton Foliot, Wiltshire, the following two lines are added :—

> " Attend the instruction which I give,
> That so you may for ever live."

The merry wedding bells have also their word to say. At Hogsthorpe, Lincolnshire, and elsewhere we meet with the following sententious couplet :—

> " When Female Virtue weds with manly worth
> We catch the rapture, and we spread it forth."

At S. Michael's, Coventry, and at Boston we have a fuller form—

> " In wedlock's bands all ye who join
> With hands your hearts unite,
> So shall our tuneful tongues combine
> To laud the nuptial rite."

An inscription at Bakewell emphasizes the extremes of joy and sorrow which the bells are called upon to mark :—

> " When men in Hymen's bands unite,
> Our merry peals produce delight ;

> But when death goes his dreary rounds,
> We send forth sad and solemn sounds."

The ordinary services of the church find frequent mention in general terms, such as

> " When I do call come serve God all,"

at Frome ; or the distinctly prosaic dictum of a bell at Thorp S. Peter, Lincolnshire, "When I call come to church." At Wainfleet S. Mary is the couplet :—

> " Come to God's house to praise his holy name,
> Those that forsake it 'tis a sin and a shame."

The sermon bell has also its appropriate legend :—

> " I ring to sermon with a lusty bome,
> That all may come, and none may stay at home."

This is found at Banbury, and at Kingsthorpe and other places in Northamptonshire.

Certain useful secular purposes for which the church bells are sometimes rung are alluded to in the following three or four quotations.

> " When backwards rung we tell of fire,
> Think how the world shall thus expire ; "

this is from a bell at S. Ives ; the Abbey Church at Sherborne has an allusion to the same use, in the form of a prayer to God and an exhortation to men,

> " Lord, quench this furious flame :
> Arise, run, help, put out the same."

The bells of Flanders in several instances have an inscription referring to their employment as alarums, the common formula being,

> " Mynem naem is Roelant,
> Als ich clippe dan is brandt,
> Als ich myde dan is storm in Vlienderland,"

which we may interpret,

'My name is Roland,
When I toll there is fire,
When I swing there is tempest in Flanders-land."

Longfellow evidently had this, or some similar bell-legend in his mind, when, in his poem on the "Belfry of Bruges," he fancies "the bell of Ghent" crying aloud,

" O'er lagoon and dike of sand,
' I am Roland, I am Roland ! there is victory in the land ! '"

Another secular use of the bells gave rise to the epigraph,

" I ring at six to let men know,
When too and from thair worke to goe ; "

which is on the fourth bell at S. John's, Coventry ; and to the terser form to be seen at S. Ives,

" Arise and go about your business."

There are still other classes of inscriptions which deserve notice. In many cases we find on the bells a record of the ecclesiastical rulers of the parish at the time of their casting. This usage is very obvious on bells of the seventeenth century, the churchwardens usually endeavouring thus to immortalize themselves, though the vicar's name is sometimes, and especially towards the end of the century, joined with theirs. At Cannings Bishops, Wiltshire, we find bells of 1602, one of which bears the name of the vicar, George Ferebe, and another that of one churchwarden, Thomas Sloper. In later times a perfect catalogue of names was sometimes placed upon the bell ; as on one cast in 1831 for Peterborough Cathedral, which bears the names of the Bishop (Dr. Marsh), the Dean (Dr. Turton), the Archdeacon of Northampton (Dr. Strong), and of six prebendaries ; and another cast in 1841 for S. Saviour's, Leeds, has the names of Dr. Hook, the vicar of Leeds, of four assistant priests, and of Thomas Mears, the founder.

The ringers of the bells are not entirely forgotten, although the inscription takes the form of a warning rather than a record of their "name and fame." At Uppingham, Rutland, and elsewhere, we find—

> " Ye ringers all who prize
> Your health and happiness
> Be sober merry wise
> And you'll the same possess."

Many bells have inscriptions expressive of the loyalty of the makers, or bearing reference to public events. A general sentiment, given in the words of holy Scripture (1 S. Peter, ii. 17), "Fear God, Honour the King," is found in many places, as on one of 1665 at Chilton, Berkshire, at Goxhill, Lincolnshire (1666), and at S. Peter's, Northampton (1734); and a doggerel rhyme founded on those words occurs at Knaresborough and several other places,

> " Our voices shall in concert ring :
> In honour both to God and King."

Church and state are linked together in the mottos in some cases, as at Ramsbury, Wiltshire, where a bell, of 1708, has, "Prosperity to the Church and Queen," and at Chippenham, where the treble bell (1734) has, " Let us ring for the Church and King. The sovereign and his people are remembered at Devizes, where a bell of 1677 bears the words, "Vivat Rex et floreat grex." The successive monarchs from the days of Elizabeth are most of them personally commemorated. At East Farndon, Northamptonshire, we meet with, "God bless our Queene Elizabeth 1587," and at Bugbrook, in the same county, "God save our Queene and her preasearve 1599." At Hemel Hempsted,

Hertfordshire, and at Wappenham, Northamptonshire, we find, " God save King James," with the dates 1604 and 1610 respectively.   Charles I. does not seem to be alluded to by name, but at Norton, near Daventry, is a bell dating from 1640, in his reign, inscribed, "God save the King," and others similarly marked hang in the steeples of various churches, and bear dates of that period.   At Banbury, the fourth bell, now recast, used to have the words, "Diu et feliciter vivat Carolus secundus Rex sic precor et opto 1664 " (Long and happily live King Charles II., so I pray and hope).   James II., who both was unpopular, and also reigned for little over three years, does not seem to be commemorated in this way, and the present writer knows of no allusion to the dual occupancy of the throne by William and Mary.   The words, "God save the King," are found however on bells of this latter reign, as at Hanley Castle, Worcestershire, on an example dated 1699.   Queen Anne is mentioned by name at Bromham, and Melksham, in Wiltshire, and at Bottesford, Lincolnshire, and is referred to by her title only at Magdalen College, Oxford.   The earlier Georges are alluded to only in the same way, by the inscription "God save the King;" a bell so marked of George II.'s time, dating from 1747, is at Kenton, Devonshire.   At Foulden, Norfolk, we find, "Long live King George the Third.   1802;" and at S. John Baptist's, Peterborough, the same words with the date 1808.   A similar prayer on behalf of George IV., and dated 1821, occurs at Poole, Dorsetshire. William IV. is another King who does not appear to have been immortalised by the bells, and our present sovereign is probably not mentioned by name, although on her behalf a modern bell at Piddington, Northamptonshire, offers the

petition, "God save our Queen and preserve our peace."
Four new bells at Cottingham show by their inscriptions
that they were added in 1897 in memory of the sexagenary
of the Queen. This event has also been commemorated at
Upottery, Devonshire, by the hanging of a new bell in the
church steeple ; it is inscribed :

> "To-day for sixty years we've been,
> The subjects of one gracious Queen,
> So as those days are ended now,
> With thanks to God this bell we vow—
> *June 22nd, 1897*."

It will be interesting to refer to some other public events
which obtain commemoration by means of these inscriptions. At Damerham, Wiltshire, the fifth bell announces,
" I was cast in the yeere of Plague, Warre, and Fire. 1666."
The long period of warfare which closed the last, and
opened the present century, has left its mark upon the bells
in many places. One at Kirton-in-Holland, Lincolnshire,
dated 1807, has the somewhat grandiloquent legend,

> " Should Battle rage, and sanguine foes contend
> We hail the Victor, when he's Britain's friend."

Another cast in the same year, and for the same place, prays,

> " May peace return to bless Britannia's shore
> And faction fall to raise her head no more."

The conclusion of the peace is celebrated at S. Giles's,
Northampton, in distinctly indifferent grammar :—

> " With joys of peace our infant voice proclaim
> With Holland, France, America, and Spain."

The illness and recovery of George III. are alluded to in
the epigraphs of two bells, dated 1789, at Eye, in Suffolk.
The seventh has the words, " O God continue thy mercies
to the King ;" and the tenor, " Let us rejoice our King's

restor'd." The first abdication of Napoleon Buonaparte, and the too enthusiastic joy of the ringers at Ashover, Derbyshire, are kept in mind by an inscription placed on a bell recast for that church, " This old bell rung the downfall of Buonaparte and broke, April, 1814." An earlier bell seems to record the finally undisputed settlement on the throne of William and Mary. It is at Stapleton, Gloucestershire, and bears the words, " Free from Rebellion. God save the King. 1694." Owmby Church, Lincolnshire, has a bell recalling the Gunpowder Plot, of November 5th, 1605.

Interesting facts in local history are occasionally recalled by the inscriptions on the bells. One at S. Peter's, at S. Albans, informs us that the tower was rebuilt in 1805 ; and another at Holyrood, Southampton, quaintly suggests the efforts required to raise the needful funds for its casting, by the words, " Long lookt for is come at last. 1742." The complete story of a parochial agitation on the question of the church bells is told by the peal at Northfield, Worcestershire, in these terms :—

TREBLE.   " Though once but five, we now are six,
    2.   And 'gainst our casting some did strive,
    3.   But when a day of meeting there was fixed,
    4.   Appeared nine 'gainst twenty-six."

The fifth and the tenor give the names of the churchwardens and the founders, Kettle and Jarvis.

Local patriotism finds expression in scores of instances. " Prosperity to this town," says a bell at Launceston, which has its parallel in " Prosperity to this parish," at S. Peter's, Northampton, at S. Lawrence's, Reading, and in other cases. A more explicit wish is " Prosperity to the town of Poole," found upon the sixth bell there; "Prosperity to New College," at that College in Oxford; and "Prosperity to this parish of S. Mary," at S. Mary's, Reading. A wider sympathy is shown in the expression of the hope of "Prosperity to the Church of England," as found at Launceston, and the corresponding prayer, "God prosper the Church of England," as at Cumnor, Berkshire, both of which are very common elsewhere; as also is the yet more general aspiration, "God save his Church," which occurs, to give one illustration out of many, at Normanton-on-Soar, Nottinghamshire.

A few inscriptions, not included under any of the above divisions, have points of interest which we may remark.

Scriptural quotations are not common on the oldest bells, the inscriptions on which were usually much more brief than is the case with modern ones. The Angelic Salutation is found, especially on Angelus bells, and the Holy Name is often expanded into the Superscription of the Cross. At Corby, Lincolnshire, we meet with a contracted Latin version of the words, "At the name of Jesus every knee shall bow, of things in heaven, and things in earth, and things under the earth." "Love horteth not," from Cranmer's rendering of Romans xiii. 10, occurs at Hannington, Northamptonshire; and S. Gabriel's declaration, "With God nothing shall be impossible" is paraphrased at Crofton, near Wakefield, in the words, "In God is al quod Gabriel." Towards the end of the seventeenth century these quotations become more frequent and more varied, among the most popular being the opening words of the several Canticles of the Church. "Gloria in excelsis," "Benedictus qui venit in nomine Domini," and "Magnificat anima mea Dominum ait

Maria," form the legends of the first three bells at S. Giles's,
Oxford, but these are all of modern date. Passages from the
Psalms, such as "Praise ye the Lord," and other expressions
of thanksgiving are very common in every county, both
Latin and English being freely employed. At Floore,
Northampton, we have "Cantate Domino cantum novum.
1679," and at Peterborough Cathedral, "Magnificate
Dominum mecum. 1709." "Dominus providebit. Anno
Domini 1665," is an inscription at Chichester Cathedral,
and "Laudate Domin.," at Hemel Hempsted, Hertfordshire,
On the other hand, "Glory be to God on high," at Marston-
on-Dove (1654), and "Sing ye merrily unto God," at
Coleby, in the same county, are but a few examples where
as many scores might easily be given. Some Scriptural
passages are very aptly chosen. "Holiness to the Lord,"
found at Orlingbury (1843), is an application to church
bells of a sacred motto, said by the prophet Zachariah
(XIV. 20) to be in the day which he foretells upon "the bells
of the horses." There is a manifest endeavour to plead a
quasi-authority from Scripture for the use of bells in the
inscription, "In timphanis laudate Dominum. 1669," found
at S. Edward's, Cambridge; and in a similar spirit the
ceremonial use of trumpets among the Jews is quoted as
having some analogy to the modern employment of bells,
in a line on a bell of 1586 at S. Alkmond's, Derby, "Ut
tuba sic resono ad templa venite pii," "I ring out like a
trumpet, come ye faithful to the temple." The diverse
occasions on which the bells are rung, are aptly recalled
by the words, adapted from those of S. Paul in the epistle
to the Romans (xii. 15), and found at Cannings Bishops,
"Gaudemus gaudentibus, Dolemus dolentibus." A passage

from the prophet Joel (ii. 15-16) sums up briefly the chief uses of church bells in the phrase, "Call a soleme assemblie, gather the people." Thus it appears at S. Martin's, Salisbury, with the date 1628. But perhaps the most striking application of a passage of Scripture to this purpose, is given us by Hemony, the Belgian bell-founder of the sixteenth century, upon some of whose bells is placed the motto, "Non sunt loquellæ neque sermones, audiuntur voces eorum," or as the Prayer Book version runs, "There is neither speech nor language, but their voices are heard." (Ps. xix. 3).

The record for length in inscriptions must surely be held by a Scottish example on the great bell of Glasgow Cathedral. It is as follows :—" In the year of grace 1583, Marcus Knox, a merchant of Glasgow, zealous for the interest of the Reformed Religion, caused me to be fabricated in Holland for the use of his fellow-citizens of Glasgow, and placed me with solemnity in the Tower of their Cathedral. My function was announced by the impress on my bosom : ' Me audito venias doctrinam sanctam ut discas,' and I was taught to proclaim the hours of unheeded time. 195 years had sounded these awful warnings when I was broken by the hands of inconsiderate and unskilful men. In the year 1790, I was cast into the furnace, refounded at London, and returned to my sacred vocation. Reader! Thou also shalt know a resurrection; may it be to eternal life. Thomas Mears fecit, London, 1790." In marked contrast to this is the series of short, pithy exhortations on the bells at Burbage, Wiltshire. The treble and the tenor are alike inscribed, "Hope well"; while the remaining three bear the words, "Love God," "Feare God," "Prayse God."

In some instances the motto seems to have been regarded as a necessary formality only, and consequently so long as something was inscribed on the bell, it did not matter what it might be. Only on such a supposition can one explain the fact that in several cases the letters of the alphabet serve the purpose of an epigraph. At Leighton Bromswold, Huntingdonshire, are bells dated 1641, with the alphabet from A to G; one at Hoby, Leicestershire, has the series as far as I; Bemerton, Wiltshire, and Elford, Staffordshire, also have from A to G; and a bell at Charwelton, Northamptonshire, has a number of meaningless letters only.

Many of these inscriptions exhibit much questionable taste, and sometimes an almost complete forgetfulness of the high and sacred purposes to which the bells are to be dedicated. One at Towcester is well nigh profane; it runs,

> " Pull on brave boys, I'm metal to the back,
> But will be hanged before I crack."

The date of the bell bearing this elegant effusion is 1725.

In style it will have been observed that these inscriptions are, when not portions of litanies or passages from Holy Scripture, usually Leonine verses in Latin, or couplets in English. As further illustrations of the first of these two classes, the following are given: from North Burlingham, Norfolk,

> " A tempestate protegas nos Petre beate,"

and again from the same county, at Aldburgh,

> " Dona repende pia rogo Magdalena Maria."

There are not wanting, however, instances of Latin verse of a more classical type. At Bletchley, Buckinghamshire, are eight bells cast by Rudhall in 1713, most of which have a Latin verse as a motto : for example, the fourth has

"Ad templum populus per me properare monetur,"

and the tenor,

"Me resonare jubent hominum mors conscio funus."

The English inscriptions occasionally expand into quatrains, or even longer stanzas ; not infrequently also one set of rhymes is divided among the whole ring. One example of this has already been given, taken from the bells of Northfield. Another instance occurs at All Saints', Oxford, and is as follows,

Treble.	" Think no cost to much
2.	That you bestow of all
3.	To bring to pass so good a thing
4.	That five bells may together ring."

The fifth bell has a Latin inscription ; the date on each is 1622.

It cannot fail to be a matter of wonder that the clergy permitted to appear such miserable doggerel as we find on church bells all over the country. The taste, or tastelessness, of the bell-founder, and the poetic skill of the parish clerk, or some other local rhyme-monger, were allowed to "run and have free course and be glorified." The only spot where the fearful poetic creations of the belfry can in any way be matched, is in the churchyard. Many of the epitaphs of the last century are at least equally horrible. Here are two more specimens of belfry doggerel, the latter one quite a modern one. At S. Benet's, Cambridge, we find a rhyme that has at least the merit of being daring :—

"John Draper made me in 1618, as plainly doth appeare,
This bell was broake and cast againe, wich tyme Churchwardens were,

Edward Dixon, for the one whoe stode close to his tacklin,
And he that was his partner then was Alexander Jacklyn."

The other example may be seen at Picton, in Devonshire, and runs thus :—

" Recast by John Taylor and Son,
Who the best prize for Church-bells won
At the Great Ex hi bi ti on
In London 1. 8. 5. and 1."

We doubt not that Messrs. Taylor would not dream of perpetrating such an abomination in the way of an inscription at the present time ; and it is at least satisfactory to know that their bells were better than their poetry.

At Little S. Mary's, Cambridge, we meet with a rare instance of an inscription of an argumentative character,—

" Non sono animabus mortuorum sed auribus viventium : "

The translation of this occurs at Hambleton :—

" I sound not for the Souls of the dead, but for the Ears
of the living."

Whether the bell-founders of old were dealing in the ecclesiastical Latin or in their mother tongue, they seem to have been equally uncertain in the matter of grammar and spelling. Numerous examples given above exhibit eccentricities in these respects ; one or two of special originality may be added.

At S. Martin's, Salisbury, we find,—

" Be mec and loly to heare the word of God. 1582."

At Upton Lovell, Wiltshire, is this original way of spelling Hallelujah :—

" Haialugeva Anno Domini, 1619."

At Clyst S. George, Devonshire, is the exhortation,

" Embrace trew museek."

Another matter in which founders were careless at times was the arrangement of the letters. We find, for instance, inscriptions entirely reversed, as at All Cannings, Wiltshire, where Anno Domini, 1626, appears as " 6261 : in : im : od : on : na." The name Sancta Helena is given on a bell at Dunsforth, Yorkshire, as " AN EL EHAT CNAS." A bell at Holton-le-Clay, Lincolnshire, has the letters mingled according to no rule, so that what was meant for Sancti Petri, appears as " SANC IRT EP IT." At Clapham, Bedfordshire, one word of the inscription is upside down, thus :—

" God save the yɔɹnyↃ "

In several places the bell-frame has its maker's name cut upon it, occasionally with the addition of those of the churchwardens. In one case, however, at least this also has its couplet. It is at Slapton, Northamptonshire, and is thus curiously expressed,

" Be-it-Kno-wen-un-to-all-th-at-see-th-is-same.
Th-at-Thomas-Cowper-of-Wood-end-made-this-frame—1634."

GREAT BELL AT MINGOON, BURMA.

CHAPTER V.

Some Noteworthy Bells.

THE popular estimate of bells seems to be based entirely on their weight and size ; and the most famous bells are consequently the largest. Without by any means conceding that this is a just, or even a reasonable, method of reckoning the relative importance of instruments of music, it will perhaps be useful to bow to public opinion so far as to begin this chapter by an account of such bells as are noteworthy by reason of their size.

It is a disputed point which country can truly claim the distinction of possessing the largest bell in the world. In Europe the record is unquestionably held by Russia ; but it is stated that China can produce yet more gigantic examples ; and it has recently been stated that the palm for actual supremacy must be given to Burmah. If this be indeed the case, it will no doubt gratify some people to feel that if the champion monster neither hang in an English belfry, nor is of English manufacture, it is nevertheless found in a British dependency.

It is at the huge padoga at Mingoon, that the bell, on whose behalf this claim is made, may be seen. It is in the open air, suspended by immense canons from several strong beams of wood, and its proportions more nearly resemble those usually adopted in the West, than those of the East, and especially in China. What its weight may be the

7

present writer knows not, and he therefore quotes with all due reserve the words of a recent traveller in Burmah, that this bell "is the largest in the world (not excepting the well-known Russian bell at Moscow), and can easily hold within it a picnic party of fifty people."*

The claim of Russia to rank at least second in the possession of big bells is apparently a sound one. The land of the Tsar is, in fact, beyond dispute the country of great bells ; for whereas single specimens notable for their size are to seen elsewhere, in Russia even small towns frequently possess bells surpassing in dimensions these locally famous examples. In a former chapter a description was given of the hauling of a bell into its place in the belfry of the Russian church of Votkinsk, which is a manufacturing town of no special mark ; the bell in this instance weighed nearly five tons, a weight exceeded in only four or five instances in England. The cities of Moscow and S. Petersburgh supply us, however, with examples compared with which all these are but toys. The Great Bell of Moscow, popularly called the Tsar Kolokol, or "King of Bells," but more correctly Ivan Kiliki or Big John, weighs nearly two hundred tons. This monster was cast in 1734, and its dimensions are as follows : the height is a little over nineteen feet, and the diameter twenty-two-and-a-half feet ; the thickness is twenty-three inches. The tongue is fourteen feet long, and six feet in circumference at the thickest part. Huge as it is, it was nevertheless suspended on a frame of immense beams near the spot where it now is, but a fire in 1737 destroyed these supports, and it fell, breaking from its side a fragment seven

* Dr. Chill, in "Travel," for October, 1896 ; p. 283.

feet high. Since then no attempt has been made to put
the bell to its proper use.   It lay just as it had fallen,
partially sunk in the earth, until 1837, when it was raised
once more to a perpendicular position, and was made the
dome of a small chapel, which was formed by excavating
beneath it.   The piece broken from its side and the tongue
lie near.   The bell is adorned with several effigies in relief.
On the one side is the Empress Anne in her coronation
robes, with above her the figure of our Lord between those
of S. Peter and S. Anne ; on the other is the Tsar Alexei
Michaelowitz, surmounted also by the Saviour between the
Blessed Virgin and S. John Baptist.   An inscription tells us
of a predecessor.   It informs us that this Tsar Kolokol was
made from the metal of a bell cast in 1654, rung for the first
time in 1658, and seriously damaged by fire in 1701.   We
learn also that this earlier bell weighed 288,000 pounds
(nearly 130 tons), but that the Empress Anne added to
this 72,000 pounds for the new bell.   This would make a
total of 360,000 pounds only, whereas Russian authorities
usually give the weight of this broken giant at 432,000
pounds.   The balance is largely, if not wholly, accounted
for by the fact that metal was brought from all directions
during the casting by the people, who were evidently stirred
by a great enthusiasm for the work, the nobles especially
vying with one another in the value of their gifts.

The " King of Bells " having been disabled by his fall,
a successor was, after an interval, cast to take his place ;
and this still hangs in the church of S. John at Moscow,
its weight being over ninety-six tons.   Another great bell in
the same city was the Bolshoi (Big), cast in 1710, at a weight
of slightly over fifty-five tons.   It was hung with thirty-two

smaller ones in the belfry of S. John's, and remained there till the great fire, which formed so dramatic an episode of the French invasion in 1812, destroyed the tower, and ruined the peal. In 1817 the Bolshoi was broken up, metal being added to raise the weight of a new bell to be cast from it to about sixty-four tons; and on the 7th March in that year this new bell was made by a Russian founder of the name of Bogdanof. It was not until February, 1819, that the bell was removed to the cathedral, a wooden sledge dragged by a vast multitude of people being the means of transport. Part of the cathedral wall was taken down to admit of its entrance, and it was finally swung into its place amid the enthusiastic transports of the populace. It bears the figures of our Blessed Lord, His Virgin Mother, and of S. John the Baptist; also of the Tsar Alexander and his Empress, the Tsar Nicholas, and other members of the imperial family.

Less than these gigantic creations of the bell-founder, yet still vast in size when compared with other western bells, are the bells of Novgorod, famous for its fairs, and of the capital, S. Petersburg. The great bell of the former weighs some thirty-one tons, and that of the latter over twenty-three-and-a-half tons. The last-named bell hangs in the magnificent cathedral of S. Isaac, and is, like the more celebrated Moscow bell, ornamented with imperial portraits; effigies of Peter the Great, Catherine II., Paul I., Alexander I., and Nicholas I., the sovereigns under whom the cathedral was built, being upon its sides. Among the Russians themselves the bells of Valdaï, a town near the capital, are famous for the richness and beauty of their tone.

Returning once more to Asia, we find immense bells at

Pekin and Nankin.   Le Comte, at the end of the seventeenth century, describes a bell which he found lying on the
ground at the latter place amid the ruins of its fallen belfry.
It was eleven feet nine inches high, and seven-and-a-half feet
in diameter; its weight being computed at twenty-two-and-
a-quarter tons.   Three lesser bells lay beside it.   The
Emperor Yong-lo, on transferring the seat of government
from Nankin to Pekin, in 1403, cast nine huge bells to
commemorate the event; and in the middle of the seventeenth century Father Verbiest saw seven of them lying in
the same forlorn condition as their brethren at the old
capital.   He measured one of them; the result in English
terms being a height of fourteen feet five inches, with
canons standing another three feet high, a diameter of nearly
thirteen feet, and a thickness of thirteen inches.   The
weight was alleged to be about fifty-three tons.   These great
bells, which are in some cases of iron, were struck by a
wooden clapper, and consequently had not so powerful a
sound as similar ones would have, if used after the European
manner.   The casting of such giants apparently went out of
fashion with the overthrow of the native Chinese dynasty
in 1644.

Japan possesses some splendid bells of great size.   Like
the Chinese examples, however, they can hardly be
compared with those of Europe without injustice to the
latter, since they are not intended to be chimed, much less
rung, in the proper sense of those terms, but are merely
struck on the outside with wooden instruments.   The late
Lady Brassey mentions one of these bells, in describing (in
the "Voyage of the Sunbeam") a visit to the Japanese
Temple of Gion Chiosiu.   "We strolled about the temple

grounds," she says, "and ascended the hill to see the famous bell, which is the second biggest in Japan. The immense beam which strikes it was unlashed from the platform for our edification, and the bell sent forth a magnificent sound, pealing over the city and through the woods."

When we come to consider the chief bells in the European states other than Russia, we at once note a considerable falling off in the matter of size. It is, however, scarcely fair to contrast Russian bells with those used further west ; for this reason, that the bells of that country also are not intended to be swung, they are merely struck. Korb, in his "Diarium Itineris in Muscovia," published in 1698, describes the method of sounding the first Tsar Kolokol at Moscow. He tells us that forty or fifty men were employed, who stood half on each side of the bell, and by means of ropes pulled the clapper to and fro. And this is the usual Russian plan to the present day ; the bells are fixed immoveably, and the clappers only swing. To a certain extent, therefore, Russian and other bells can scarcely be called examples of the same kind of instrument, their use being so entirely different ; and to compare them is almost as unreasonable as it would be to compare a harp with a pianoforte.

Nevertheless, one or two of the largest of the European bells do not fall much below some of the smaller examples quoted above. The great bell of Cologne Cathedral weighs twenty-five tons, and replaces one cast in 1448, at a weight of eleven tons. There is one at Olmutz of eighteen tons, and another at Vienna which weighs seventeen tons fourteen cwt., and was cast in 1711. The famous bell at Erfurt, dating from the fifteenth century, and long reputed

"TSAR KOLOKOL," MOSCOW.

to be the largest in Europe, weighs thirteen and three-
quarter tons ; it is ten and a quarter feet in height and eight
and a half feet in diameter.   The Low Countries are
represented by the great bell of Bruges, dating from 1680,
which, however, only weighs ten and a quarter tons.
France has several examples of noteworthy proportions.
The old " Jacqueline " of Paris, cast in 1400, attained only
the modest weight of six tons, but the modern great bell of
Notre Dame in that city weighs seventeen tons.   Rouen
had one, the George d'Amboise, of sixteen tons, dating
from 1501.   At Toulouse the bell of Cardaillac is of a
great size, as also is the largest of the ring at Lyons.   Of
Italian bells one at Florence holds the premier place ; it
weighs about seven and a half tons, and has been swung up
into the tower of the Palazzio Veccio, 275 feet from the
ground.

We turn now to English bells, first among which in the
matter of size is " Great Paul," of London, said to be the
largest bell in the world which is actually rung, in the
technical sense of being revolved in the usual manner of
English bells.

One or two facts in connection with the casting of this
splendid bell have been already given in illustration of the
methods employed in modern bell-foundries ; but a brief
account of the making and hanging of it should be given.
On the 23rd November, 1881, the foundry of Messrs. Taylor
& Co., Loughborough, witnessed the casting of the largest
bell ever made in England.   Over eight hours were occupied
in melting the twenty tons of metal in the three furnaces
devoted to the work, and it was past ten o'clock on the
night named, when the molten streams ran into the gigantic

cast iron mould, and in about four minutes filled it with the glowing metal. Six days were allowed for the thorough cooling of the mass, and it was not until November 29th, that eager eyes and ears could satisfy the many anxious minds of the beauty and the soundness of the work. The dimensions of the bell are: height, eight feet ten inches, diameter, nine feet six-and-three-quarter inches, and thickness at the sound-bow, eight-and-three-quarter inches; and the actual weight is sixteen tons, fourteen cwt., two quarters, nineteen lbs. The tongue is seven feet nine inches long and weighs nearly four-and-a-quarter cwt. The inscriptions and ornaments upon the bell are simple but appropriate; consisting of the name of the founders and the date, "John Taylor & Co., founders, Loughborough, MDCCCLXXXI," of the arms of the Dean and Chapter of S. Paul's Cathedral, and the motto, 'Vae. Mihi. Si. Non. Evangelisavero." (1. Corinthians ix. 16). "Great Paul" from first to last cost about £3,000. The note given out by it is E flat, "the upper partials B flat, E flat, and G being just audible, with the sonorous ground-tone." So wrote Dr. Stainer, and speaking of the intention of using the bell for the first time on the following Easter Day, he added, "I shall be surprised if Londoners do not realize the fact that 'Great Paul' is worthy alike of their ancient city and splendid cathedral."

The public interest shown in the conveyance of the monster to its home in the metropolis was very great; church bells rang out to greet it, and in some cases the Volunteers turned out to escort it. A carriage of massive timber was specially constructed for it, the weight of the car being five tons, and this was drawn by a traction engine;

a second being in attendance to assist if needful on bad
roads and in hilly districts.   Many difficulties had to be
faced during the journey;   bridges had to be inspected
before the engines with their load of twenty-two tons could
be suffered to venture on them; in one place a piece of soft
road had to be covered with boiler-plates, two inches in
thickness, to allow of the passage of the car; and as
London was approached the ever-increasing stream of traffic
compelled those in charge to travel chiefly by night.   The
final stage of the journey, from Highgate to S. Paul's,
was made between midnight and eight o'clock in the
morning of May 22nd, 1882, and preparations for getting
the bell into the cathedral were at once commenced.   The
chains which had secured it to its carriage were removed,
and some of the stonework having been taken out so
as to enlarge the doorway, "Great Paul" was at last
successfully swung up by means of pulleys into its place
in one of the western towers.

S. Paul's Cathedral possesses, in addition to this English
" King of Bells," a fine ring of twelve, the tenor of which
weighs three tons two hundred weight.   Their dedication in
the year 1878 was described in an earlier chapter.   Up
to that date S. Paul's, alone among the cathedrals of
England, and probably of Europe, possessed no peal of
bells.   The twelve were cast by the same firm which
afterwards was entrusted with " Great Paul," and they were
given for the most part by the various city companies, the
total cost being about £5,000.   The treble and the second
bell were given by the Drapers' Company; the next four
by the Turners and the Baroness Burdett-Coutts, who
is a member of that company;   the seventh bell by the

Salters, the eighth by the Merchant Taylors, the ninth by the Fishmongers, the tenth by the Clothworkers, the eleventh by the Grocers, and the tenor by the City Corporation. Each bell of the ring, which weighs in the aggregate about eleven tons, bears the armorial shield of the Dean and Chapter, and also that of the company presenting it, with the motto of the latter.

The old "great bell" of S. Paul's was cast in the reign of Edward I., and hung in Westminster Hall Gate, where it was used for sounding the hours for the information of the judges. In those days it was popularly named first " Edward of Westminster," and later " Westminster Tom." William III. presented it to the cathedral, and thither it was conveyed on New Year's Day, 1699; but at Temple Bar, the boundary of the city, " Tom " rolled off his car and cracked himself. It was recast in 1708, by Philip Wightman, and again in 1716 by Richard Phelps. It is the hour-bell, and otherwise was formerly used, and only used, to toll for the death of a member of the Royal Family, of the Bishop, the Dean, or of the Lord Mayor.

Having given precedence to London's great bell, it is but right that the next place, at any rate, should be given to those of Canterbury and York, each of which, and especially the latter, is of no mean reputation.

The largest bell at Canterbury is "S. Dunstan," the casting of which in the Cathedral yard, in 1762, has already been referred to. The present "S. Dunstan" is the successor of a more ancient one, and not improbably the name dates back almost to the days of the great artist and archbishop from whom it is borrowed. The dimensions of this bell are: diameter five feet eight-and-a-half inches, and thickness at the sound-bow five-and-a-half inches; its inscription merely records the names of the dean, Dr. William Friend, of the founders, Messrs. Lester and Pack, and of William Chapman, who superintended the work; together with the date, 1762. Among the records preserved by the Dean and Chapter of Lincoln is an account of the expenditure in the casting of this bell. Several of the items will be of interest, as illustrating the price of labour and of materials in the middle of the eighteenth century. The account runs as follows :—

Dr.   The Dean and Chapter of the Cathedral of Canterbury.

1762, Sep. 10.					£	s.	d.
To Bell Metal, 10-cwt. 0-qrs. 0-lbs. at 14d. per lbs.					65	6	8
200 Windsor Bricks at £4 per 1,000 ...	...	...			0	16	0
250 Large Bricks Compos	...	...	...	...	0	10	0
For Tackle Ropes and Collar Ropes, 7-cwt. 2-qrs.							
16-lbs. @ 3d.	...	...	...	...	10	14	0
4 Hogsheads	...	...	..	...	1	4	0
2 Casks ..	...	...	...	..	0	10	0
Cartage ...	...	...	..	..	0	12	0
Wharfage and Porterage	...	...	...	0	8	0
1 Clapper 85½ lbs.—10d.	..	...	...	...	3	11	3
Tackle ropes which remain, 20 @ 6d. lbs.	...	...	0	10	0
1 Brass Roller, 30½ @ 12d.	...	...	...	...	1	10	6
To recasting one large Bell	...	..	...	....	100	0	0
Coachhire for Wm. Chapman ...	...	.	...	3	0	0
Freight and Land Carriage	...	...	...	...	5	7	2
Over paid	...	...	...	...	...	0	0	4

£193 19 11

On the other side we find :—

1762.	The Dean and Chapter	**Crs.**			£	s.	d.
By deducted for a brass Rowler	...	...	...	1	0	4
Do. for old Clapper, 1-qr. 5½ lbs. @ 2d.	...	1	4	3
Do. for waste of metal	...	...	...	...	4	13	4
Dec. 10, by cash in full	...	...	...	...	187	2	0

£193 19 11

"S. Dunstan" is the clock-bell of the Cathedral.
The bell of state and ceremony, whose voice warns the
citizens of the death of the Sovereign or of the Archbishop,
and which is rung on other occasions of special solemnity,
is "Harry" or the "Bell Harry," hanging in the central
tower to which it has given its name. This is also
Canterbury's Curfew-bell.

The Northern Metropolis can boast a much heavier bell
than any in the possession of her Southern sister, "Peter
of York" ranking third in size of the bells of the kingdom,
the heavier ones being both in London, "Great Paul" and
"Big Ben." "Peter" is reputed to weigh twelve tons,
ten cwt, and was cast by Messrs. Mears of Whitechapel
on January 18th, 1845. Its diameter is eight feet four
inches, its height, seven feet two inches, and its thickness
at the sound-bow, seven inches. Its note is F, or as some
say F sharp. The cost was about £2,000. On the 21st,
August, 1845, it was rung by sixteen men, but it is now
never sounded in the regular way. Every day at noon,
Sundays excepted, it is struck twelve times by means
of a hammer worked by a manual lever, after the clock
has sounded the hour upon the tenor bell of the ring;
and once a year, on the 31st December, it tolls midnight
in the same way. Otherwise it is only used occasionally
as a passing, or a funeral bell.

The ring of bells at York is known as the "Beckwith
Peal," having been purchased from a bequest left for
the purpose by Dr. Beckwith, of York, in 1843. They were
cast in the following year by Messrs. Mears, and were
placed in the south tower. The bells are twelve in number,
ranging from a treble weighing about seven and half cwts,

to the tenor of two tons, thirteen cwts, three quarters. The diameter of this latter bell is five feet five inches, and its note is C.

The bells of the parish churches in the city of York are none of them remarkable in the matter of size, although several of them are interesting in other ways, especially as illustrations of the once famous local industry of bell-founding. The church of S. Maurice has a couple of memorial bells, which may be noted in passing. They were given to the church in memory of John Henry Cattley, a chorister, who was accidentally drowned on November 2nd, 1882, and bear the apt quotations :—" Misit de summo et accepit me," "Sumpsit me de aquis multis," (" He sent from on high and took me, He drew me out of many waters,") from Psalm xviii., 16.

One of the most famous bells in England is " Mighty Tom" of Oxford. At the dissolution and plunder of the monastic foundations, the great bell of Oseney Abbey was taken to S. Frideswide's, at Oxford, and became the original " Mighty Tom," its inscription being one already quoted, " In Thomæ Laude Resono Bim Bom Sine Fraude." Among other accounts in reference to the transference of the bell, we learn that in 1546 there was "payd to Wellbye of Ensham for caryege of the great bell to Fryswids, 26 September, xxs.," and also fourpence for " ale to theym laboreres at ye wyndyng up of the great bell into Friswides steple." In the reign of Mary it was re-dedicated in the name of the Queen, but the old name has always continued in popular use. In 1612 it was damaged by an accident, and was consequently re-cast, on which occasion Richard Corbet, subsequently Dean of Christ Church, and later

Bishop of Norwich, celebrated the event in some verses full of rather ponderous humour. In 1680 the bell was again re-cast, the work being entrusted to Richard Keene, of Woodstock, who was exceptionally unfortunate, or remarkably incompetent. Anyhow it was cast three times unsuccessfully; twice there was not enough metal allowed, so that the moulds for the cannons were not filled, and the third time the mould burst, and the molten metal ran into the ground. The College authorities took pity on the poor bell-founder, and "made him amends;" but they transferred the work to Christopher Hodson, of London, who carried it through satisfactorily. Soon after Sir Christopher Wren had completed the Gatehouse, this bell was removed to the tower there. The diameter of "Mighty Tom" is 7 feet 2 inches, the height 6 feet 9 inches, and the thickness $6\frac{1}{2}$ inches. The clapper weighs 342 pounds and the bell 7 tons, 11 cwts, 3 qrs, 4 lbs. Its inscription sets forth that "Magnus Thomas" was re-cast on April 8, 1680, in the reign of Charles II., and gives the names of the College authorities, and of the founder. It was first rung on the 29th May, 1684, and its voice has ever since been familiar to each successive generation of undergraduates, since it is the signal that all must at once betake themselves to their respective colleges. For this purpose it rings at five minutes past nine o'clock at night one hundred-and-one strokes, whereby it also commemorates the original number of the scholars on the foundation.

It has been pointed out† that the various bells of the city of Oxford form, by a curious accident, a complete chromatic

---

† By the Rev. Wm. C. Lukis in "An Account of Church Bells." Parker, London and Oxford, 1857.

scale. Christchurch peal is said to have as its key-note the
"vocal D," and S. Mary's the D of the concert pitch.
Merton and New College have E flat, Magdalen E natural,
Carfax and S. Mary Magdalen F, S. Michael's and S. Giles's
F sharp, All Saints G, S. Aldate's A flat, S. Peter-in-the-
East A natural, and Holywell B flat. The scale, is not,
however, accurately in tune throughout.

Of the origin of "Great Tom" of Lincoln there are
several legends, most of which are not over-creditable to
the ecclesiastics of the day.   One story has it that it was
stolen from Beauchief Abbey, Derbyshire, another that it
was "conveyed" in a similar way from the Abbey of Peterborough, and a third says that no less a personage than
Bishop Longland (1521-1547) stole it from the suppressed
priory of Markby, in Lincolnshire.   Tradition seems to
have determined that at any rate the bell was stolen, though
there are that aver that the Abbot of Peterborough gave it as
a present ; and as it is known that Geoffry Plantagenet gave
two fine bells to Lincoln Minster in the twelfth century, it
is possible that all these accounts are incorrect, and that
"Tom" is a descendant from one of these. The first
authentic allusion to this bell is in a document among the
archives of the Dean and Chapter bearing date January 30,
1610, or, in the new style, 1611. This informs us that it
was re-cast in the Minster Yard, by Oldfield, of Nottingham,
and Newcombe, of Leicester, and that "upon Sunday
the xxvij of this month" it was "ronge oute and all
safe and well."   The former bell had weighed rather more
than 3 tons 18 cwt. ; the new one was slightly heavier, and
measured in circumference "seven yards and a half and two
inches." In 1827 Great Tom cracked, and nothing was

done to repair the damage until 1834. In that year Mr. Thomas Mears took down and broke up not only the great bell, but also six small ones which hung in the Rood Tower, and were known as the Lady Bells; and from the metal of them all three bells were cast, the present "Great Tom" and two quarter bells. The casting was done on November 15th, 1834, and on the sixth of the following April the bell commenced its journey to Lincoln, being taken by road on a wooden car drawn by eight horses. It reached its destination on 13th April, 1835, and was suspended in the Rood Tower. It is used as the clock bell, and is also tolled on special occasions. It alone rings for services on Good Friday, and it announces the death of persons of special note in the city or the country, and is employed as the "sermon bell" on great festivals. The diameter of Great Tom is 6 feet 10½ inches, and the weight 5 tons 8 cwt. It gives out the note A

The western Cathedral of Exeter boasts two noteworthy bells, "Great Peter" and "Grandison"; the first named from the dedication of the church, with perhaps an allusion to the original donor of the bell; the second from John de Grandison, bishop of the see from 1327 to 1367. "Peter" is the clock bell, and also sounds daily for mattins and the curfew, being struck with a hammer. An inscription sets forth the fact that the bell was given by Bishop Peter Courtenay (who ruled the see from 1478 to 1487) in 1484, and that it was recast by Thomas Purdue in 1676 at the cost of the Dean and Chapter. It is six feet four inches in diameter, and five inches thick at the sound-bow, and weighs 5-tons 2-cwt.; its note is A. "Grandison" is the tenor in the peal of ten. As far back as 1396 Exeter Cathedral possessed a bell of this name, and it (or a successor) is mentioned in 1552, the weight being given as "XL^C waight by estimacon." It has been twice since then recast; by Pennington in 1629, and by William Evans, of Chepstow, in 1729. It still bears a legend announcing that it is the gift of Bishop Grandison. It is six feet in diameter, and nearly five inches thick at the sound-bow, and weighs 3-tons 7-cwt. 1-qr. 18-lbs., being, it is said, the heaviest bell in England that is regularly rung in a peal. Its note is B flat.

The largest bell at Gloucester, although smaller than those already spoken of, is remarkable as being the only old example of a heavy bell that we now possess. It is supposed to date from about 1400. Its inscription asserts " Me fecit fieri conventus nomine Petri " (the convent had me made in the name of Peter), the arms of the abbey and the founder's trade-mark being used as stops. It is five feet eight-and-a-half inches in diameter, and weighs 2-tons 18-cwt., giving out the note C sharp. It was formerly customary for nine men to ring this bell, eight pulling the rope as they stood in the choir, while the ninth, stationed in the ringing-chamber, steadied it. Since 1827, however, "Great Peter" has not been raised, but it is still sounded by means of a hammer at nine every night. It also tolls a knell on the death of a member of the Royal Family.

Before leaving the great bells of England, one or two secular examples demand notice, first among which, by right of size, situation, and fame, is "Big Ben," of Westminster. The first bell of the name was cast in 1856, by Messrs. Warner & Son, of Stockton-on-Tees, and was, according to the design of Sir E. B. Denison (now Lord Grimthorpe) to be nine feet in diameter, and fourteen tons in weight, the

hammer for striking it weighing a ton. It was brought up
to London, but on trial it was found not only to have a flaw
in its metal, but to be actually cracked. It was consequently
broken up, and recast at Whitechapel by Messrs. Mears, in
1858. The weight was this time reduced to 13-tons 10-cwt.
3-qrs. 15-lbs., and the new hammer was only 6-cwt. This
bell also cracked after a time, and for a considerable period
it was not used. Subsequently it was patched up, and still
serves its original purpose of an hour-bell. The Westminster
quarter bells, on which are sounded the famous Westminster
chimes, are of no despicable size. The first weighs four-
and-a-half tons, the second two tons, the third one-and-a-half
tons, and the fourth a ton; the notes sounded being
respectively B, E, F sharp, and G sharp. They all hang in
the clock tower of the Palace of Westminster. The two
Bens cost £4,000.

Several provincial towns have fine bells, used generally as
clock bells, in their Town Halls. Manchester has one, cast
in 1876, which weighs 6-tons 9-cwt.; Preston's Town Hall
bell was cast in 1878, at a weight of 4-tons 16-cwt.; at
Bradford is a similar one, dating from 1873, and weighing
4-tons, 7-cwt.; Leeds Town Hall has a bell, dated 1859,
and named Victoria, which weighs 4-tons 1-cwt.; and the
Halifax bell weighs just three tons. "Big Ben" is the
largest of our secular bells, and second only to "Great Paul"
in the list of all the English bells.

A record of famous English bells would be indeed
incomplete were no mention made of Bow Bells. These
are celebrated, not from anything remarkable in their size or
tone, but because the church of S. Mary-le-Bow has long
been reckoned the very heart and centre of London, so that

it is essential to the being of a true cockney that he should have been born within the sound of Bow Bells. Alexander Pope has two allusions to them. In the Dunciad (Book III., line 278) he defines the limits of London, or "Lud's old walls," as being

"Far as loud Bow's stupendous bells resound";

while in the "Rape of the Lock" (Canto IV., line 118) he contrasts the mercantile city with the environs of the court, by suggesting that it is impossible that

"— wits take lodgings in the sound of Bow."

The old story of the hopes of which Bow bells sung in the ears of young Dick Whittington, and of their strange fulfilment, need scarcely be recalled to anyone. The modern bells are not, however, precisely those to which the future Lord Mayor listened, nor even those of which the poet sung; for of the original ten, the tenor was recast in 1738, and the rest in 1762, two more being added in 1881. The central position of Bow Church was recognised by the authorities when they ordained that from its steeple should sound the curfew for the city.

Dorchester Abbey has a tenor bell which is noteworthy for its donor's sake. It was originally cast in Tournai, and presented to Dorchester Abbey by Cardinal Wolsey. It is slightly under three tons in weight, and although it has been twice recast, it still bears the legend,—

"By Wolsey's gift I measure time for all,
To mirth, to grief, to church I serve to call."

Other bells in the country claim to have been the gifts of the great Cardinal, as, for example, the third bell at Hilmarton, Wiltshire.

In the parish church of Great Hampden are three bells

dated 1625, which it is suggested were probably given by John Hampden, who lived at the manor-house, and was the patron of the living.

The bells of S. Andrew's, Plymouth, are said to have originally commemorated the return of Drake, after his circumnavigation of the globe, in 1594. The existing peal was cast, however, with the exception of the tenor, by Bilbie in 1749. The tenor dates only from 1840, and came from the foundry of Thomas Mears.

Wales possesses several noteworthy peals of bells. Wrexham has a fine ring of ten, already mentioned; and Llanbadarn bells, near Aberystwith, are exceptionally sweet and mellow. The "bells of Aberdovey," so famous in song, probably owe their reputation chiefly to the fancy of the poet who sang of them; and the same may be said of the Cornish peal, "the bells of S. Michael's Tower," whose merry music rang out so joyfully "when Richard Penlake and Rebecca his wife arrived at the church door."

Of Scottish bells, one at Glasgow Cathedral, and the quaintly-inscribed ring of four at Orkney Cathedral, have already been mentioned. Of these latter, the tenor was recast in 1682, at Amsterdam, at a cost of "1,303 merks Scots," equal to about £72 7s. 9d. The weight of the bell is only 13-cwt. 2-qrs. 16-lbs. "S. Lawrence," an old bell at S. Nicholas, Aberdeen, was a fine one, but it was unfortunately destroyed, owing to the burning of the steeple, in 1874. The Cathedral of S. Mary, Edinburgh, has a good peal.

The Limerick bells are justly celebrated for the sweetness of their tone; they are said to have been brought from Italy, and into their history is woven the following romantic episode. A young Italian, so runs the legend, had devoted himself to the art of bell-founding, and with such success that he at last produced a peal of bells whose tones almost realized his ideal of the perfection of belfry music. This wonderful ring was sold to the abbot of a neighbouring convent; and the artist, now living in a state of modest affluence, bought a small villa in the district, where day by day the sweet voices of his own creation might sing their songs of joy and sadness, of sacred duty and heavenly hope, in his listening ears. But such a time of peace was not to last. Warfare swept across the land ; and when the tide of fire and rapine had subsided, all was changed. The young artist found himself homeless and ruined, and even his loved bells had gone, sold in a moment of necessity by the reverend abbot, and carried into far-distant Ireland. For a long time the wretched man was an outcast and a wanderer throughout Europe ; his heart was crushed within him, hope seemed to him as much devastated as was his home. At last after long and weary journeyings he found himself on board a little bark bound for the unknown Hibernian coast. Evening, clear and calm, was shining around them with a mellow light, as their keel silently cut the glistening waters of the Shannon, for the voyage's end was near. Suddenly filling and thrilling the throbbing air came a sound of heavenly music, rising and falling on the evening breeze. " Limerick bells !" cried the rough skipper, " we shall be able to drop anchor, lads, ere dark to-night." But that lonely Italian passenger, starting at the first boom of those bells, moved not, nor answered. Speedily the bark made her way homeward ; hoarsely the shout of the skipper was answered from the shore, and at last, amid the rattling of blocks and the grinding of chains, the little vessel lay still, her voyage o'er. But still the lonely Italian stirred not, and when they went to him they realized that a strange thing had happened ; for his soul had gone out to meet the singing of his bells, and was by them upborne, as on the wings of angels, to the Paradise of God. His voyage too was o'er.

Father Prout's verses have established the fame of the Shandon bells. One stanza may be quoted to illustrate both the enthusiasm of the Irishman, and the ingenuity of the poet :—

> " I've heard bells chiming
> Full many a clime in,
> Tolling sublime in
>   Cathedral shrine,
> While at a glibe rate
> Brass tongues would vibrate—
> But all their music
>   Spoke naught like thine ;
> For memory dwelling
> On each proud swelling
> Of the belfry knelling
>   Its bold notes free,
> Made the bells of Shandon
> Sound far more grand on
> The pleasant waters
>   Of the river Lee."

Whether the bells have degenerated, or whether they were never so splendid as their bard would have us believe, it would perhaps be dangerous for an Englishman to attempt to decide. That, at any rate, opinions may differ on the subject even of the beauty of Shandon bells, is abundantly proved by comparing the foregoing stanza with the following from the pen of another Irishman, the late A. M. Sullivan, M.P. :—

> " I've heard bells rattle
>   Round the necks of cattle ;
> The Chinese in battle
>   Use hideous gongs ;
> And down in Galway
> The natives alway
> Enswarm their bees
>   To the beat of tongs.
> But there's something sadder
> To drive one madder
> Than gongs or tongs
>   Struck discordantly,
> 'Tis the bells of Shandon,
> With discord dinned on,
> The roaring waters
>   Of the river Lee !"

S. Patrick's Cathedral, Dublin, has recently had a fine peal of ten bells presented to it by Lord Iveagh. The total weight of the metal is over nine tons, the tenor weighing 2 tons, 5 cwt., 1 qr., 18 lbs. : and the founders were the firm of Taylor, Loughborough. The inscriptions are for the most part taken from the Canticles of the Church, and are as follows :—

" Treble. Sursum corda.
   2.   Venite adoremus et procidamus.
   3.   Te laudamus.
   4.   Tibi benedicimus.
   5.   Te adoramus.
   6.   Te glorificamus.
   7.   Per singulos dies benedicimus Te.
   8.   Omnis spiritus laudet Dominum.
   9.   Gloria in excelsis Deo.
   Tenor. Ad majorem Dei gloriam. This peal of ten bells was
           erected at the expense of Edward Cecil, Baron Iveagh,
           K.P., A.D. 1897. Henry Jellett, Dean."

One or two more continental examples, besides those quoted above for their size and weight, deserve mention. Strasburg has a famous ring of nine bells, among which are several devoted to special duties. The Storm-bell dates in its present form from 1774, and was rung to warn travellers of approaching storms, and to guide them to the city gates. The Gate-bell, dated 1618, but recast in 1651, informs the citizens of the opening and closing of the gates at morning and evening. "Mittags" sounds the hours of noon and midnight. One of the most beautiful of continental bells is "Carolus" at Antwerp. This was given to the city by the Emperor Charles V., and has ever since been held in special honour by the citizens. Amongst its belfry comrades are "Horrida," the tocsin, dated 1316, now seldom used, "S. Maria," dating from 1467, "S. Antoine," and the "Curfew," which rings thrice daily.

Crossing the Atlantic, we find the city of Montreal laying claim to the possession of the heaviest bell on the American continent. This hangs in the Roman Catholic Cathedral, and weighs 13½ tons ; but the tenor bell of the chimes in Trinity Church, New York, has the reputation of being the sweetest in tone. The United States have made a point of casting large and sonorous bells for secular use, and especially as alarm-bells. The alarum of the Old City Hall, New York, weighed over 10 tons, but having been broken in removal, the metal was recast as five small bells. An example, specially interesting to American citizens, is the "Liberty Bell" in the Philadelphia State House. This was cast in 1752, in England, but having been cracked by a trial stroke, was recast at Philadelphia by Isaac Norris. It bears an inscription taken from Leviticus xxv. 10 :—" Proclaim Liberty throughout all the land to all the inhabitants thereof ;" and, in 1776, as if in fulfilment of its unconscious prophecy, it rang in celebration of the Declaration of the Independence of the United States. It was again cracked in ringing a welcome to Henry Clay, and has since been preserved as an honoured relic only.

An interesting peal of bells, consisting of twenty-five, hangs in the cathedral at Zanzibar, their tones forming a chromatic scale of two octaves. They were presented by various schools and colleges which support the English mission to that district, and bear appropriate names. Thus Durham gives "S. Cuthbert;" London, "S. Paul;" Canterbury, "S. Augustine;" Dublin, "S. Patrick," and so forth. They were cast by Messrs. Warner.

The British Colonies have not so far provided their churches with any very noteworthy bells. South Africa, for example, has only two full peals of eight, namely, those in the cathedrals of Capetown and of Grahamstown ; and in neither instance can they be rung, one or two bells in the former case being damaged, and the bell-frame in the latter being faulty. The love of bell-music may be a mere matter of sentiment, yet sentiment is a powerful factor in human action ; and one cannot but think that the cost and trouble involved in producing in the New World the old familiar chimes of the English village church, would be amply repaid in their influence for good.

CHAPTER VI.

The Loss of Old Bells.

IN view of the fact that the churches of mediaeval England were so well furnished with bells, it may appear strange that so few really ancient specimens are left to us. A few words of explanation are therefore offered. The extent of the loss which has to be accounted for is illustrated by the following facts supplied by two works already quoted.* In Leicestershire, 147 bells only out of 998 are of dates earlier than the year 1600; in Northamptonshire there are 137 out of 1,317; in Lincolnshire, 353 out of 2,036; and in Rutland 31 out of 191. In Wiltshire, out of 698 bells recorded by the Rev. W. C. Lukis, 63 were older than the year 1500, 23 dated from that period to 1600, 273 belonged to the seventeenth century, 239 to the eighteenth, and 46 to the nineteenth; the date of the remaining 26 being doubtful. No doubt, could we obtain statistics of the whole country, the proportions of ancient and modern bells would not be found materially different from those which we obtain in these five counties.

In the course of the centuries a great many bells have been destroyed through what may be called natural causes, the accidents to which all earthly things are liable; and how simple a matter may fracture a bell is not probably realized by those unfamiliar with belfry lore. One sees a

---

North's "English Bells," and Lukis's "Church Bells."

ponderous mass of metal, weighing some hundredweights, or even tons, and measuring several inches in thickness; and the uninitiated is apt to imagine that nothing short of very violent ill-usage could damage it; and yet, as a matter of fact, when that sonorous metal is all throbbing beneath the stroke of its clapper, the sudden checking of its vibrations by a very little thing may cause it to crack. It has even been said that a piece of string tied tightly round the sound-bow of a large bell may be sufficent to ruin it. At Hanbury, Burton-on-Trent, a new bell was being sounded, when a workman in play sprang on to it, and clung to it by clasping his legs around it, with the result that it cracked. Many a sweet-toned bell has been destroyed by a careless sexton, in his endeavours to make the tolling of it easier. In many places instead of swinging the bell, the sexton fastens a cord to the clapper, and pulls it against the sound-bow, as he stands beside the bell. In tolling a minute-bell, or any slow strokes, this avoids the necessity of "raising" and "setting" the bell, that is, ringing it in the orthodox way, but the extra labour is only saved at the risk of cracking the bell; for if the clapper be brought smartly against the sound-bow, and for a moment held there tightly (as in this process is very likely to be done), the vibrations may be hindered with fatal results. Neither the custom nor its consequences are of modern date, for the authorities of S. Laurence's, Reading, found it needful long since to decree that, "Whereas there was, through the slothfulness of the sextine in times past, a kind of tolling ye bell by ye clapper rope: yt was now fforbedden and taken awaye; & that the bell should be told: as in times past: & not in anie such idle sorte."

The same unfortunate effect has also been frequently

produced in the case of small bells by the practice of
"getting the double" on them; that is, by swinging them
like factory bells, the clappers striking both sides in quick
succession.

Would that in all places as much thought had been given
to the care of the bells as was evidently the case at Barrow-
on-Humber, where, among other rules for the parish clerk's
guidance "as recorded in the Town's Book, 1713," we
read:—" He must be Careful that no Boys or Idle persons
Jangle the Bells or abuse the Church or the Windows; he
is to grease or oil the Bells, and to keep them in good
order, and if they be defected in anything he shall let the
Churchwardens know, that they may be mended in convenient time."

It must, however, be admitted that wilful destruction
accounts for the disappearance of a great number of old
bells. We have already alluded to the story of that
sacrilegious monarch, King Henry VIII., staking a ring of
bells over a game of dice with Sir Miles Partridge, and
losing them. It is some little satisfaction to be able to add
that the knight was hanged in the following reign. But
this was not a solitary act of the kind on the part of the
monarch. In the little Sanctuary at Westminster hung
three large bells given by Edward III. for the use of
S. Stephen's Chapel, around .he heaviest of which ran, so it
is reported, the following legend :—

> "King Edward made me thirtie thousand weight and three,
> Take mee down and wey mee and more ye shall fynd me."

So notorious was the greed of the Tudor sovereign that
someone scrawled beneath this "with a coale":—

> " But Henry the Eight
> Will bait me of my weight."

Sir Henry Spelman gives us more than one instance of the sacrilegious robbery of church bells during the Reformation period. Sir Hugh Paulet despoiled the Jersey churches of their bells, and sold them into France. The county of Norfolk suffered severely in this respect, but a singular fatality is alleged to have attended the godless traffic in these consecrated articles of church furniture. " In sending them over the sea, some were drowned in one haven, some in another, as at Lynn, Wells, or Yarmouth ;" fourteen of the Jersey bells sunk in the harbour of S. Malo, and at Hunstanton a bell was seen, at an exceptionally low tide, half-buried in the sands, in Spelman's days. Even the clergy were not always ashamed to seek these ill-gotten gains. The same chronicler informs us that, " in the year of our Lord 1541, Arthur Bulkley, Bishop of Bangor, sacrilegiously sold the five fair bells belonging to his cathedral, and went to the sea-side to see them shipped away ; but at that instant was stricken blind, and so continued to the day of his death."

In the present year (1897) an interesting discovery was made in Suffolk, which seems to point to this time of destruction. In cleaning an old pond at Rooksie Farm, Preston, in that county, it was found necessary to pump out the water and to dig out a considerable depth of mud at the bottom, in which process a bell bearing the date 1133 was laid bare, embedded in the clay which formed the subsoil. One wonders was it flung there by the despoilers, or by some friendly hands endeavouring to save it from desecration, who failed afterwards to recover it.

The traffic with the continent in bell-metal became sufficiently large to attract attention, and in 1547 such export was forbidden, not from any scruple of conscience, but lest there should be a lack of material in the country for the casting of cannon! In 1549, the rising in the West against the innovations in religion, was made the excuse for the wholesale spoliation of the belfries of Devon and Cornwall. According to Strype, "it was remembered how the bells in the churches served by ringing to summon and call in the disaffected unto their arms," and consequently Lord Russell was ordered "to take away all the bells" in those counties, "leaving only one in each steeple, the least in the ring, which was to call the people to church." When the wholesale robbery of church plate, and the sale of church lands, is remembered, it seems very questionable whether the plundering of the steeples was not part of a policy of lawless greed, the rebellion affording an excuse, rather than a reason for it.

The following extract from a letter written by Richard Bellycys to Thomas Cromwell deals with this traffic in bells. The writer is superintending the demolition of certain abbeys in Yorkshire; and thus expresses himself: "as concerning the selling of the bells, I cannot sell them above fifteen shillings the hundredth, wherein I would gladly know your lordship's pleasure, whether I should sell them after that price or send them up to London; and if they be sent up surely the carriage wolbe costly frome that place to the water . . . And thus the Holy Ghost ever preserve your lordshipp in honour." Surely blasphemous effrontery could go no further!

In some few cases the bells carried off from the monastic houses at their suppression were given or sold to parish churches, but to what extent the spoliation was carried on is illustrated by an indenture of 1540-1, by which Henry VIII. sold to John Core, a citizen and grocer of London, one hundred thousand pounds weight of bell-metal for nine hundred pounds, giving him at the same time leave to export it.

This traffic in church bells was checked under Edward VI. and Elizabeth, although it is evident that it was not entirely stopped, from the fact that Thomas Egerton made the former sovereign an offer to buy "all the bell metal that his Highnesse nowe hathe in the realme at the price of xx$^{s.}$ euerie hunderith weighte." Among the articles stolen (by authority) from S. Mary's, Reading, and sold in this reign, were " Two belles weighing 38 cwt. 4 lb. at 30s. the cwt."

Where the example is set by the great ones of the earth, there are not wanting plenty of lesser note who are ready to follow. Thus in 1552 complaint is made that the church-wardens of Devizes had in their private possession two of the church bells, which they refused to surrender : while the people of Sidmouth, Devon, gave a bell towards the cost of Ottermouth Haven ; and those of Skidbrook, Lincoln-shire, sold two bells to raise money to clear out their sand-choked haven, as well as to make some repairs in the church.

In Scotland the destruction of bells was far more thorough at this period than in the southern kingdom. There it was not a matter of mere covetousness, but was a systematic attack upon what the reformers denounced as a superstitious practice. Abbot, afterwards Archbishop of Canterbury, visited Scotland in 1605, and was astonished at the almost complete lack of bells : "at Dunbar, he asked how they chanced to be without such a commodity, when

the minister, a crumpt unseemly person, thinking the
question as strange, replied, 'It was one of the Reformed
Churches!'" Here, too, people were not wanting to argue
that what was right for the state could not be very wrong in
the individual, and so about 1560 we have the authority of
the Baillies of Dundee invoked in two cases concerning
bells; James Young had in his house "the bell of Kynspindie," which he refused to part with; and William
Carmichell was ordered "to deliver to the parishioners of
Lyff their bell, taken by him frae certain persons wha
wrangously intromittit therewith."

Spain, when under the dominion of the Moors, witnessed
a curious misuse of some of her church bells. The
victorious Mohammedans captured in battle the bells,
evidently small ones, of S. Jago de Compostella; and
having no use for them as such, they turned them upside
down, and suspended them by chains in the splendid
Mosque, now the Cathedral, of Cordova, making use of
them as lamps. There surely is a moral in the fact that
even these "infidels," as Mediaeval Christendom always
called them, in their momentary triumph over Christianity,
still devoted the captured treasures of the Church to the
service of religion.

Several bells exist in England which have had their inscriptions mutilated by the hand of some fanatic of the sixteenth
or of the seventeenth century. At Apethorpe, Northamptonshire, the name of the saint has been cut from the bell;
at South Lopham only the word "Vocor" has been left on
one of the bells, and at S. Michael Coslany, Norwich, only
the word "ora." No doubt if this process of chipping with
hammer and chisel at the bells was general in any district,

some examples must have fallen victims to this display of misplaced zeal.

In not a few cases church bells have been taken down and sold in order to raise funds for repairs to the fabric. This was specially characteristic of the parsimony in such matters of the last century, an age when chancels were pulled down to save the cost of repair, and towers were truncated for the same reason. In the single county of Lincoln church funds were raised by the sale of the bells at Cadney, Fosdyke, Fulletby, Howell, South Reston, Skegness, Strubby, Sturton Magna, Low Toynton, and elsewhere.

The destruction, partial or complete, of the church, has naturally, when it has taken place, involved the bells in the general ruin. All through the Middle Ages the great enemy of the property of the church was fire. There is hardly an old cathedral in the country that has not suffered from this cause, in some cases more than once. The peal at Croyland, famous as being the first in England, was destroyed through the burning of the abbey at an early chapter in its history. The bells of old S. Paul's perished in the general conflagration of the cathedral, and other cases might be quoted.

One great cause of the disappearance of old bells remains still to be mentioned. The introduction of the art and mystery of change-ringing is answerable probably more than anything else for the rarity in England of ancient examples in our belfries. We have seen that in mediæval times, although no churches had less than two bells, few had more than three or four. Early in the seventeenth century change-ringing was introduced into the country, or more properly was invented, and about the middle of that century it grew rapidly into increasing popularity.   A ring of three or four bells was, however, quite useless for the practice of the new art, and thus every church in a parish of any pretensions became ambitious of possessing a larger ring of bells, six being the minimum required for the purpose.   In any case where the bells already in the belfry were heavy ones, the simplest and cheapest way of meeting the difficulty was found in melting them down, and making a larger ring of smaller bells ; and unfortunately this was done all over the country in almost countless instances.   The practice has received some illustration already in considering the inscriptions upon bells, some of which allude to it.

One cannot but feel a certain sentimental regret at the disappearance, from one or another of these many causes, of so large a number of our ancient bells.   On other grounds, however, there does not seem to be any ground for special regret.   The art of bell-founding not having, like so many others in the service of the church, fallen behind its older self.   There is no reason to suppose that the best founders of to-day cannot turn out as good bells as any of their predecessors.

CHAPTER VII.

Towers and Campaniles.

BEFORE leaving the questions connected with the making and hanging of the bells, a few words may appropriately be added on the provision made for their accommodation in the church and elsewhere.

Belfries did not form part of the structure of churches until the seventh or eighth century, the earliest mention of them being in the latter period by the monk of S. Gall and Amalarius ; and the first of whose erection we have a record was built either by Pope Stephen III. in 770, or by his successor two years later. The precise reason for this form of addition to ecclesiastical architecture has been debated, but whatever it may have been, it may be taken as fairly certain that the introduction of large bells, and especially of complete peals, into the service of the church must sooner or later have led to some such building.

By a law of Athelstan in 926, the possession of a bell-tower at the church on his estate conferred on the thane the right to sit in the town-gate, or, in modern phrase, to take his place on the grand jury. This fact, taken in connection with the gift to the abbey of Croyland of the first peal in the country by Abbot Turketyl about the middle of the tenth century, seems to point to the period at which towers began to become usual in England. Such bells, few and small, as the churches possessed before that time may have been hung, as is still the case in many village churches, in a mere turret or bell-cote ; but in some cases they were most likely suspended in a timber frame hard by.   Such was certainly the use in several instances at a much later date.   At Aberdeen and at Glasgow, and at several places in Kincardineshire and elsewhere in Scotland, the bells were hung on trees ; and in the churchyard of S. Helens, in Brittany, may still be seen a kind of gallows within which hang the two church bells.   The wit of the Irish Roman Catholics suggested a similar practice by way of evading the oppressive law which at one time forbade their erecting steeples to their churches and placing bells therein.

Probably most of the earlier towers, when erected specially to contain bells, were built detached from the churches. Belfries thus situated it has become the custom to speak of in England as *campaniles*, though it will be obvious that the word strictly implies merely a bell-tower, no matter of what kind or in what position.   We still have several of these detached towers, that of Chichester Cathedral being perhaps the best known.   Worcester formerly had such a "clocherium," crowned with a wooden spire, near the north-east transept ; Little Snoring, Norfolk, has an ancient example, and others are found at East Dereham, Spalding, Torrington, Woburn, Bronellys, and other places.   At the restoration of Holy Trinity Church, Coventry, the bells were removed to a wooden campanile in the churchyard, their position in the tower not being deemed safe.

The country most famous for its campaniles is undoubtedly Italy.   That of S. Mark, at Venice, is of brick, and rises to a height of 350 feet without buttresses, and without pinnacles ; the splendid campanile of Florence was

BELLS AT ST. HELENE, BRITTANY

begun in 1324 by Giotto, and attains a height of 267 feet; the tallest in Italy is at Cremona, its elevation being 395 feet.   Other fine examples are met with at Ravenna, Padua, Bologna, Siena, and Pisa.   Spain has also a beautiful campanile in the work of Guever the Moor at Seville, begun in 1568, and standing 350 feet in height.   A church in the Italian style of architecture was built at Wilton, near Salisbury, about half a century ago, the belfry of which is a tall campanile connected with the main building by a covered arcade.   The need of some protection of this kind for the ringers as they passed between the belfry and the church, must soon have become obvious to everyone in our northern climate; and this probably accounts for the fact that the detached tower is chiefly found in southern Europe. With us the western, or the central, tower forming an integral part of the plan of the church, was probably the most usual design almost from the first.

It is alleged, however (as by Grose in his "Antiquities"), that the old central towers were at first intended merely as lanterns to give light to the body of the church, and that it is for this reason that old examples are generally raised so little above the nave roof.   Where we find, as is so frequently the case, that other storeys have been added to the "squat" original tower, it tells of the time when room was required for a peal of bells.

Occasionally all the bells are not hung in one tower; at Beverley, for instance, the peal hangs in the north tower, while the southern one contains the deep-toned funeral bell.   The same is true of St. Paul's, and in other instances.   A small turret over the chancel-arch frequently contained the "sacring-bell," when the rest of the bells hung in a western tower.

In the sister kingdom of Scotland, towers were never the rule in the case of ordinary parish churches, but a type of bell-gable of more imposing proportions and more elaborate design than the bell-cote of the English hamlet was evolved by their builders. Several good specimens of these still exist. There are mediæval ones at Abdie, in Fifeshire, Dyce, in Aberdeenshire, and Corsragnel, in Ayrshire; others of a more classic design, dating from the Renaissance period, may be found at Kinneff and Garvoc in Kincardineshire, and elsewhere. The form which these take has been called a "bird-cage belfry:" they consist of four stone pillars on an oblong ground plan, or of two side-walls pierced, surmounted with a stone roof with mouldings; the whole generally finished off with a stone ball, or other similar finial, bearing a weather-vane.

A peculiarity with respect to Scottish steeples in the towns, is that they are frequently the property, not of the church, but of the municipality; the bells in these cases belong to the civil authorities, and are used by them for civil purposes during the week, though the church has the use of them on Sundays. It seems that in past times it was not unusual for the burgh to advance money for the repair of the edifice on the security of the steeple and bells; hence the present state of things. In 1778, the council of the Burgh of Peebles agreed that the town should bear the cost of the steeple, clock, and bells of the new church there; and in return for this should continue to hold them as its property. Aberdeen, Dundee, Forfar, Stirling, and Montrose, all supply instances of the same arrangement. Occasionally, however, the church owns one bell absolutely, though that one does not always hang in the church steeple

at all, but in the tower of the Tolbooth, or some other
public building.   A somewhat similar case exists at the
curious church in Berwick-on-Tweed.   There is no belfry to
this building, but only two little "ornamental" cupolas;
but the Town Hall bells ring the people to church.
Colonel Fenwicke, one of Cromwell's officers, and governor
of Berwick during the Commonwealth, was the leading
spirit in the erection of this church, and probably he shared
the Puritan dislike to "steeple houses."

The introduction of change-ringing has had a serious
effect upon the stability of some of our old towers.   An
erection that was thoroughly capable of withstanding wind
and weather, and of bearing the weight of its two or three
bells, gently swung as they were on their half-wheels, has
frequently been put to a test beyond its strength when
required to endure the swaying caused by eight or ten bells
revolved in rapid succession, and that occasionally for an
hour or more at a time.   The ancient church of S. Leonard,
Middleton, Lancashire, has a tower, the upper storey of which,
erected in 1709, is of wood; probably because it was feared
that the foundations were unequal to the weight of a heavier
superstructure, such as was required for effectively hanging
the peal of bells.   In arranging a ring of bells in the bell-
frame, care is always taken to make them swing in different
directions, so as to neutralize to some extent the force of
their revolutions; but even so a distinct oscillation is
imparted to the tower.   The mischief has often been
increased by ignorant joiners wedging the bell-frame tightly
between the walls, when disaster can scarcely ever be more
than a question of time.   No serious evil need result where
the frame is fixed in a reasonable way, clear of all the walls,

and the peal is not too heavy for the structure in which it hangs.

Many English churches anciently had a small bell-cote for one or two bells, over the gable between the nave and the chancel, in addition to their belfry. In these hung the bells rung at the Elevation in the Mass. Such bell-cotes, now without their bells, may be seen at Isham, Rothwell, and Desborough, Northamptonshire, at Bloxham, Brize-Norton, Coombe, and Swalcliffe, Oxfordshire, and at Boston, in Lincolnshire. One complete in the possession of its bell is found at Long Compton, Warwickshire.

CHAPTER VIII.

Bell-ringing and Bell-ringers.

HAVING devoted considerable space to the consideration of the bells themselves, we turn to the question of their use; and, as is natural, the human agents in such employment of them first demand some attention. There is not much of interest, however, to record concerning these until comparatively modern times; for although bells, as we have seen, are very ancient, bell-ringing as it is understood in England to-day is a thing of the last three hundred years only. In the days when churches usually had two or three bells only, and these were chimed or tolled singly, the bell-ringers' art was not one to attract notice. Charlemagne ordained that the clergy themselves were to sound the bells as a summons to divine worship, and as late as the last century the custom was regularly observed in some places; at Notre Dame, in Paris, for instance, the priests, arrayed in surplices, rang the bells, and such is still the rule among the Carthusians. The churchwardens' accounts for the parish of Ludlow in 1551 have an entry of the sum of twelvepence paid to "the dekyns for rynginge of day belle;" and a trace of the same usage is to be found at Holy Trinity, Coventry, a century earlier. At Exeter, in 1511, the chantry priests were bidden to toll the bells, first one and then all, at the canonical hours. Among the figures carved on one of the shafts of the chancel arch at Stoke Dry Church, Rutland, and on the font at Belton, Lincolnshire, are men in albs ringing church bells. These do not, however, necessarily represent clergy, but more probably members of the separate order, as it was in some cases accounted, of bell-ringers. The Council of Cologne, held in 1310, decreed concerning these, that "those persons whose office it is to ring the church bells, shall know how to read, in order that they may be able to make the responses; and also that they shall wear the alb during divine service." From this it would seem that they filled to some extent the place of our now almost extinct parish-clerks.

It is said, however, that a gild of ringers existed at Westminster as early as the reign of S. Edward the Confessor, and that it can be traced at least as late as the time of King Henry III., from whom it received a royal patent. It may reasonably be supposed that such a society was not absolutely unique, though the absence of any records forbids our supposing that such provision for the ringing of the bells was common.

By the middle of the sixteenth century, ringing had become well known in the country, although it was probably of a somewhat unscientific sort; and already the ringers had gained that evil reputation for irregularity of life which so long, and it is to be feared to some extent justly in past days, clung to them. "The people of England," says Paul Hentzner, who travelled among them about the year 1550, "are vastly fond of great noises that fill the ear, such as firing cannon, beating of drums, and the ringing of bells; so that it is common for a number of them that have got a glass in their heads to get up into the belfry and ring the bells for hours together for the sake of exercise."

Early in the following century more system and science were introduced into the art by the foundation of societies for the special study and practice of it. The "Scholars of Cheapside" came into existence in 1603, but the fraternity was probably not long-lived. In 1637 the far more famous "Ancient Society of College Youths" was established, taking its name from S. Martin's Vintry, on College Hill, London, where the "youths" practised. Other societies with a similar object quickly came into being; Oxford, Cambridge, Norwich, and other places had their "scholars" or "youths," all eager to learn the intricacies of change ringing, and London saw others of these companies formed. The "Union Scholars" were founded about 1715, and lasted nearly half a century, and there still survives the society of the "Royal Cumberland Youths," so called from the Duke of Cumberland, but originally named the "London Scholars." Whether the existing "College Youths" can trace their pedigree in an unbroken line from the Ancient Society of 1637, is a debated question, some authorities maintaining that the original body died out in 1788.

The "College Youths" started their career under distinguished auspices, Lord Brereton and Sir Cliffe Clifton being among the founders, but their special claim to recollection in the history of bell-ringing lies in the fact that to them was dedicated Stedman's "Tintinalogia," the earliest book on the principles of change-ringing, published in 1667.

Fabian Stedman, of Cambridge, is looked upon as the father of all modern bell-ringers, for to him is due that complex system of changes which makes a "peal." But little had been attempted in this direction before the year 1657, which date is assigned to the invention of "Stedman's principle" by him whose name it has ever since borne. In his "Tintinalogia" he thus refers to the art of ringing as practiced up to and at that time: "for the Art of Ringing, it is admirable to conceive in how short a time it hath increased, that the very depth of its intricacy is found out; for within these fifty or sixty years last past changes were not known, or thought possible to be rang: then were invented the sixes, being the very ground of a six-score: then the twenty, and twenty-four, with several other changes. But Cambridge forty-eight for many years was the greatest peal that was rang or invented; but now, neither forty-eight, nor a hundred, nor seven hundred and twenty, nor any number, can confine us; for we ring changes *ad infinitum*."

Stedman's system, as originally devised, was intended for application to a ring of five bells only, but it was very soon adopted to rings of seven, nine, and other uneven numbers.

It would be out of place to insert here anything in the way of an elaborate treatise on change ringing; some account of what is meant by the term, is, however, necessary to the completion of our subject. The number of permutations possible in any given series of things is found by a well-known rule of arithmetic, namely by multiplying the consecutive numbers together. Thus, two things can stand only in two ways: three in thrice as many, or six ways; four in four times as many again, or twenty-four ways, and so forth.   Briefly, then, change-ringing consists of sounding a ring of bells according to every possible combination, each of which must be used once only.   It is usual to commence with a "round," or the simple sounding of the bells in regular scale from treble to tenor ; the order must then be continually changed, without repetition, until every permutation possible to a ring of that size has been used.

This would be a perfect and complete peal, but it will be obvious that in a ring of many bells it is impossible to actually ring all the changes.   A ring of twelve bells, for instance, will allow of the astonishing number of 479,001,600 ; changes which at the average of 24 changes per minute, would take nearly 38 years in execution.   In dealing with such rings, therefore, a certain section only of the possible changes is employed at one time.   Five thousand changes, which it is only possible to ring with seven or more bells, is the smallest number to which the name of a peal is technically allowed, less than that number merely constitutes a "touch."

From the intricacy of the work, it will at once be obvious that both deft hands and clear heads are needed for it : the former to keep the bell in such perfect control as to insure its sounding only in the right place, and the latter to determine that place amid the continually changing variations.

Several different systems have been composed for arranging the possible changes in rings of various numbers ; and each ringer must know by heart the course which his own bell is to take among the others, according to the special system employed.   The oldest system is that known as a "Grandsire Bob," for five bells only.   "Grandsire Triples" were invented by Benjamin Anable, who died in

1755, and further elaborated by Mr. Holt. A manufacturer of barometers in the early eighteenth century, Patrick by name, was also a composer of peals. The names by which peals of different kinds are distinguished are curious. The Piain Bob, the Treble Bob, the Alliance (a combination of the preceeding two), and the Court Bob are all systems differing chiefly in the method in which the treble bell passes through the order of the changes. Another set of terms tells the experienced ringer the number of the bells in the ring; those consisting of the odd numbers, three, five, seven, nine, and eleven, being denominated respectively, Singles, Doubles, Triples, Caters, and Cinques; while the even numbers, four, six, eight, ten, and twelve, are called Minimus, Minor, Major, Royal, and Maximus. A Bob Major, that is a peal consisting of every possible permutation of eight bells, consists of no less than 40,320 changes, and this is the fullest complete peal that has ever been rung. An epitaph in Leeds Churchyard, Kent, records the accomplishment of this extraordinary feat:—"In memory of James Barham, of this parish, who departed this life Jan. 14, 1818, aged 93 years: who from the year 1744 to the year 1804 rung in Kent and elsewhere 112 peals, not less than 5,040 changes in each peal, and called Bobs, etc., for most of the peals; and April 7th and 8th, 1761, assisted in ringing 40,320 Bob Major in 27 hours." This took place in the belfry of the church of the said parish of Leeds, and was performed by thirteen men, one of whom rang for eleven hours, and another for nine, out of the twenty-seven. The average rate at which this peal was rung was, as will be seen, rather over twenty-five changes per minute.

The longest peal rung by one set of men only is said to

have been a Kent Treble Bob Major, which was rung at St. Matthew's, Bethnal Green, on April 27th, 1868. It consisted of 15,840 changes, and was completed under the conductorship of Mr. H. Haley, in nine hours and twelve minutes. Oxford has records of notable peals rung on the bells of Christ Church, New College and Magdalen; as, for instance, one dated March 27 (Easter Monday) 1815, when ten thousand and eight Grandsire Caters were rung at New College in six hours and forty-two minutes. It is probably well that these exhibitions of skill cannot very frequently be given: for our fallen nature cannot always endure even sweet music for a quarter of a day, or more, without rest or respite. Many old churches with fine rings of bells have some record of past exploits by their ringers, the details of the peal being not infrequently painted on a board in the belfry.

Allusion has already been made to the fact that bell-ringers in the past bore anything but the best of reputations. In the general carelessness concerning the fabric and furniture of the church, the belfry almost ceased at one time to be considered part of the consecrated building; the clergy seldom entered it, and the ringers and their friends went in and out much as they pleased, and rang their touches and peals for mere amusement; until it became almost proverbial that even after calling the parishioners to divine worship the ringers usually turned their backs upon the church and sought the neighbouring ale-house. John Bunyan, some will perhaps remember, was in his early days one of the bell-ringers at Elstow; but an employment which in better regulated times ought, from its sturdy exercise for the body, and its summons of the soul to prayer and praise, to be a help to a man, was found in those days to be a hindrance, and was abandoned by Bunyan as he grew more thoughtful, together with profanity and Sunday "tip-cat," dancing and evil company. A curious illustration of the customs of the belfry in bygone days is the existence in several places of "ringers' jugs," which are generally careful to tell us by means of an inscription that they were intended for something stronger than water. At Hinderclay is one inscribed as follows : "By Samuel Moss this pitcher was given to the noble society of ringers at Hinderclay, in Suffolk, viz: Tho. Sturgeon, Ed. Loch, John Haw, Ric. Ruddock, and Ralf Chapman, to which society he once belonged, and left in the year 1702.

> From London I was sent,
> As plainly doth appear ;
> It was with this intent,
> To be filled with strong beer.
> Pray remember the pitcher when empty."

Thomas Sturgeon and his four brethren of the "noble society" must have been thirsty souls, for the pitcher will hold sixteen quarts. At Clare is a similar jug of a slightly larger size. These are still preserved in the church ; another belonging to Hadleigh is kept at the "Eight Bells" Inn. It is dated 1715, and has the following lines, in addition to the names of the eight ringers of that date, roughly engraved upon it :—

> "If yov love me doe not lend me,
> Evse me often and keep me clenly,
> Fvll me fvll, or not at all,
> If it be strovng, and not with small.
> Hadly."

George Fox, the Quaker, sent in 1650, the following letter to the ringers of S. Peter's, Derby, his reason for so doing being no doubt the general reputation for careless lives which such men then unfortunately bore :—

"Friends,—Take heed of pleasures and prize your time now, while you have it, and do not spend it in pleasures or earthliness. The time may come, that you will say, you had time, when it is past. Therefore, look at the love of God now, while you have time ; for it bringeth to loathe all vanities and wordly pleasures. O consider! Time is precious. Fear God, and rejoice in Him, who hath made heaven and earth." An old proverb which declares that

> " Singers and Ringers
> Are little home-bringers,"

obviously alludes to the fact that they were notorious for spending their earnings too readily and too selfishly.

Some attempt was early made to keep the belfry in order by means of more or less elaborate rules, a copy of which was hung therein, or painted on the wall. The two oldest examples now extant are those to be found at Scotter, Lincolnshire, and at Dunmer, Basingstoke. The former painted in black and red Gothic letters, runs as follows :—

> " Yow ringers All
> who heare doe fall
> And doe cast over
> a bell doe forfeit
> to the Clarke theirfore
> A Groute I doe yow
> tell & if yow
> thinck it be to
> little & beare
> A valliant minde
> ymore yow give
> vnto him then
> you prove to him
> more kinde."

10

The rules at Basingstoke, dating from the sixteenth century, are imperfect; they now appear in this fragmentary form :—

> . . . Bless the King . . .
> To the Sexton thay belong.
> pay him tharefore, do him no rong.
> Stand from the ringers a yard at least . . .
> 26 years pay i do not jest
> if any bell you over throw it cost you p . . . you
> So put of your hats else pay . . ."

It may not be unnecessary to explain that overturning a bell, which is punished with a fine in these and other rules hereafter to be quoted, consists in raising it with such force as to break either the slide or the stay, so that the bell instead of resting mouth upward until brought back in the reverse direction, makes a complete circle and comes down on the wrong side. It is a serious belfry offence, because it renders the correct ringing of the overturned bell impossible without the repair of the broken timber.

Here is a fuller form of rules found at Hathersage, Derbyshire, and with little alteration at Chapel-en-le-Firth, and at Tideswell :—

> " You gentlemen that here wish to ring,
> See that these laws you keep in everything ;
> Or else be sure you must without delay
> The penalty thereof to the ringers pay.
>
> First, when you do into the bell-house come
> Look if the ringers have convenient room ;
> For if you do be an hindrance unto them
> Fourpence you forfeit unto these gentlemen.
>
> Next, if you do here intend to ring,
> With hat or spur do not touch a string ;
> For if you do, your forfeit is for that
> Just fourpence down to pay, lose your hat.

If you a bell turn over, without delay
Fourpence unto the ringers you must pay ;
Or if you strike, miscall, or do abuse
You must pay fourpence for the ringers' use

For every oath here sworn, ere you go hence
Unto the poor then you must pay twelve-pence ;
And if that you desire to be enrolled
A ringer here, these words keep and hold !

But whoso doth these orders disobey
Unto the stocks we will take him straitway ;
There to remain until he be willing
To pay his forfeit and the clerk a shilling."

The parish stocks frequently stood in the churchyard, and were therefore " convenient " for the application of summary punishment on an obstinate offender. Fourpence was long the traditional fine for the violation of belfry-law. The ancient rules at Scotter demand a " groute," and so do these just quoted, whose date is about 1650, and others at Culmington, Shropshire, which have the date 1663 affixed.

The following regulations were in force at Tong, in the last named county, but whether they were calculated to improve the moral tone of the ringers may be questioned.

" If that to ring you doe come here
You must ring well with hand and eare,
Keep stroak of time and goe not out
or else you forfeit out of doubt.
Our law is so concluded here ;
For every fault a jugg of beer.
if that you ring with spur or hat
a jugg of bear must pay for that.
If that you take a rope in hand
these forfeits you must not withstand,
or if a bell you ov'rthrow,
it must cost sixpence ere you goe.
If in this place you sweare or curse,
sixpence you pay, out with your purse :

Come pay the clerk, it is his fee
for one that swears shall not go free.
These laws are old and are not new,
therefore the clerk must have his due.

GEORGE HARRISON, 1694."

At S. Andrew's, Plymouth, and at Landulph, in Cornwall, we meet with verses of a more ambitious character. They are dated 1700, and headed with the words, " Nos resonare jubent Pietas, Mors atque Voluptas." (Loudly we sound at the call of Gladness, Devotion, and Death.)

" Lett awfull silence first proclaimed be,
And praise unto the holy Trinity,
Then honour give unto our valiant King,
So with a blessing raise this noble ring.

Hark ! how the chirping Treble sings most clear,
And covering Tom comes rowling in the rear.
Now up on end at stay, come let us see
What Laws are best to keep sobriety,
Then all agree and make this their decree.

Who swear or curses or in hasty mood
Quarrell and strikes altho' they draw no blood,
Who wears his hatt or spurs, or turns a bell,
Or by unskillfull handling marrs a peale,
Lett him pay sixpence for each single crime,
'Twill make him cautious 'gainst another time.
But if the Sexton's fault an hindrance be,
We call from him a double penalty.

If any should our Parson disrespect,
Or warden's orders any time neglect,
Lett him be always held in foul disgrace,
And ever after banished this place.

Now round let goe with pleasures to the ear,
And pierce with echo through the yielding air,
And when the bells are ceas'd, then let us sing
God bless our holy Church, God save the King.

Other places in Cornwall adopted these rules, with certain omissions and alterations; they are to be found at Fowey, Wendron, Lanlivery, and elsewhere.

At Southill, Bedfordshire, is a set of rules, partly in rhyme, partly in prose. It is entitled " Rules to be strictly observed by everyone who enters this belfry."

> " We ring the Quick to Church, the Dead to grave,
> Good is our use, such usage let us have.
> He who wears Spur, or Hat, or Cap, or breaks a stay,
> Or from the floor does from a bell rope sway,
> Or leaves his rope down careless on the floor,
> Or nuisance makes within the Belfry Door,
> Shall sixpence forfeit for each single crime,
> 'Twill make him carefull at another time.

Whoever breaks or injures any of the Handbells shall make the damage good.

> We Gentlemen Ringers are nobody's foes,
> We disturb none but those who want too much repose,
> Our music's so sweet, so enchanting to hear,
> We wish there was ringing each Day in the Year.

To call the folks to church in Time we chime three seven minute peals, stop one minute between; toll the Tenor four minutes; ring the Ting Tang three minutes.   Total ½ an hour.

> When mirth and pleasure is on the wing we ring,
> At the departure of a Soul we Toll."

One of the longest forms of these rhymed belfry rules is that found at Grantham, the date being 1764.

> " He that in Ringing takes delight
>   And to this place draws near
> These Articles set in his sight
>   Must keep if he Rings here.
>
> The first he must observe with care
>   Who comes within the door
> Must if he chance to curse or swear
>   Pay sixpence to the poor.

And whoso'er a noise does make
   Or idle story tells
Must sixpence to the Ringers take
   For melting of the Bells.

If any like to smoke or drink
   They must not do so here
Good reason why—just let them think
   This is God's House of Prayer.

Young men that come to see and try
   And do not Ringing use
Must Six Pence give the company
   And that shall them excuse.

So that his hat on's head does keep
   Within this sacred place
Must pay his Six Pence ere he sleep ;
   Or turn out with disgrace.

If any one with spurs to's heels
   Ring here at any time
He must for breaking articles
   Pay Six Pence for his crime.

If any overthrow a Bell
   As that by chance he may
Because he minds not Ringing well
   He must his Six Pence pay.

Or if a noble minded man
   Come here to Ring a bell
A shilling is the Sexton's fee
   Who keeps the church so well.

If any should our Parson sneer
   Or wardens' rules deride
It is a rule of old most clear
   That such sha'nt here abide.

The Sabbath day we wish to keep
   And come to church to pray
The man who breaks this ancient rule
   Shall never share our pay.

> And when the bells are down and ceased
> It should be said or sung
> May God preserve the Church and King
> And guide us safely home."

Some of the lines in the above sets of rules seem to have become almost traditional, and they are found combined with various other doggerel "tags" all over the country. The following, from S. Mary's, Stow, Lincolnshire, is concerned rather with the apprenticeship of the novice in the art of ringing than with offences committed in the belfry, and is in other respects different from those already given

	s.	d.
"All you who hath a mind to Larn to Ring		
Must to the Sexton Admission money Bring - - -	2	6
Those Articles observed strict must be		
Or your expelled this Society.		
Two nights a week, Sirs, you must meet, or pay		
This forfeiture to us without delay - - - - -	0	2
Or when the Sexton for you tools a bell		
You must appear, or else this Forfit tell - - - -	0	2
And when you come upon this Bellfrey		
If that you noise or talk, this Forfeit pay - - -	0	1
When you Round peals can Ring, you must pay down		
To be a change man, Sirs, just half-a-crown - - -	2	6
On the first change that you have Learned to Ring		
One shilling more must pay, Sirs, that's the thing - -	1	0
And every Ringer must spend more or Less		
As he thinks meet, to wish you good Success - - -	0	2
If you would learn to prick a peal in Score		
Unto those Colledge youths you must pay more - -	1	0
When you know Bob, Hunt, Single, Dodge compleat		
You'll not deny our Colledge youths a Treat - - -	2	6
On our Feast-Day, the Twenty-ninth of May,		
Each member must, Sirs, just one shilling pay • -	1	0
When our accompts are passed, Sirs, for truth		
And you are stiled then a Colledge youth,		
New Stewards then are chose, and, by the by,		
If that you do the Stewardship deny		

Your fine must pay—as in the margin see   -   -   - 1 6
Then from your Stewardship one year are free.
Those Rules peruse well before you enter,
Its a hard task on which you venture.
When once a member you are freely made
Those Articles must justly be obey'd.
So now, my Lads, admission money bring   -   -   - 2 6
And we will Learn you presently to ring."

These articles are attested by John Marshall, Master, and William Smith, Notary, and bear date March, 1st, 1770. One cannot but feel in reading them that a novice in the belfry at Stow was made the most of by his elders.

In some instances no attempt was made at weaving the code of belfry laws into verse. In the church at Clee are a set of " Orders to be observed kept by yᶜ Bell Ringers in yᵉ town of Clee, in yᵉ County of Lincoln, from this 27th day of Novr. 1793, with the consent of the Rev. J. Stockdale Vicar." They cover most of the offences already noticed, such as ringing in hat or spurs, breaking the stay, leaving the rope's end lying upon the floor, and so forth ; the last two orders are :—

" Any person or persons who shall swear, lay wagers, etc., in yᵉ ringing room, shall forfeit for every offence 3d, to yᵉ use of yᵉ ringers.
Any person yᵗ shall read any of these orders with his hat upon his head shall pay 6d to ye use, etc."

Several other "codes" contain this last regulation, and since in each case it stands last of the list, so that the unwary would be unlikely to see it until the offence in question had already been committed, it seems probable that it was inserted, not out of reverence to the rules, but as a trap for obtaining sixpences from strangers.*

In spite of all these rules and regulations—(most of which, it must be confessed, aim rather at making the man a good ringer, than at making the ringer a good man), the art of bell-ringing was at a very low ebb in the early part of the present century.   Thus despondently does the Rev. Wm. C. Lukis speaks of it in a book already quoted—(published as late as 1857):—"There are sets of men who ring for what they can get, which they consume in drink ; but there is very little love for the science or its music : and, alas ! much irreverence and profanation of the House of God.   There is no 'plucking at the bells' for recreation and exercise.   Church-ringers with us have degenerated into mercenary performers. In more than one parish where there are beautiful bells, I was told that the village youths took no interest whatever in bell-ringing, and had no desire to enter upon change-ringing."   The complaint is made specially concerning Wiltshire, but it was equally applicable to many, if not most, other counties.   Here, however, as everywhere else, the revived Church life of the last half century has shown its power.   The belfry is no longer used as a lumber-room for the sexton, nor as a lounge for the village idlers.   Almost everywhere it is as well cared for within and without, in its degree, as any part of the church ; and week after week from hundreds of steeples the music of the bells is sent throbbing across town and country by bands of willing workers, who throw head and heart and hands into the work

---

* That little collection of notes on bells, "Curiosities of the Belfry," by John Potter Briscoe, F.R.H.S. (London : Hamilton, Adams & Co., 1883), contains some two score examples of these belfry rules.   The present writer is indebted to the book for several interesting facts.

for the love of God and of His Church. That there are no
neglected belfries left, and no drunken ringers still to be
seen, amid the thousands of the former and the myriads
of the latter in England, were too bold an assertion; but
this may be said without fear of contradiction, that the ill-
repute of bell-ringers as a class has gone; it has been lived
down.

An epitaph, which contains a record of a famous peal,
has already been quoted; it is by no means the only
instance in which reference is made upon a tombstone to
the ringer's love of his art. In the chancel of the church
of Wainfleet S. Mary, Lincolnshire, is a slab with these
words :—

"Under this stone there is a vault and therein lyes the Remains of
Adlard Thorpe, Gent., a Sinner and a Ringer, who departed this
life on the 24th of January, 1770, aged 58 years."

In the same county, at Scothorne, the old sexton, John
Blackburn, is thus commemorated :—

> "Alas poor John
> Is dead and gone
> Who often toll'd the Bell,
> And with a spade
> Dug many a grave
> And said Amen as well."

At Pett, near Hastings, is a brass tablet immortalizing the
name of George Theobald, "a lover of bells," who "gave a
bell freely to grace the new steeple;" but instances are not
rare of ringers giving, not only their time and talents to their
art, but their means also to provide the instruments required
by it. The inscription on the treble and second bells at
S. Peter's, Nottingham, records that they were given by the
Society of Northern Youths in 1672, and re-cast by the

Sherwood Youths in 1771.   At Aldbourne, Wiltshire, is a
bell with the inscription :—

> " The gift of Jos. Pizzie & Wm. Gwynn.
>   Music & ringing we like so well
>   And for that reason we gave this bell.
> Robt. Wells, of Aldbourn, fecit.   1787."

By a quaint conceit, similar to that by which all drivers of
post-horses were called "boys," all ringers of bells anciently
considered themselves "youths."   In each case the exercise
indulged in was of so health-giving a nature, that the characteristics of youth, if not of boyhood, might well gain from it
an unusually extended life.   Old James Barham, whose
ringing at Leeds and elsewhere has been noticed, lived to
the age of 93 years, and cases are often quoted in proof of
the longevity of bell-ringers.   For example, at Painswick, in
Gloucestershire, on May 5th, 1817, the longest peal of caters
on record, consisting of 12,312 changes, was rung by ten
men in seven hours and forty-nine minutes, and of these
ringers one still survived in 1883 at the age of 91 years, and
the rest had died at the respective ages of 89, 87, 85, 84,
80, 78, 71, 70, and 50.   A modern instance of long-
continued service in the belfry is sufficiently remarkable
to deserve mention.   Samuel Mayers, who still survives,
took part in ringing a muffled peal at Christleton Church,
Cheshire, on the occasion of the death of William IV. ; he
also helped to celebrate the accession of Queen Victoria,
and was present at his place in the belfry when a loyal
peal was rung in 1887 to commemorate her Jubilee ; and at
the rejoicings for the sexagenary anniversary of her accession
on June 22, 1897, he assisted in ringing a set of Holt's

Grandsire Triples of 5,040 changes, which occupied nearly three hours.

Even in the belfry, however, the "youths" have not been suffered to maintain an absolute monopoly, and the "gentler sex" has tried its hand here and there at tolling and chiming; but a company of female change-ringers has apparently not yet arisen. At Spalding, at the beginning of this century, and at S. Benedict's, Lincoln, at the same period, the widows of the sextons held their late husbands' offices for some years, and regularly tolled the morning bell. At Spring-thorpe, Lincolnshire, a funeral wreath and gloves, made of white paper, hang in the chancel, commemorating the sad death of a girl who was killed in unskilfully handling a bell, allowing herself to be drawn up by it, and dashed against the floor of the bell-chamber. Such tragedies, though happily uncommon, have happened elsewhere. In June, 1778, a ringer named Lilley was killed at Doncaster in a similar way.

Some unknown hand has sought to immortalize the "youths" who rang the bells at Ecton, Northampton-shire, some hundred and fifty years ago. The belfry con-tains the portraits of the six, each holding the rope of his bell: they wear knee-breeches, with stockings and buckled shoes, their shirts are open at the neck, and their coats and vests lie upon the floor. The leader is represented as dressed in a somewhat better style than his companions, from which we may judge that he occupied a social position more or less in advance of theirs. The manners and customs allowed in the belfry in those days in too many instances, are illustrated by this quaint old painting, which represents, upon a bench on one side, a jug of beer, a mug, and five tobacco-pipes.

During recent years the old Societies of "College youths" and others have been supplemented by the establishment of county or diocesan associations, under whose auspices the art and mystery of change-ringing have become more widely popular, and the status of the ringers deservedly improved. Occasionally the use of the church bells for peal-ringing is criticized, as if it were a secularizing of sacred things ; but the complaint is surely made somewhat thoughtlessly. If abuses are removed, so that the sacred character of the belfry, as part of the church, is neither forgotten nor ignored ; if the ringers be men whose conduct in the belfry and out of it be such as to bring no scandal on the Church, whose humble ministers they are ; and if they who ring for exercise and pleasure are those who also sound the summons to worship, and obey the summons which they sound ; there can be no more objection urged against peal-ringing, at proper times and within reasonable limits, than against a "voluntary" on the organ, or, to quote a closer parallel, against a "recital" thereon. And the belfry is not devoid of its spiritual force any more than the organ-chamber : he is indeed dense of soul, or hard of heart, that can hear unmoved the mellow music of the pealing bells across the green fields of Old England as the summer sun sinks westward to his rest ; and who has not felt his blood tingle and his spirit stir within him, as amid the hurry and bustle of the busy, selfish town, the mad clash and clangour of the bells on Christmas Eve, echoing from a dozen quivering steeples, tell him that "Christ is born" to bring on earth goodwill and peace ?

The names of several distinguished men are to be found among those who have used the exercise of bell-ringing. In

the roll of the Society of College Youths are reckoned Sir
Michael Hicks (in 1699), Sir Watkin Williams Wynn (in
1717), and Lord Mayor Slingsby Bethell (in 1756).   Sir
Matthew Hale, the Lord Chief Justice, was a bell-ringer;
and Anthony Wood, the Oxford antiquary of the seventeenth century, tells us that he "often plucked at them (the
bells of Merton) with his fellow colleagues for recreation."
Perhaps the most distinguished name of all, however, so far
at least as worldly position goes, is that of the Tsar Ivan
Vasilievitch, known as the Terrible.   It was his delight to
mount the belfry of his favourite monastery at Moscow, and
toll the bell for Mattins at three or four in the morning.
But in his case, at least, the music that fell from the
throbbing metal was powerless "to soothe the savage breast."
Ivan was both a fanatic and a tyrant, and turned, as if for
relaxation, from Mattins to murder, and from villany to
Vespers.

The Ancient Society of College Youths assumed almost
the dignity of a company; they had their own beadle, who,
armed with a staff surmounted by a silver bell, preceded
them as they went in procession to Bow Church once a
year.

Now and again a bequest proves that the sweetly
modulated music of the bells has found an echo in some
grateful heart.   Nell Gwynne, the frail and fair, left money
for a "weekly entertainment" for the ringers of S. Martin's-
in-the-Fields; and in 1603, a worthy of Harleigh,
Middlesex, remembered the ringers of that parish in a way,
which, if not appealing to their poetic sentiments, perhaps
touched their feelings in a more tender place—he provided
for them an annual feast of roast pork.

CHAPTER IX.

The Church-Going Bell.

IN dealing with the uses of bells it is natural to speak first of that employment of them which was the original cause of their introduction into our churches, and still remains the most familiar evidence of their presence there ; namely, the ringing of the bells as a notification to the people of the ordinary services of their parish church.

Amongst the Jews, it will be remembered, although small bells were known, solemn assemblies were summoned by a blast of silver trumpets. Thus ran the divine command : "Make thee two trumpets of silver, of a whole piece shalt thou make them : that thou mayest use them for the calling of the assembly, and for the journeying of the camps." (Num. x. 2.) Trumpet music in other respects also took, among that ancient people, the place filled among us by bell-music. In a later verse of the chapter just quoted, we read, "In the day of your gladness, and in your solemn days, and in the beginnings of your months, ye shall blow with the trumpets over your burnt offerings, and over the sacrifices of your peace offerings." The ark of God was brought up to Jerusalem amid the sound of trumpets, and in a similar way the fall of Jericho was celebrated ; in a word, in circumstances where we look for the clash of bells, the Jews were familiar with the blare of clarions.

Huc, the Lazarist priest, who travelled in Mongolia in

1844, found the same means employed for summoning the worshippers in Thibet. Among them also bells are known and used, but the calling of an assembly is thus described : "When the hour for prayer is come, a Lama whose office it is to summon the guests of the convent, proceeds to the great gate of the Temple, and blows as loud as he can a sea-conch, successively towards the four cardinal points ; upon hearing this powerful instrument, audible for a league round, the Lamas put on the mantle and cap of ceremony and assemble in the great inner court ; when the time is come the sea-conch sounds again, the great gate is opened, and the living Fô enters the Temple." At Willoughton and at Thorney are preserved tin trumpets, which are said to have served at one time for calling the people together.

In the primitive Church during the times of persecution the use of bells, or any other public announcement of divine worship, was, of course, impossible ; but in their stead trusty messengers, called "runners," passed from house to house of the faithful, briefly stating the time and place appointed for their next meeting. To this custom Tertullian seems to allude in the last chapter of his "De Fuga in Persecutione," "If you cannot assemble by day," he says, "you have the night, the light of Christ luminous against its darkness ; you cannot run about among them one after another, be content with a church of threes."

In the eighth century the Greeks began to employ sonorous pieces of wood, much as we now use bells ; on high festivals, at solemn litanies, and when carrying the blessed sacrament to the sick, they struck upon these "holy boards." At a later time a plate of metal came to be used in a similar way, under the name of *hagiosideron*, or "holy iron." The employment of such rude methods of announcing a public service came later into vogue, and is still the usage in Greek monasteries. Dr. Neale describes one of these "semantra" as a board or log, twelve feet long, one and a half feet broad, and nine inches in thickness ; the priest, he tells us, "strikes it with a mallet in various parts, various angles eliciting sounds not altogether unmusical." By the constitutions of Lanfranc a blow on the cloister door with a mallet summoned the convent at Canterbury to attend a dying monk.

The earliest allusions to bells in this connection have reference to Western monasteries. S. Gregory of Tours speaks of a "signum" for assembling the monks to say mattins, and the Venerable Bede tells of a bell at the abbey of S. Hilda, at Whitby. The first English rule upon the subject is found in the " Excerptions " of S. Egbert, Archbishop of York, of which the date is 750 :—" Let all priests at the appointed hours of the day and night toll the bells of their churches (*sonent ecclesiarum signa*), and then celebrate the divine offices." In monastic houses the *signum* was the bell rung for the offices of the hours, namely, Mattins, Lauds, Prime, Terce, Sext, Nones, Vespers, and Compline. The large bell, *campana*, rang out the summons for the laity without the abbey walls to attend such services as were not meant primarily, or perhaps exclusively, for the brethren.

Mention of the "signum" ringing as a call to public prayer is made in the Canons of the second Council of Cealcythe, held in 816, by the Emperor Charlemagne in reference to mass, and in the Chronicle of Battle Abbey of the twelfth century. The small hand-bells described in the

11

first chapter of this book, and associated with the names of
S. Patrick, S. Gall, and others, were probably used to gather
listeners to the teaching of those apostolic men.   Such was
the method used in India by S. Francis Xavier, as Turselini,
in the life of the saint published in 1594, tells us.   "He, a
man of grave years and authority," he writes, "went up and
down the highways and streets with a little bell in his hand,
calling the children and servants together to Christian
doctrine."   In Italy, also, S. Francis Borgia used a hand-
bell to collect the children to the catechism ; and the same
was done, in the days of S. Vincent de Paul, at the commencement of the catechism at S. Sulpice, Paris.   S. Francis
Xavier tells us that the native Christians whom he found at
Socotra, the descendants of the disciples of the apostle
S. Thomas, "used no bells, but wooden rattles to call the
people together."

The law for the use of "the church-going bell" in England
at the present time, is found in the following rubric in the
Prayer-Book, at the conclusion of the preface "Concerning
the Service of the Church ;" "The Curate that ministereth
in every Parish-Church or Chapel, being at home, and not
being otherwise reasonably hindered, shall say the same (the
Morning and Evening Prayer) in the Parish-Church or
Chapel where he ministereth, and shall cause a bell to be
tolled thereunto a convenient time before he begin, that the
people may come to hear God's Word, and to pray with
him."   The Prayer-Book of 1552 suggests the old custom,
whereby the priest himself was the ringer, for the direction
therein runs that he "shall toll the bell."

The method of ringing differs in various places, according
to local custom and the number of bells in the church.

Where there is a full ring the usage is usually somewhat on the lines laid down in the belfry rules of Southill already quoted. The peal or chime sometimes concludes with the tolling of a number of strokes corresponding with the day of the month.

The "Sermon Bell" is the special tolling of a single bell to give notice that a sermon is to be preached in the course of the following service. It is sometimes rung considerably before the service, sometimes at the close of the peal which announces the service, and occasionally immediately before the sermon itself. Its use is very ancient, dating from days previous to the Reformation. The "Rites of Durham" mention the fact that on Sunday afternoons a sermon was preached in the Galilee of the Cathedral, and that the great bell was tolled to give notice of it. The Injunctions issued by King Edward VI. in 1547, order that "in the time of the Litany, of the Mass, of the Sermon, and when the priest readeth the scripture to the parishioners . . . all manner of ringing of bells shall be utterly forborne at that time, except one bell in convenient time to be rung or knolled before the sermon." The Churchwardens' Accounts for Melton Mowbray, in the years 1547 and 1553, mention the ringing of bells when the Bishop of Lincoln and Hugh Latimer preached there; but these seem to be cases of summoning the people at an unusual occasion, and not instances of the "Sermon Bell" proper.

In Leicestershire and Rutland the tenor bell is still very commonly rung before the service if a sermon forms part of it, and the same is true of Lincolnshire; though in some few cases the treble bell is used. In many instances a bell rung at seven, eight, or nine in the morning is called the Sermon

Bell ; and in others it is rung at two or three in the afternoon. In a great many places the rapid growth of the custom of celebrating the Holy Eucharist at eight o'clock on each Sunday morning, while happily restoring to the early bell its utility, has concealed the fact that that bell was formerly rung at the same hour for another purpose. On the other hand, the almost universal use now of evening, instead of afternoon, services has left the afternoon Sermon Bell, which usually rang about an hour before the service, a mere survival of a bygone usage.

A regulation in force at Exeter during the seventeenth century was to the effect that the Sermon Bell should be tolled "every Sunday after the second lesson of the quire service in ye morning when there is a sermon." It is said that as late as 1703 a bell was rung each Sunday at Ravenstondale, Westmoreland, at the conclusion of the Nicene Creed, to summon the Dissenters to hear the sermon.

A small bell hung in the belfry was occasionally, in olden times, called the "Priest's Bell," its purpose being described in the return of the Church goods at Ware, Herefordshire, as being "to calle for ye priste, clarke, or sexton when they are absent." This purpose is still often kept in view in the tolling of a small bell just before service, but the name is not so commonly used; "early bells," "minute bells," or "Tantony bells," are more familiar titles. The last expression, properly S. Anthony bells, is derived from the fact that that saint is usually represented with a small bell, sometimes at the end of his staff, and sometimes suspended from the neck of his strange companion, a pig.

The fact that the Holy Eucharist is to be offered, is in some places notified, just as the expected sermon is, by the employment of a special bell, hence called the Sacrament Bell. At Lutterworth the ancient Sanctus Bell concludes the peal on this occasion, instead of the sermon bell. In several places, as for example at Uppingham and in more than one church at Stamford, a smaller bell than that usually rung similarly gives the final tolls before the service. An excellent custom at one time prevailed, and has recently been in many instances revived, of marking the passage from Mattins to the Eucharist by the tolling of a bell, so that those who feel unequal to attending the series of services (as Mattins, Litany, Eucharist and Sermon) often inconsiderately strung together into one wearisome whole, might know when to come for the highest and most important of them. Archbishop Whitgift speaks of " ringing when mattens is done." Hooper, Bishop of Gloucester, in his injunctions to his diocese in 1551, gives orders concerning both the use of the Sacrament Bell and also the more general employment of these parochial " signa." From henceforth, he enjoins, " in no parish in the diocese shall the bells be rung . . . . but before service, as well in the morning as at even, to warn the people by as many peals or ringings as they think good ; and in case there be any pause between the morning prayer and the communion, then to advertise and signify unto the people of the ministration of the holy sacrament, to toll one bell, such as the parish shall think most meet and convenient." Hooper also makes enquiry at his visitation, " whether they ring or knoll the bells at the time of the communion, or between the morning prayers, which is commonly called matins, and the communion, as they were wont to ring out of matins to mass before this order was brought in."

It is a curious fact that in not a few instances the custom of ringing the bells at a certain hour has survived the service for which it was originally a summons. The early bell on Sunday mornings, though in some cases a " sermon bell," probably in others called the people to mass in years gone by, and has happily been restored to its early use in many places. The so-called " Pancake-Bell " on Shrove Tuesday, which announced that the parish priest was waiting to shrive his people before the solemnity of Lent began, is a striking case in point, that will hereafter be again noticed. Most remarkable is the extent to which this fact is true of Scotland. Religion has there not been subject only to " reform," but to revolution, the old services have gone, the old ecclesiastical order has been abolished ; yet the bells, as if in protest against the change, keep up their constant chiming for offices which the people know not. Mr. F. C. Eeles has tabulated a number of instances of this in his work on the " Bells of Kincardineshire." In that county the usual times for the Sunday morning service are eleven, half-past eleven, or twelve o'clock. Yet in a dozen instances the bells ring at eight or nine o'clock, and again at ten or half-past ten. At Johnshaven the chapel bell was formerly rung daily at six in the morning and eight in the evening, and at Drumlithe and Stonehaven the bells sound daily. The local people, have, of course, their own reasons to give for these customs ; as that they are to give notice of the coming of the " Sabbath " for instance ; and in some cases probably the ten o'clock bell is a relic of a time when there was a " Scripture Reading " before the regular service. But this does not account for the earlier bells, or for those on the weekdays, concerning which we may safely conclude that they still ring for mattins or for early mass, as they did centuries ago.

In some places it is the custom to ring the good folk out of church, as well as into it. At Culworth, Northampton-shire, a bell is tolled as the congregation leaves after a celebration of the Holy Eucharist. In the Midlands and in Lincolnshire a similar rule obtains, not infrequently, in country parishes, as regards every Sunday morning service. At Louth, the third bell used to be rung after both mattins and evensong, under the name of the " Leaving-off Bell ;" and at Gedney Hill a bell is always rung at the end of a service, no matter what or when. The name given to this tolling is sometimes the " Pudding Bell," the idea being that as the congregation breaks up after the Sunday morning service, notice is thus given to the housewives at home to commence their final preparations for dinner. In some country churches it is unquestionably a reminder to the congregation that there is to be another service at night ; and if evensong is not to be said there, the bell is not rung. It is suggested, how-ever, by Mr. North, in his " English Bells and Bell Lore," that, as a rule, the tollings, as distinct from the peals, both before and after the service, are really the Angelus or " Ave Bell."

The children of the Church have not been ignored in the definite rules concerning the bells. In fulfilment of the canon of the Council of Trent, which enjoined the regular catechising of the young, several provincial synods gave directions for furthering the work, and several, those of Salerno and Milan among others, specially ordered that the

bell should be rung to summon the children. Among ourselves, evensong having been very generally transferred from
the afternoon to the evening, the old afternoon ringing
frequently is now a call to the young people of the parish to
their special service.

One summons to the parishioners which the bell gives
forth, and which is felt by all to be of peculiar interest, is
on the occasion of the induction of a new incumbent into
his benefice. This ceremony, which, on the mandate of the
bishop, is performed by the archdeacon or his deputy, forms
the legal installation of the parish priest into the possession
of the temporalities of his living. It commences by the
formal unlocking of the church-door, and concludes with
the ringing of the bell by the incumbent, as a summons to
the people to come and meet their new spiritual head. It
is a tradition that as many tolls as the priest gives, for so
many years will he occupy that cure ; but whether death or
promotion will cause him to vacate it, time alone can
show.

That intensity of Puritanical feeling which led to a general,
but not quite universal, destruction of bells in Scotland, was
not without sympathizers in England also. It is amusing,
and yet somewhat humiliating, to find Tyndale admitting, as
if it were rather a concession concerning the ringing of bells,
that "while the world is out of order, it is not damnable to
do it ;" while in the same spirit Whitgift allows that bells
are not marks of Antichrist. These, and such as these,
would surely have agreed with the Moslem infidels, who feel
the strongest prejudice against the use of bells. As is well
known, throughout Islam the muezzin, from the summit of
the minaret, summons the people to prayer by a musical

chant, which, in that clear oriental air, is said to ring out to a surprising distance. Some of the melodies declaimed by these sacred watchmen are very striking ; and heard as the Eastern sun leaps up at dawn, or as the evening shadows are swiftly falling, are full of power and pathos.

CHAPTER X.

Bells at Christian Festivals and Fasts.

IT has for ages been customary to mark the chief festivals and fasts of the Christian year by means of the bells, now pealing merrily, now simply chiming, and anon tolling mournfully, or perhaps hushed altogether into an unwonted silence. The details of such usages probably always differed considerably in different countries, and were, it may be, nowhere so full as in England, which has been called "the ringing island;" and among ourselves there must always have been local peculiarities, which have been accentuated by time. Customs have survived in one district which another has entirely forgotten; here modern convenience has been allowed to modify the ancient practice; while there the most rigid conservatism has prevailed, and occasionally new ideas have given a fresh purpose to peals which are really an echo of the past.

It will be useful to follow the course of the Church's year and mark the varying uses of the bells.

As the civil year draws towards its close, it is a common thing to hear, once or twice a week, the bells pealing forth right lustily from the steeple of the parish church; and if the enquiry be made as to their meaning, the answer will generally be, both from ringers and the other parishioners, that it is merely practice for the merry ringing of the Christmas bells. If, however, one cares to look a little deeper into things, he cannot but be struck with the fact, singular indeed if this explanation be the only one, that these "practices" are governed in many cases not by the convenience of the ringers of to-day, but by immemorial custom. We find, for instance, that at Claxby, Lincolnshire, the bells are rung each year once in the first week in Advent, twice in the second, three times in the third, and four times in the week immediately preceding Christmas; at Epworth the ringing commences on the Saturday following Martinmas, and is continued on each succeeding Thursday and Saturday until Shrove Tuesday; at Blakesley, Northamptonshire, the bells are always rung at this season on a Monday, and in the same county at Dodford, Pottersbury, Culworth, and Staverton, they are rung at five o'clock in the morning of each Monday in Advent. Other cases might be quoted, in which certain days and hours have been long associated with the ringing of the bells at this time of the year. All these instances point conclusively to the idea that these peals are not merely "practices," but a formal recognition of the season of Advent as the precursor of the glad festival of the Nativity; and this fully explains the custom, found elsewhere than in Claxby, of ringing with increasing frequency as that day draws nearer. Thus, at Moreton Pinkney, in Northampton-shire, during the last week in Advent, peals are rung nightly, and each morning also on the last three days before Christmas. Is it not possible that the early peals in the Northamptonshire parishes named, and elsewhere, may have originally had an allusion to the words of the epistle for Advent Sunday (Rom. xiii. 2), " Now it is high time to awake out of sleep?" In the unreformed missal the epistle for the day began with this verse, not as now three verses earlier, and it consequently gave more obviously than at present the key-note to the season.

Throughout a great part of England, S. Thomas's Day has long been sacred to the cause of charity. The poor, and especially women, have a traditional right to seek alms from their richer neighbours on this festival, presumably as a help towards keeping the Christmas feast. The custom has various names, as *gooding* or *goodening*, *mumpsing*, and Thomasing. Only in a few places has the assistance of the bells been invoked on the occasion. In Warwickshire, at Wellesbourne, a peal is rung at six in the morning, perhaps to remind the poor of the privilege of the day; and until recently the tolling of the tenor bell at Wragby, Lincolnshire, notified them that a dole of bread and meat was about to be distributed.

Of all times in the year none has become so closely associated in popular fancy with the pealing of the bells as the joyous season of Christmas. The merry music of the belfry is recognised as forming as essential a part of the Yuletide festivity as the decking of church and home with evergreens, or the provision of the time-honoured good cheer. A custom so well known and so natural needs little comment or illustration, but in some localities there are usages in connection with it that are worthy of notice. One of the most curious is that of the ringing of the "Devil's Knell" on Christmas Eve, which is done at Horbury and at Duesbury, in Yorkshire, in commemoration, it is alleged, of the fact that the incarnation of Christ broke the power of the Evil One. The Rev. Anthony Sterry left by will, in 1598, a sum of money to pay the ringers at Ricardean, Gloucester, for ringing each Christmas Eve from

midnight until two in the morning.   Peals late on the eve
or very early in the morning are very common everywhere.   A phrase in the rule given by S. Dunstan for
the monasteries of his own time illustrates the antiquity
of these Christmas peals, and shows, moreover, that it
was customary to ring them at intervals during the
whole octave; "at mass, nocturns, and vespers from
the Feast of the Innocents to the Circumcision," he
orders, "all the bells should be rung as was the custom
in England."

It is a very ancient usage on the feast of Childermas, or
of the Holy Innocents, to mingle certain signs of sorrow
with the tokens of joy; which is accounted for on the ground
of the tender age of the little martyrs, and also by the fact
that the victory of Christ over "the sharpness of death"
had not, at that time, "opened the Kingdom of Heaven to
all believers."   Thus, according to the chief Western usage,
the vestments of the day are not red, as for a martyr, or
white, as for a high festival, but of the penitential violet.
In the same spirit it is, or at any rate was, the practice to
ring a muffled peal on this day in many places, especially in
the West of England, at Salworthy, Somersetshire, Ross,
Herefordshire, and elsewhere.

The belfry's celebration of the octave of the Nativity,
the feast of the Circumcision, is obscured by the fact that
the civil year now commences on that day, so that for the
most part New Year's Day, and not the Christian festival, is
the anniversary commemorated.   The old year's knell is
solemnly tolled in many places, and the new year greeted
with a merry peal; a muffled peal occasionally takes the
place of the more funereal tolling.   It is to this custom that

the late Poet Laureate alludes in the stanzas quoted in the
first chapter :—

> " The year is dying in the night ;
> Ring out wild bells and let him die."

In the churchwardens' accounts for Kirton-in-Lindsey
in the year 1632, we find an entry proving that the usage
has been recognised for at least two centuries and a half:
" Item, to the ringers of the new year day morninge, xijd."
But the solemn and joyous commemoration of the
commencement of a new period of time is far older than
the Christian dispensation.   Among the Jews the seventh
month began the civil year, and the first day was
observed even more ceremoniously than the monthly feast
of the new moon.   The law prescribed on that day a
"sabbath, a memorial of blowing of trumpets, an holy
convocation," the sacred clarions, here, as on other occasions,
fulfilling much the same office as that now consigned to
church bells.

The next important festivals in the Christian year are
Epiphany and Candlemas.   No special use of the bells,
however, distinguishes these, though there are even here
exceptions to "prove the rule."   Swineshead, Lincolnshire,
still gives forth special Epiphany peals, and down to the
seventeenth century the same was done at Loughborough at
Candlemas.   It is extremely probable that many ancient
customs of the belfry died out during that century ; almost
all use of the bells was stopped during the Commonwealth,
and the bells themselves, in some cases, were stolen or
destroyed ; and many practices which depended solely on
tradition would, doubtless, lack vitality to survive the
interruption of a dozen years.

We now approach the season of Lent, the special time of meditation, penitence, and prayer. To such thoughts human nature turns with only too obvious a reluctance, and the outward manifestation of this is seen in the Continental carnival on Shrove Tuesday, the round of revelry and folly, with which the world says its farewell to pleasure before plunging into the forty days of penance. The Church calls the faithful to a far different method of preparation for Lent; with her Shrove Tuesday is a day for contrition and confession, and its English name still bears witness to the fact. With us, however, although the carnival, in the Continental sense, was probably unknown, feasting and frivolity bore equally strong evidence to our forefathers' regret at the privations enjoined in Lent; and many to-day are careful to observe the feast, who are heedless of the following fast. Thus has it come to pass that in so many parishes the Pancake Bell still rings on Shrove Tuesday. In its origin it was a summons to the parishioners to come to confession as a preparation for the solemnity of the coming season; but as that practice has so largely dropt out of the experience of the English people, the sound of the bell has come to be associated with the preparation of the traditional delicacy of that day. The pancakes themselves were at first not without their laudable connection with the Lenten fast. If we may trust a writer in *Notes and Queries* (3rd Series, vi. 404), " they were chiefly made in order to use up ere Lent began such lard and other ingredients as were in the house and could not be used during the fast." The connection between the day and the confection is certainly old. In Shakespeare's day it was already proverbial; the clown in "All's well that ends well" (Act 2 Sc. ii.), among

his many similes for aptness, says, "as a pancake for Shrove
Tuesday." Taylor, the Water Poet, in his "Jack-a-Lent,"
published in 1630, mentions not only the cake, but the bell
also. "On Shrove Tuesday," he says, "there is a bell rung
called Pancake Bell, the sound whereof makes thousands
of people distracted and forgetful either of manners or
humanitie. Then there is a thing called wheaten floure,
which the sulphury necromanticke cookes doe mingle with
water, egges, spice, and tragicall magicall inchantments;
and then they put it little by little into a frying-pan of
boyling suet." In 1684 we find another allusion in "Poor
Robin's Almanack," in the words,

> "But harke ! I hear the Pancake Bell,
> And fritters make a gallant smell."

The usual hour for ringing the Pancake Bell is eleven in
the morning; at some places, however, it is twelve. The
custom is unfortunately dying out; many parishes have dis-
continued it within living memory, although it is still kept
up in scattered places all over the country, and in the
county of Lincoln it is frequently found. The tenor, or one
of the heavier bells, is commonly the one used; in a few
cases two bells are rung; and at Belgrave, Leicestershire, the
tolling of the tenor is followed by a full peal. At Daventry it
is called the "Pan-burn Bell," and at All Saints', Maidstone,
the "Fritter Bell."

The sound of this was in times past the signal for many
forms of revelry, as well as the feasting on pancakes.
School children and apprentices usually had a holiday for
the rest of the day; football was played in a tumultuous
and unscientific fashion at Derby, and in many other towns;
the cruel amusements of cock-fighting and cock-throwing,

and other pastimes, were commonly indulged in ; and in not
a few places the belfry itself was practically thrown open to
the public, who clashed and clanged the bells at their
pleasure.   An order of the corporation of Grantham, dated
1646, orders the belfry door to be locked on Shrove
Tuesday, on the ground that "an innumerable concourse of
old and young," in the course of their Shrovetide jollity,
used to "jangle the bells and break the chime wires."

With the coming of Ash Wednesday, ushering in Lent,
all signs and sounds of joy are for a time suspended, and
the belfry shares the solemn feeling that prevails.   In many
parishes it is a rule to chime only, and not ring, during
these six weeks ; and in view of the fact that merry peals are
so commonly employed to mark the great festivals of the
Church, it would probably be found useful, as well as
reasonable, to distinguish the great annual fast in this way
more generally than is the case.

In pre-Reformation times the bells were altogether silent
from the mass on Maundy Thursday until Easter morning.
In many places, however, wooden clappers or rattles were
substituted.   S. Francis Xavier alludes to the custom, when,
in describing the usages of the Christians whom he found at
Socotra, he says, "They use no bells ; but wooden rattles,
such as we use during Holy Week, serve to call the people
together."   A wooden bell is preserved in a chest at S.
Mary Magdalen, Ripon, and there are several, already
referred to in an earlier chapter, at Lenton ; and it has been
suggested that these were possibly used, in place of the
sonorous metal, during this solemn time.   In some places,
as in Mexico, the people, on the last days of Holy Week,
carry wooden clacks, which they rattle as they go about the

12

streets ; the idea probably being to scare away evil spirits, which are for the time undisturbed by the bells, as a farmer's boy scares off the rooks from his master's wheat.   The Hon. Margaret Collier (Mme. Galletti di Cadilhac) describes the custom as witnessed by her on Holy Saturday in an Italian village.   "The next morning early," she says, in her account of her "Home by the Adriatic," "men go about hammering bits of wood, and crying, 'Come to mass in memory of Christ's death ;' this is called the *tric-a-trac.*" Aubrey, in the Lansdowne Manuscript (quoted in Brand's "Popular Antiquities "), describes what seems to have been a survival of a similar practice in England.   "It is the custom for the boys and girls in country schools, in several parts of Oxfordshire, at their breaking up in the week before Easter, to goe in a gang from house to house, with little clacks of wood, and when they come to any door, there they fall a-beating their clacks, and singing" a doggerel ditty, which he gives.   The wooden clacks for church use are mentioned in some of the inventories of the churches of mediæval Lincolnshire.   At Rouen, during Holy Week, the blast of a horn used to be substituted for the sound of the bells ; and it is very probable that the usage was not unknown in England.   Possibly the tin horns at Willoughton and at Thorney, mentioned in the preceding chapter, were used for this purpose.   The modern Roman usage, which anticipates the dawn of Easter Day in several ceremonial matters, is to discontinue all use of church bells of every kind, from the singing of the *Gloria in excelsis* at the Maundy Thursday mass until the same place in the mass of Holy Saturday.   It is usual in many places in England (and surely would be only seemly in all) to toll only for the service of Good Friday ; and in not a few places the older custom of observing a solemn silence in the belfry has been revived.   At Lincoln, "Great Tom" is tolled for service on this day, and in several instances the tenor bell alone is sounded.   At Caistor, Lincolnshire, a muffled peal is rung at three o'clock in the afternoon, the hour when the Redeemer "gave up the ghost," and at Aisthorpe, and elsewhere, it is usual to toll a knell at that hour.

At Easter, the "Queen of Festivals," the bells, of course, join in the rejoicings of the faithful.   Very early peals are common on this morning, though the old practice, once found in some churches, of ringing a peal at midnight seems to have died entirely out.   Easter Monday and Tuesday have also, in some instances, their traditional peals.

Early ringing of the bells, moreover, ushers in the other chief festivals of the Christian Church, as Ascension Day, Whitsun Day, and Trinity Sunday ; and in belfries where the custom is to chime on ordinary Sundays, the bells are usually rung for service on these high days.

In addition to these belfry observances of the greater feast-days, several of the days dedicated to the memorials of the Saints had their peculiar usages.

For some reason not very obvious S. Andrew's Day was specially honoured by the bell-ringers.   The "Tandrew (S. Andrew) Bell" is rung at noon at Bozeat, Northamptonshire ; and at Hallaton, Leicestershire, the school children, within the present century, were permitted on this day to lock themselves in the belfry and to jangle the bells ; in neither of these cases is S. Andrew the patron saint of the church.   An item in the churchwardens' accounts at

Kirton-in-Lindsey shows that in that parish, whereof this saint is the patron, the ringing on his day was not intermitted even during the Commonwealth; under the date 1658, we read, "It' to the ringers on Saint Andrew's Day o. 1. o."

Of the two great festivals of the Blessed Virgin, the Annunciation and the Assumption, the latter seems to have been observed with greater fervour in Old England; partly perhaps because the former not only falls frequently in Lent, but also at a time (March 25th) when open-air ceremonies and festivities are scarcely seasonable in our northern climate; whereas the date of the latter (August 15th) is eminently suitable for them. Peals no doubt were rung in many, or most, places on these festivals, but there is nothing calling for particular notice concerning them, except with regard to the ringing at Lincoln Minster. The bells are still rung there on Lady Day, the Cathedral being dedicated in honour of Our Lady; but a special chime was rung by the choristers on the six Lady Bells, until their destruction in 1834. Speaking of the manner in which these bells were rung, the late Sir Charles H. J. Anderson says, "I am more and more convinced that the chiming on Lady Day was the *Ave Maria*," and he shows how naturally the words "Ave Maria, ora pro nobis" might be suggested by the chime.

S. George has not obtained so much public recognition as the patron of England as he deserves. At the present day the difference between the observance of S. Patrick's Day by the Irish, and of S. Andrew's Day by the Scots, Presbyterians though they be, is in marked contrast to the little notice paid to S. George's Day (April 23rd) in England.

This neglect, however, does not appear to be of modern growth only, for there are few records (yet there are a few) of peals rung on that festival.

One or two holy days have gained a kind of fictitious prominence from the fact that events of public importance, and giving rise to national rejoicings, have occurred upon them. Thus S. James's Day (July 25th) became associated with the defeat of the Spanish Armada in 1588, and with the coronation of King James I., as is illustrated by entries in the churchwardens' accounts at Bishop Stortford and elsewhere. Similarly the accession of Queen Elizabeth on S. Hugh's Day (Nov. 17th) was the occasion of much ringing of bells throughout her reign, which had no reference to the saintly Bishop of Lincoln, although the payment for it is often simply entered in the parish accounts as for "ringing on S. Hugh's Day." Such uses of the bells will be included more appropriately in a later chapter, dealing with the secular, and semi-secular, usages connected with them.

No season, next to the highest festivals, was so marked by bell-ringing as Hallowmass, when the eves of All Saints and of All Souls were celebrated with almost continuous peals throughout the night. The accounts of more than one parish contain records of this; the amount of work required of the bells and their tackling often necessitating repairs in preparation of the event. At Bishop Stortford, in 1546, they paid "iiijs." "for makyng of a bell wheele ayenst All haluntyde;" in 1526 "Rodlay ye wright," of Leverton, in Lincolnshire, was paid "for me'dyng of ye bells agayns halomes, iiij^d.;" and at Heybridge, Essex, we find the following entries in 1517 :—

"Item, payed to Andrew Elyott, of Maldon, for
 newe mendinge of the third bell knappell
 agenste Hallowmasse - - - - - o£ is. 8d.
Item, payed to John Gidney, of Maldon, for a
 new bell-rope agenste Hallowmasse - - o£ os. 8d."

In the year 1546 the following injunction was issued by
Henry VIII. through Cranmer :—" Forasmuch as all the
vigils of our Lady and the apostles, and all other vigils,
which in the beginning of the church were godly used, yet
for the manifold superstition and abuses which after did
grow up by means of the same, they be many years passed
taken away throughout all Christendom, and there remaineth
nothing but the name of the vigil in the calendar, the thing
clearly abolished and put away, saving only upon Allhallow-
day at night, upon which night is kept vigil, watching, and
ringing of bells all the night long ; forasmuch as that vigil is
abused as other vigils were, our pleasure is, as you require,
that the said vigils shall be abolished as the other be, and
that there be no watching, nor ringing, but as be commonly
used upon other holy days at night."

If this order obtained universal obedience, the accession
of Mary no doubt restored the ancient custom, and it continued, at any rate for a considerable time, under Elizabeth.
Perceval Wiburn, writing to his friends at Zurich an account
of the Church of England during this latter reign, mentions,
among other things still retained, "the tolling of bells . . . .
on the vigils of saints, and especially on that of the feast of
All Saints, when it continues during the whole night."
The opposition to the practice still, however, found support
in high places. Grindal, as Archbishop of York, issued
certain "Injunctions to the Laity" in 1571, one of which is
"that neither on All Saints' day after evening prayer, nor

the day next after, of late called All Souls' day, there be any
ringing at all then (than) to Common Prayer, when the same
shall happen to fall on the Sunday."   Subsequently Grindal
was translated to Canterbury, and he made haste to carry on
in the southern province the crusade which he had begun
in the north ; in 1576 he published certain "Articles of
Enquiry" for the province, covering much the same ground
as did his Injunctions, this bell-ringing appearing among the
rest.   Either through the efforts of Grindal, or by other
means, the custom was finally eradicated, for no trace of it
appears to exist at the present time.

CHAPTER XI.

The Epochs of Man's Life Marked by the Bells.

WE have seen how the bells follow the course of the Christian year, tolling or pealing as the various mysteries commemorated seem to demand. We turn now to the life of the individual Christian, and we shall find that, with equal fidelity, the bells accompany him from the cradle to the grave, and even beyond, rejoicing with him in merry peals when he rejoices, and sobbing forth their dreary tolling amid the gloom of human sorrows.

We gather from a Spanish romance of the last century,* quoted by Brand in his "Popular Antiquities," that in Spain it was customary at that time to greet "the little stranger," even before his actual entrance on the stage of this world. " I remember once," says the hero of the story, "that in the dead time of the night there came a country fellow to my uncle in a great haste, intreating him to give order for knocking the bells, his wife being in labour (a thing usual in Spain); my good curate then waked me out of a sound sleep, saying, 'Rise, Pedro, instantly, and ring the bells for child-birth quickly, quickly.' I got up immediately, and as fools have good memories, I retained tne words 'quickly, quickly,' and knocked the bells so nimbly, that the inhabitants of the town really believed it

* "The Lucky Idiot: or, Fools have Fortune," by Don Quevedo de Alcala, 1734.

had been for fire." An analogous custom is cited in Thiers'
"Traité des Superstitions":—"When a woman is about to
be delivered," he tells us, "they take her girdle, go to the
church, tie the bell with this girdle, and ring it three
times, in order that the woman in question may be happily
delivered;" and he proceeds to quote to the same effect an
Archdeacon of Pampeluna, who says that "this superstition
is largely observed throughout the whole of his country."

The actual birth of a child is seldom hailed with bell-
ringing, unless it be a birth of local or national importance:
the coming of an heir to a royal house, or to that of a lord
of the manor, is not infrequently treated as a matter for
rejoicing, in which the bells, as usual, play their part. Two
parishes in Lincolnshire, however, have special methods of
celebrating the baptism of an infant; at Fulbeck the fourth
bell is rung before the service, and at Searby a short peal
follows it.

Peals are rung in most English parishes on the occasion
of the administration of Confirmation; but this is not so
much in celebration of the service as in welcome to the
bishop, just as in many places a flag flies on the church
tower when the "Father of the Diocese" comes to visit
some of his people. Latimer tells a quaint story of this
(though the occasion in this case was an episcopal visitation,
not a Confirmation) in a sermon preached before King
Edward VI., on April 12th, 1549. "I heard," says he, "of
a bishop of England that went on visitation, and as it was
the custom, when the bishop should come, and be rung into
the town, the great bell's clapper was fallen down, the tyall
was broken, so that the bishop could not be rung into the
town. There was a great matter made of this, and the chief

of the parish were much blamed for it in the visitation.
The bishop was somewhat quick with them, and signified
that he was much offended. They made their answers, and
excused themselves as well as they could : ' It was a chance,'
said they, 'that the clapper brake, and we could not get it
mended by and by ; we must tarry till we can have it done :
it shall be amended as shortly as may be.' Among the
other there was one wiser than the rest, and he comes me
to the bishop: 'Why, my lord,' saith he, 'doth your lordship make so great a matter of the bell that lacketh his
clapper? Here is a bell,' saith he, and pointed to the
pulpit, 'that hath lacked a clapper this twenty years. We
have a parson that fetcheth out of this benefice fifty pound
every year, but we never see him.'" In this connection
also we may quote one of the regulations promulged by
Bishop Alnewick of Lincoln in 1444, to the effect that
"not to ring the bells on the arrival of the bishop is a
manifest mark of contempt, for which the vicar may be
summoned to give account."

The next leading event in the lives of most of the male
portion of the population is the conclusion of their apprenticeship, and this is noted by the ringers in at least one
parish in England ; the tenor bell being sounded for a few
minutes at Waddington, in Lincolnshire, to notify to all
whom it may concern that another youth is "out of his
time."

Our hero having been thus confirmed and also trained for
his life's work, may be considered now to have attained to
man's estate ; and to be fitted, so far as may be, for the
responsibilities of life in things sacred and secular. His
thoughts turn naturally next to the finding of a fitting

partner for his home; and "the course of true love"
running to its desired end, in due time the banns of
marriage are "put up." The custom of ringing "Banns
Peals," as a kind of foreshadowing of the coming "Wedding
Bells," was at one time common, and though now dying
out, it is still found in several districts. In Lincolnshire,
which is conspicuous for its retention of bell customs, the
bells are still rung in over fifty parishes on the publication
of the banns. In some cases the peal follows the service at
which the contracting parties have been "asked" for the
first time; this is the usual practice in Lincolnshire, and
also at Owston, in Leicestershire, at Bulwick, in Northamptonshire, and other places. The "third time of asking" is,
however, the favoured occasion at Asterby, Cotes Magna,
and elsewhere in the first named county. The first and
third "askings" are both marked in this way at Ingoldsby,
Westborough, and in other Lincolnshire parishes; and all
three publications are honoured at North Cockerington,
Elsham, Searby, and in some other instances. At North
Kelsey the Monday morning after the last Sunday is marked
by a peal; and until the year 1867 a disorderly custom
prevailed at Sutton, in Northamptonshire, whereby any
young man from the congregation was suffered to make a
rush for the bell-rope, and tug at it according to his own
sweet will, at the conclusion of the service at which the first
publication had taken place. Ringing these peals is called
in some places "giving their spurring" to the young couple,
the term being derived, it has been suggested, from the old
Danish "*sporge*," meaning "asking."

The joyous peals which signalize the celebration of a
wedding have become proverbial among us; "merry as a

marriage bell" is accepted as a simile for the acme of mirth
and gaiety. Several bells, as we have already seen, bear
inscriptions allusive to their matrimonial usage, and another
instance may be added to those already cited ; on the fifth
bell at Kendal are the words :—

> " In wedlock bands
> All ye who join with hands
> Your hearts unite ;
> So shall our tuneful tongues combine
> To laud the nuptial rite."

In his "Epithalamium," or Bridal Song, Edmund Spencer
exclaims :—

> " Ring ye the bels, ye yong men of the towne,
> And leave your wonted labours for this day."

The number of the peals rung on the occasion differs in
different places, and is also considerably affected by the
popularity of the bride and bridegroom, or by the amount
of the fee given to the ringers by the latter. In the year 1612
the churchwardens of S. Martin's, Leicester, endeavoured
to regulate the matter in that parish by ordaining that three
peals should be rung for half-a-crown, and any more that
might be desired on payment of sixpence for each one ; a
charge that was certainly reasonable enough. Thirty years
earlier, in 1588, a shilling was the fee for a peal at Loughborough, in the same county, according to the following
minute in the churchwardens' book :—"Agreed at this
accompt that every marridge haveing or reqring to have
the bells rung shall paye vjd. to the poremen's boxe and vjd.
towards repairinge of the bells."

Parishes, whose churches possess but one bell, find it
almost impossible to produce a very joyous effect with such

limited means ; but the good folk of Stroxton, Lincolnshire,
which in past days was so situated, made a masterful
attempt to surmount the difficulty.   Three men stood
round the single bell, each armed with a hammer, where-
with they beat out a "three-bell-peal."   Wonderful to
relate, the long-suffering bell survived the process, but it
bears to this day the marks of all it has suffered on behalf
of the wedded joys of the parishioners.

Custom at one time required that the bells should be
rung to greet the bridal party as they went to church, as
well as to celebrate the completion of the rite.   To this Ben
Jonson refers in his "Tale of a Tub" (Act II., sc. 1), published in 1633 :—

> " We are going to church in the way of matrimony.   .   .   .
> They have rung all in already."

A somewhat pathetic usage prevailed of old at Barwell,
Leicestershire, which was to ring the body of a spinster to
her funeral with " her wedding peal ;" but the practice there
was probably unique.

It was an ancient tradition to wake the wedded pair on
the morning after their marriage with music of a more or less
boisterous kind.   Gay, in his " Trivia " (published in 1715),
speaks of it :—

> " Here rows of drummers stand in martial file,
> And with their vellum thunder shake the pile,
> To greet the new-made bride.   Are sounds like these
> The proper preludes to a state of peace ?"

Another writer tells us how " the drums rattle, the shaumes
tote, the trumpets sound tan-ta-ra, ra, ra, and the whole street
rings with the benedictions and good wishes of fiddlers,
drummers, pipers, and trumpetters."   Such a scene of

noisy jubilation Hogarth has given us in his print of Goodchild, the "Industrious Apprentice," married to his master's daughter. We are not surprised, therefore, to find that frequently the bell-ringers took their part with the other musicians of the town in the rude awakening of the bridal couple. At Rushton, Northamptonshire, at Mumby, Lincolnshire, and elsewhere, it was the practice until recently to ring a peal early on the morrow of the marriage ; and at Scotter, in the latter county, it is still occasionally done. In other parishes, as at Hogsthorpe, the ringing takes place at a later hour.

The bells have not even yet, however, contributed their full quota to the nuptial rejoicings. On the Sunday following the wedding it was the use in days gone by for the bridal party to make a kind of state attendance at church. "On the Sunday after marriage," says Pennant, speaking of the custom in North Wales, "the company who were at it come to church, *i.e.*, the friends and relations of the party make the most splendid appearance." On this occasion in many places the bells once more hailed them as they came to the church, and sent them home again after the service with another joyous peal ringing in their ears.

When the bride and groom happen to be people of local importance, or a couple exceptionally well known in the place, a merry peal usually greets them yet once more when they return home after their honeymoon. And with this last booming of the wedding bells, the excitement of the marriage festivities subsides, and life for the wife and husband drifts on "the even tenour of its way."

From this time forward to the end of life, though lights and shadows checker his pathway, the ordinary man

celebrates no epochs in his career which evoke the
throbbing voices of the bells; until, sobered down from
merry peal to solemn toll, they announce to the world
the conclusion of this mortal segment of his existence.
Of all the many uses of the church bells not one is more
thrilling than the slow booming of their deep tones in token
of a death.   In the village or the country town, where every
inhabitant is known to every other one at least by sight, the
melancholy music comes home to every heart, with its
message that some familiar face and figure, some one whose
life's web has been knit more or less closely, in joy or
sorrow, in friendship or in enmity, into those of all his
neighbours, will never more be seen coming down the
village street, never more be met in the haunts where he
was known so well.   And even in the busy city, when above
the hum of voices and the ceaseless tramp of feet, the tolling
of the bell tells of one more voice that is hushed for ever in
this world, of feet, once tramping life's march with the rest,
now stark and still in their winding-sheet, few are the hearts
so callous that the slow-measured knell does not, if but for a
moment, "give them pause."

In days gone by, when it can hardly be denied that men
took a more brotherly interest in each other's spiritual
welfare than is common at the present time, the good
offices of the bells were invoked, not as a mere signal that
a soul had departed, but as a summons to the faithful to
remember in prayer the sinner struggling in his last conflict.
The name "Passing Bell" is still frequently used, but inap-
propriately now; of old it actually spoke of a soul about to
"pass" into the mysterious "Land of the Hereafter."

When the custom of tolling this "Soul-bell," as it was

also called, first arose, it is impossible to say; the usage
is certainly very ancient.   The Venerable Bede, in relating
the circumstances of the death of S. Hilda at Whitby in 680,
tells us that S. Bees (Begu) heard, at the moment of her
departure, the well-known sound of a bell, such as was wont
to call them to prayers when a soul was passing away.
Durand, writing at the close of the twelfth century, says
very definitely, "when anyone is dying, bells should be
tolled that the people may offer up prayers; twice for a
woman, thrice for a man; and if for one of the clergy as
many times as he had orders; and at the end, a peal of
all the bells to signify the position of the person for whom
the people are to pray."   At the Reformation many even of
the most extreme men were compelled to acknowledge the
Christian charity of this godly practice.   Hooper issued this
among other injunctions to the diocese of Gloucester in
1551; "in case they that be sick and in danger, or any
of their friends, will demand to have the bell toll whilst the
sick is in extremes, to admonish the people of their danger,
and by that means to solicitate the hearers of the same to
pray for the sick person, they may use it."   Archbishop
Grindal, whose strenuous opposition to the ringing on All-
hallow E'en has been noticed, speaks even more strongly
than Hooper in favour of the passing bell.   In his injunctions to the northern province, he orders that "when any
man or woman, dwelling near to the church in any city,
borough, or great town, is in passing out of this life, the
parish clerk or sexton shall knoll the bell, to move the
people to pray for the sick person."   This order was
subsequently issued, in almost identical words, to the
southern province also.   Royal Injunctions enjoined the

tolling of this bell in 1559; and in 1564 the "advertisements" bade "that where anye Christian bodie be passing,
that the bell be tolled, and that the curate be specially called
for to comforte the sicke person." The canons of 1603
employ very similar words, the sixty-seventh concluding
thus; "when any is passing out of this life, a bell shall be
tolled, and the minister shall not then be slack to do his last
duty." About the middle of the seventeenth century it
would appear that the use of the "Soul-bell" began to drop
into abeyance, for at that time it is frequently found needful
to make enquiries concerning it in articles of diocesan visitation; in the Archdeaconry of York it is asked "whether
doth your clarke or sexton when anyone is passing out of
this life neglect to toll a bell, having notice thereof?"
Similar queries are put to the clergy of Chichester, Worcester, and other dioceses.

As illustrations of local rules concerning the passing-bell,
this may be quoted from the parish accounts of Wolchurch
in 1526:—"Item, the clerke to have for tollynge of the
passynge belle, for manne, womanne, or childes, if it be in
the day, iiijd. Item, if it be in the night, for the same,
viijd. ;" and this from the Corporation Records of Boston for
1588:—"Every person that shall have the great bell rung
for him in their extremity of sickness to pay 4d. to the
church over and beside the usual fee to the clock keeper."
A similar fee was charged in 1713 for the clerk's
duty in this respect at Barrow-on-Humber. An interesting
note in the accounts at Peterborough for 1572 tells us
that a gown was given to Scarlet, the celebrated old
sexton of the cathedral, on the ground of his "beyng
a poore olde man and rysyng oft in the nyghte to

13

tolle the bell for sicke persons, the wether beynge grevous."

Wheatley, in his work on the Book of Common Prayer, published in 1755, says, " The passing-bell is now generally disused." It is recorded that the first person in Melton Mowbray for whom it was not rung was one Mr. Crane, who died in 1738 ; yet Mrs. Law, who died so late as 1874, at about the age of 94, remembered the ringing of the passing-bell as a regular custom at King's Cliffe, Northamptonshire. In any case it survived even the Puritan regime ; it was, in fact, a custom to which even they could not, as a rule, find any objection ; and Fuller relates that John Rainolds, one of the representative Puritans at the Hampton Court Conference, when he felt death approaching, " expressed by signs that he would have the passing-bell toll for him."

English literature has frequent allusions to this beautiful custom. Shakespeare says of the " first bringer of un-welcome news " that

> " His tongue
> Sounds ever after as a sullen bell
> Remember'd tolling a departing friend."
> —Henry IV. (2nd pt.), i. 1.

And again (Henry VI. ; 1st pt. ; iv. 2) :—

> " Hark ! hark ! the Dauphin's drum, a warning bell,
> Sings heavy music to thy timorous soul ;
> And mine shall ring thy dire departure out."

Beaumont and Fletcher, in the " Beggar's Bush " (iii. 2), speak of " him that waits his sentence, or hears his passing-bell." Hall, Bishop of Norwich, who died in 1656, in referring to it, explains one of its names :—" We call them," he says, " *Soul-bells*, for that they signify the departure of

the soul, not for that they help the passage of the soul."
Nelson, in his well-known "Fasts and Festivals of the
Church" (1732), contemplates a Christian man having so
far subdued his passions, that, "if his sense hold out so
long, he can even hear his passing-bell without disturbance."
Pennant, who died at the end of the last century, tells us
that at Whiteford and Holywell "that excellent memento to
the living, the passing-bell, is punctually sounded." Many
other illustrations from writers of all kinds might easily be
added, but these will suffice.

The tenor bell, having the most solemn tone in the
peal, was naturally the one almost universally selected for
sounding this "memento mori," but probably a smaller bell,
with brighter note, would sometimes be used for the passing-
bell of a child, as is now occasionally the case with a death-
knell.

Several of the authorities above quoted as justifying the
ringing of the passing-bell, allude to other belfry usages
in connection with a death. Not to weary the reader by
detailing them all once more, the latter part of the sixty-
seventh Canon may be cited, as a specimen of them all :—
"After the party's death, if it so fall out," we are told,
"there shall be rung no more than one short peal, and one
other before the burial, and one other after the burial."
The first of the three "peals" here authorized is still rung
practically everywhere in England, although it is not now
a peal in any technical sense, but rather a tolling of one
bell, usually the tenor. A singular exception to this is
found at Marbury, Cheshire, where the bells are chimed to
the melody of the "Old Fourth Psalm."

It is usual in the manner of ringing this bell, the Death

Knell, or "Dead Bell," as it is sometimes called, to give some intimation of the sex, and occasionally of the condition, of the deceased; though this part of the ringing seems to have been originally connected with the passing-bell proper, and not with the knell. The details of this ringing are very various, the county of Lincoln alone having more than seventy methods in different parishes of performing it. A quotation given above from the "Rationale" of Durandus, gives one way of distinguishing the sexes, which still largely prevails, namely, by three strokes for a man, and two for a woman. A singular reason for this is alleged in a quaint old Homily for Trinity Sunday, quoted in Strutt's "Manners and Customs":—"The fourme of the Trinity was founden in manne, that was Adam our forefadir, of earth oon personne, and Eve of Adam the secunde persone, and of them both was the third persone: at the death of a manne three bellis shulde be ronge, as his knyll, in worscheppe of the Trinetee, and for a womanne, who was the secunde persone of the Trinetee two bellis should be rungen." The series is completed in many places by giving a single stroke to mark the death of a child. These "signs" vary very considerably in the way of their ringing. In some cases the required strokes follow the knell, in some they precede it, and in yet others they both begin and conclude it. Again there are instances where the chime of one, two, or three, is given in succession upon each bell of the peal, a knell on the tenor following. The most elaborate rendering of the usage is the one in vogue at Morton-by-Gainsborough, where the whole knell is rung in triplets, couples, or single strokes, as the case requires. The strokes are, however, very generally increased, keeping the same proportion; thrice three for a

man, thrice two for a woman, and thrice one for a child ;
but in many cases the sex only is marked, and no distinction of children is made.   This system was not sufficiently
detailed for some tastes, and more elaborate ones were
evolved.   Thus at Skirbeck and at Swineshead, both in
Lincolnshire, thrice four marks a married man, twice four a
single man, and four separate strokes a male child ; similarly
thrice three indicate a married woman, twice three a spinster,
and three strokes a female child.   At Marsham, Norfolk,
the following directions were at one time hung up in the
belfry, headed " Knocks for the Dead ;" three for a girl, and
four for a boy ; six for a spinster, and seven for a matron ;
eight for a bachelor, and nine for a married man.   The line
at which childhood was to be reckoned as ceasing was
fixed, so far as the parish of Leverton was concerned, by the
following entry in the Constable's Accounts for 1692 :—" In
ringing the passing-bell it has been, time out of mind, customary for a man that dies to toll 12 tolls : for a woman 9
tolls : they are accounted man or woman at the age of 16 or
18 years : for younger persons, a male 7 tolls, a female 6
tolls."   These strokes, or knocks, are called " tellers " in
some parts of Leicestershire and elsewhere, and it has been
suggested that the old saying " Nine tailors make a man,"
is simply a corruption of the words " Nine *tellers mark* a
•man."

The time for ringing the knell is fixed within certain
limits in some districts.   In Hertfordshire it takes place
twelve hours after the death ; in Bedfordshire, Buckinghamshire, Leicestershire, Northamptonshire, Lincolnshire, and
some other counties, it is rung as soon as the body is laid
out for burial ; but in some parishes in North Lincolnshire

it is never rung between eight o'clock at night and eight in the morning. At Collingtree, Northamptonshire, the hour fixed is nine, on the morning following the death. In cases where a coroner's inquest is held it is usual not to ring until after the finding of the verdict; as should that be of a nature to preclude Christian burial, the knell is not rung at all. Occasionally the tolling concludes with a number of strokes corresponding with the age of the deceased. At Great Yarmouth the bell is tolled daily from the day of death to that of burial.

There can be no question that as the intention of the passing-bell was to call the faithful to prayer for the dying, so the knell originally was a summons to prayer for the dead. In this spirit is one of the Constitutions of William de Bleys, Bishop of Worcester, issued in 1219 :—" When a parson, vicar, or ministering priest, shall die, let his death be immediately announced to the dean of the place, who shall make it known to all the mother churches in his deanery, in each of which the bells shall be tolled for the deceased : and every chaplain shall immediately say a commendation, and on the following morning a mass for his soul." So also the " Book of Ceremonies," of 1539, thus explains the use of the knell :—" Bells are ordained to give knowledge of our Christian brother or sister departed out of this world, that both we may call to remembrance our own mortality, and also be moved with charity to pray for them so departed." In connection with this practice it will not be out of place to briefly cite one or two authorities of the post-reformation Church in England. "The Church prays for all persons that died in the Christian and Catholic Faith," is definitely stated by Bishop Jeremy Taylor, while Overall calls the

GREAT PAUL, ST. PAUL'S CATHEDRAL, LONDON.

practice "pious and Christian," and Heber "natural and comfortable."

Charges for ringing the knell frequently appear in church-wardens' accounts, the fee varying considerably in different parishes, or perhaps the amount of ringing depending on the amount of the fee.   In 1498 six shillings was paid to the parish of S. Margaret's, Westminster, "for the knell of Jane Grey of Wilton," the great bell being used ; while fourpence only was paid for a knell at Stratton, Cornwall, in 1512.   The knell, as distinct from the passing-bell, is alluded to in Shakespeare's seventy-first sonnet :—

> "No longer mourn for me when I am dead,
> Than ye shall hear the surly sullen bell
> Give warning to the world that I am fled
> From this vile world, with vilest worms to dwell."

This bell, like the passing-bell, was sometimes called also the *soul-bell*, as in a statement of the clerk's fees at Barrow-on-Humber for 1713, where fourpence is charged "for every passing-bell and for every soul-bell."

Scarcely a trace remains now of the "short peal" ordered to be rung immediately after the death of a parishioner, except that in some churches a bell is "rung" in the technical sense, for a few minutes after the conclusion of the tolling of the knell.

It has been already remarked that the "great bell" of S. Paul's (the old "great bell," not the new Great Paul,) rings the knell only of the royal family, and of a few persons of special official distinction.   A very weird and striking effect is said to have been produced by the S. Paul's bells when they alternated with a solemn knell, tolled for the death of Nelson, a joyous peal for the victory of Trafalgar.

At King's Cliffe, a bell known as the "Winding Bell" used to be rung while a dead person was being put into his shroud ; the same name is given to the ringing of the second bell immediately after the usual mid-day bell, on the morning of a funeral at Moreton, in the same county of Northampton. It is said that the great bell of the church is always tolled in Russia, while the body of a deceased ecclesiastic is being laid out.

In a good many parishes in Lincolnshire, and in other counties, it is usual to toll the tenor bell for a few minutes at or about eight o'clock on the morning of a funeral ; which, it may be suggested, was originally a summons to the funeral mass.   Also an hour or so before the time fixed for the funeral to leave the house of mourning, a bell is tolled for a short time in many places, as a signal to the bearers and friends.   It is sometimes known as an "Invitation Peal," sometimes as the "Company Bell."

We come now to the actual ringing for the interment, in connection with which the Canon already quoted, and other authorities of about the same date, allow a short peal both before and after.

The custom of ringing at a funeral is very ancient, Grandison, Bishop of Exeter, finding it needful to check the abuses to which it had run so long ago as 1339; it seems that at that time the peals were so frequent and prolonged as to be "an annoyance to the living, and injurious to the fabrick and the bells."   The method of ringing these peals is thus described in "Campanólogia, or the Art of Ringing" (1753):—"It being customary not only in this city of London, upon the death of any person that is a member of any of the honourable societies of ringers therein, but likewise in most counties and towns in England (not only upon the death of a ringer, but likewise of any young man or woman), at the funeral of every such person to ring a peal: which peal ought to be different from those for mirth and recreation (as the musick at the funeral of any master of musick, or the ceremony at the funeral of any person belonging to military discipline), and may be performed two different ways: the one is by ringing the bells round at a set pull, thereby keeping them up so as to delay their striking, that there may be the distance of three notes at least (according to the true compass of ringing upon other occasions) between bell and bell; and having gone round one whole pull every bell (except the tenor), to set and stand, whilst the tenor rings one pull in the same compass as before; and this is to be done whilst the person deceased is bringing to the ground; and after he is interred, to ring a short peal of round ringing, or changes, in the true time and compass, and so conclude. The other way is called buffeting the bells, that is, by tying pieces of leather, old hat, or any other thing that is pretty thick, round the ball of the clapper of each bell, and then by ringing them as before is shown, they make a most doleful and mournful sound; concluding with a short peal after the funeral is over (the clappers being clear as at other times); which way of buffeting is most practised in this city of London."

Shakespeare, in " Titus Andionicus " (Act v., Sc. 3) refers to the funeral peal, "no mournful bell shall ring her funeral," and Beaumont and Fletcher in " Bondnea " (Act v., Sc. 3) allude more definitely to the peal preliminary to the act of interment;

"They ring a strange sad knell, a preparation
To some near funeral of state."

It is now almost universally customary to toll a bell, generally the tenor, as the funeral procession approaches the church; but the use of more than one bell, and the ringing after the funeral, are both found only in scattered instances. It is not unusual for the tolling to give way to a chime just as the funeral comes to the churchyard; this is the usage at Saxelby, Leicestershire, and a chime proceeds the interment at Cradley and elsewhere in Herefordshire. Similar cases are found in Lincolnshire, Yorkshire, Northamptonshire, and Rutland, though in some instances the chime is only given in response to a special request, or as a mark of more than ordinary respect. Almost the same may be said of the peal after the funeral, except that this is becoming even more rare. Both peals may be heard at King's Sutton and at Benefield, Northamptonshire; the final peal was rung at Hatherleigh, Devonshire, at least as late as 1816, and is so still occasionally at Helidon.

In several instances the "tellers" which mark the age, and in some those indicating the sex, of the dead are added to one or other of these funeral peals. At Hempsted, in Gloucestershire, the age is given out by the bell, after tolling subsequently to the funeral, in periods of twenty strokes with a pause after each period; at Almely, Herefordshire, they mark the sex with the unusual numbers of thirteen tellers for a man, and fourteen for a woman; at Burley-on-the-Hill, Rutland, the sex is indicated both before and after the funeral.

Muffled peals, described above as "buffeting" the bells,

are not unusually rung in the evening after the funeral of
any one of local distinction.

During the Commonwealth some scruples were raised
as to the " lawfulness " (in a religious sense) of the use
of bells at all at funerals.   In 1655 "the ministers of the
town (of Newcastle-on-Tyne) were desired to come before
the Mayor and Aldermen to give their opinion concerning
the legality of ringing bells at funerals, as had hitherto been
the custom."   There is abundant evidence, however, that
in many places the funeral knell was still frequently rung
during that unsettled period.

On the rare occasions on which a body was disinterred
for burial in some other place, it was customary for the
churches which the remains passed on their way to toll
as for a fresh funeral.   The corpse of Richard, Duke of
York, was thus transported in 1476 from Pontefract, where
he was buried after the Battle of Wakefield in 1460, to
Fotheringhay ;   which gave occasion for the following
curiously-worded entry in the accounts of S. John Baptist's
Church, Peterborough, " Itm payd the ryngers to the
wursthypp of God and for the Duke of York Sowle and
bonys comyng to Fodrynghey, iiijd."

Many bell inscriptions, as already shown, refer to their
usage on the mournful occasions of deaths and funerals.

Even the funeral peals were not always, however, the
last commemoration of the dead by the bells.   It was
formerly usual to make a special memorial of the
dead at the end of the month, and of the year, from their
decease : these were called in England the month's mind,
and the year's mind.   Fabyan, the chronicler, who died
in 1512, gives minute directions in his will for the keeping

of his month's mind, ordaining among other things that
" my knyll be rongyn at my monethes mynde after the
guyse of London." These concluding words, when
compared with the final assertion in the above quotation
from the " Campanologia," at least suggest that " the
guyse of London " may have been a muffled peal. Barnabe
Googe, in his translation of the " Popish Kingdome,"
(1570) says—

> " Give money and thou shalt be blest with store of Trentals soong
> And yearely in remembrance had, with soule peales duely roong."

An instance of this is afforded by the will of Sir Adam
Outlaw, a priest, who, in 1501, devised three acres of land
to the parish clerk of Lynn, "so that he do ring in pele on
the vigil" of Sir Adam's year-day.

These year's minds were also called " Obits," and as
such often appear in churchwardens' accounts ; at S.
Martin's, Leicester, for instance, in 1544, there is an entry,
" Rychard Fynnes obbyt iiij bels, xxd.," and others similar.

One or two instances of Commemorative Peals still
exist in England. The Ancient Society of Ringers at
S. Stephen's, Bristol, have it as a rule to ring nine peals
each year in memory of past benefactors. Mr. Matthew
Wyldbore, at one time Member of Parliament for Peterborough, left, at his death in 1781, an annual sum of five
pounds for the entertainment of the ringers at S. John
Baptist's Church, in the said city, on condition that they
rang a peal each year on the anniversary of his death, which
took place on March 15th. Nicholas Hardy, dying on
January 11th, 1826, left £25 for a similar purpose to the
ringers of Harloxton, Lincolnshire ; and similarly £5 was
left by Edward Trapnill, who died November 26th, 1710, to

the ringers of Clyst-Honiton, Devonshire.   Until recently a muffled peal was rung each year on January 30th at New-castle-on-Tyne, in memory of the death of King Charles I.

Hand-bells have from time to time had their part to play in ringing for the dead.   In ancient Rome a bell was sounded at the head of a funeral procession, not in this case as a note of sorrow, but as a warning to the priests, whose office forbade their ceremonial defilement by contact with the dead, to turn aside, and thus avoid meeting it. Similarly a criminal going to execution was preceded by a bell, the act of death being anticipated in this particular, just as with us a portion of the funeral service is read in the hearing of a condemned man on his way to the scaffold. Again a striking and somewhat dramatic incident, alluding to this usage, at the triumph of a Roman conqueror, was provided by a scourge and a bell attached to the hero's chariot, which by sight and sound conveyed to him in the hour of his highest glory the lesson taught us by the Apostle, " Let him that thinketh he standeth take heed lest he fall."

In Paris, and probably elsewhere on the Continent, it was at one time customary for a man, titled the "bell-man of the dead," to perambulate the streets at night, summoning the people by the sound of a hand-bell which he carried, to pray for the dead and the dying.   A similar English custom is spoken of by Henry Machyn, in whose diary (1557) we read that "in Alderman Draper ward, called Chordwenerstrett Ward, a bell-man went about with a bell at every lane end and every ward end, to gyff warning of ffyre and candell lyght, and to help the powre, and pray for the ded."

Hand-bells were also anciently used at Christian funerals. The scene in the Bayeux tapestry which represents the approach of the bier of S. Edward the Confessor to West-minster Abbey, shows us two lads walking beside it carrying small bells ; and the prohibition of them by Grindal proves their use in the sixteenth century. Chaucer alludes to this practice in "The Pardoneres Tale":—

> " These riottoures thre, of which I telle,
> Long erst than prime rong of eny bell,
> Were set hem in a tavern for to drynke ;
> And as thay sat they herd a bell clinke,
> Biforn a corps, was carried to the grave."

The "Company Bell," as known in England, was also at one time represented in some parts of Scotland by a hand-bell. In a "Statistical Account of Scotland," Sir John Sinclair tells us, concerning the parish of Borrowstowness, county Linlithgow, that "at the burials of the poor people, a custom, almost obsolete in other parts of Scotland, is continued here ; the beadle perambulates the streets with a bell, and intimates the death of the individual in the following language, 'All brethren and sisters, I let ye to wit there is a *brother* (or *sister*) departed at the pleasure of the Almighty (here he lifts his hat), called . . . All those that come to the burial, come at . . . of clock. The corpse is at . . .' He also walks before the corpse to the churchyard, ringing his bell." Similarly it was part of the duty of the "bedel," or bell man, in the pre-reformation gilds, to go round the town and summon the members to attend the funeral of a brother or sister deceased.

The services of the bell-man were also frequently invoked in commemoration of the year's mind of the dead. William Motte, in 1349, bequeathed to the bell-man of Great

Yarmouth, and to his successors, the sum of sixpence per
annum, to pray for the soul of the testator and his relatives
"about the town as the manner and custom was." The
same amount was left by Simon de Stalham, on behalf of
himself and his wife, to the bell-man of the same town.
Sir Adam Outlaw recompensed the bell-man of West Lynn
more generously, when he left him by will a tenement on
condition that on the vigil of his "yere-day" the said bell-
man should "pray for the souls of Thomas of Acre and
Muriel, his wife, Sir Adam's soul and the souls of his
benefactors, with his bell going round the town." One more
illustration is given us by the statutes of Magdalen College,
Oxford, founded by William of Waynflete, in 1458; "every
year," so that prelate ordained, "on the day of the said
burial service (that is, his own year's mind) fourpence for
his trouble shall be paid to the common bell-man, who is
accustomed to make public proclamation after the Oxford
practice."

A death-bell of special sadness and solemnity is that
which tells of a death which comes neither in the course
of nature, nor by mere accident, but by the hand of human
justice. Walter Halton, prior of Spalding in the middle of
the fourteenth century, erected a high tower for his monastery, and hung therein a large bell, which was tolled at
executions, as well as on other more than usually mournful
occasions. At Chester the bells of S. Mary's and of Holy
Trinity used formerly to toll as a condemned criminal was
taken from the castle through their respective parishes to
the place of execution ; a similar custom prevailed at
S. Helen's, Worcester, and no doubt at other places also.
The most celebrated instance of this usage, however, was in

connection with S. Sepulchre's Church, London. In the year 1605, Robert Dowe, or Dove, bequeathed £50 to this parish on condition of its undertaking certain duties on behalf of condemned prisoners in Newgate. In the first place, on the night before an execution, some person, armed with a large hand-bell, was to get as near as possible to the window of the condemned cell, and there, after sounding twelve solemn double strokes with his bell, was to recite as follows :—

> " All you that in the condemned hold do lie,
> Prepare you, for to-morrow you shall die.
> Watch all, and pray, the hour is drawing near
> That you before the Almighty must appear ;
> Examine well yourselves, in time repent,
> That you may not to eternal flames be sent,
> And when S. Sepulchre's Bell to-morrow tolls,
> The Lord have mercy on your souls.
>   Past twelve o'clock !"

The bell which was used on these gruesome occasions was discovered in the year 1895 in an old chest in the church, the custom described have been allowed to lapse long since. It is a bell of rough and simple make, standing nine inches high, and being five inches wide at the mouth. Its shape is almost exactly that of an ordinary flower-pot, with a short handle to it. Since its discovery it has been used on the occasion of the annual picnic of the parish school-children, to collect the children for the homeward journey ; truly a startling change from its original purpose !

The other requirement, under Dowe's will, was that the great bell of S. Sepulchre's should toll as the prisoners passed from Newgate to Tyburn, and that the sexton, or bellman, should look over the wall, and cry, "All good people, cry heartily unto God for these poor sinners, who

are now going to their death !" For this service the cryer
was to receive the sum of £1 6s. 8d. When Tyburn
ceased to be the place of public execution the processions
no longer passed S. Sepulchre's, and consequently the latter
part of this direction could not be fulfilled; but the great
bell of the church continued to ring for every execution
until 1890, when the Charity Commissioners diverted the
legacy from its original purpose, and directed the trustees
(the Rector and Churchwardens) to employ it in some way
on behalf of deserving and necessitous prisoners on their
discharge. The only bell which now announces an
execution at Newgate, is one in a wooden bell-cote on
the roof of the prison.

CHAPTER XII.

𝕿𝖍𝖊 𝕭𝖑𝖊𝖘𝖘𝖎𝖓𝖌𝖘 𝖆𝖓𝖉 𝕮𝖚𝖗𝖘𝖎𝖓𝖌𝖘 𝖔𝖋 𝖙𝖍𝖊 𝕭𝖊𝖑𝖑𝖘.

OUR forefathers had great faith in the power of the
bells to help them in dangers ghostly and bodily.
It was of old held as an undoubted fact that evil spirits
hated and feared the sound of church bells, and could
therefore be put to flight by it. This idea was largely
mixed with others of a more devout character in the ringing
of passing and funeral bells. Grose thus speaks of the
former of these; "the passing-bell was anciently rung for
two purposes; one to bespeak the prayers of all good
Christians for a soul just departing; the other to drive away
the evil spirits who stood at the bed's foot and about the
house, ready to seize their prey, or at least to molest and
terrify the soul in its passage; but by the ringing of that
bell (for Durandus informs us evil spirits are much afraid of
bells) they were kept aloof; and the soul, like a hunted
hare, gained the start, or had what is by sportsmen called
law. Hence, perhaps, exclusive of the additional labour,
was occasioned the high price demanded for tolling the
greatest bell of the church, for, that being louder, the evil
spirits must go farther off to be clear of the sound, by which
the poor soul got so much more the start of them; besides,
being heard farther off, it would likewise procure the dying
man a greater number of prayers. This dislike of spirits to

bells is mentioned in the Golden Legend by Wynkyn de Worde."

No theory of the beneficent power of bells was more wide-spread than the belief that they were a protection against lightning and storm. In the translation by Barnabe Googe of the "Popish Kingdome" of Naogeorgus, is the following scornful allusion to this opinion :—

> "If that the thunder chance to rore, and stormy tempest shake,
> A wonder is it for to see the wretches how they quake,
> Howe that no fayth at all they have, nor trust in anything ;
> The clarke doth all the belles forthwith at once in steeple ring,
> With wond'rous sound and deeper farre than he was wont before,
> Till in the loftie heavens darke the thunder bray no more.
> For in these christned belles they thinke doth lie such power and
>   might,
> As able is the tempests great and storms to vanquish quight.
> I saw myself at Numburg once, a towne in Toring coast,
> A bell that with this title bold hirself did proudly boast :—
> By name I Mary called am, with sound I put to flight
> The thunder crackes and hurtfull stormes, and every wicked spright.
> Such things whenas these belles can do, no wonder certainlie
> It is, if that the Papistes to their tolling alwayes flie,
> When haile, or any raging storme, or tempest comes in sight,
> Or thunderboltes, or lightning fierce, that every place doth smight."

Henry Bullinger seems to think that this idea arose from the people being summoned to prayer by the voice of the bell in time of any severe storm, and that afterwards the sound of the bell itself came to be counted efficacious in such cases. In the fifth of his "Decades" (published in 1551) he says, "About bells there is a wonderful superstition. They are christened by bishops, and it is thought that they have power to put away any great tempest. In the old time men were stirred up to prayer by the ringing of them, what time any sore tempest did rise ; but now the very ringing of bells, by reason of their consecration, seemeth to have a peculiar kind of virtue in it."

Pilkington, Bishop of Durham, speaks, in more than one of his writings, of "ringing the hallowed bell in great tempests," as an "unlawful thing." Archbishop Whitgift also alludes to the practice.

In 1464 a charge was made in the churchwardens' accounts for the parish of Sandwich for refreshments for the "ryngers in the great thundering;" a similar entry occurs in the accounts at Spalding for 1519 :—"Itm pd for ryngyng when the Tempest was, iijd " The storm-bell of Malmesbury Abbey was the one known as S. Adelm's ; in Paris the great bell of S. Germain's Abbey rang during storms ; and there is said to have been a special endowment given to old S. Paul's "for ringing the hallowed belle in great tempestes or lighteninges."

Bacon gives a theory, but without committing himself to it, to explain by natural causes the alleged dispersal of tempests by this means. "It has anciently been reported," he says, "and is still received, that extreme applauses and shouting of people assembled in multitudes, have so rarified and broken the air, that birds flying over have fallen down, the air not being able to support them ; and it is believed by some that great ringing of bells in populous cities have chased away thunder, and also dissipated pestilent air ; all which may be also from the concussion of the air, and not from the sound." Fuller however, disputes the whole position. "Bells," he confidently declares, "are no effectual charm against lightning, the frequent firing of abbey churches by lightning confuteth the proud motto commonly written on the bells

in their steeples. . . . 'Lightning and thunder I break
asunder' : whereas it appears that Abbey steeples, though
quilted with bells almost cap-à-pie, were not proof against
the sword of God's lightning." A violent storm is recorded
to have broken over Brittany on Good Friday in 1718, when
twenty-four churches where the bells were ringing were all
struck by lightning ; while, curiously enough, not a steeple
whose bells were silent was touched. Even these facts have
not, however, been felt by everyone to prove the case against
the bells, if it be true, as is alleged, that so recently as 1852
the Bishop of Malta set the church bells a-ringing to
lay a gale of wind.

The passage quoted above from Bacon refers to the
scattering of pestilence, as well as storm. Of this we may
call medical testimony. Dr. Francis Hering issued in 1625
"Certaine Rules, Directions, or Advertisements for this
time of pestilential Contagion," in which he writes, "Let
the bells in cities and townes be rung often, and the great
ordnance discharged; thereby the aire is purified." Whether
the good doctor's advice was generally acted upon or not we
have no record ; but certainly the pestilence was not driven
from the country for nearly half-a-century after the date given.

S. Anthony the Hermit was reputed to have obtained a
singular power over spirits of evil ; and in art this trait in
his character is typified by the presence of a small bell.
Sometimes it is suspended from his crutched staff, sometimes
it hangs from a cross near him, at others he carries it in his
hand. Bale, in his comedy of "Three Lawes" (published
in 1538), seems to have both this fact, and the virtue usually
ascribed to bells, in his mind, when he introduces the
character of Infidelity as saying :—

" Good Christen people, I am come hyther verelye
  As a true proctoure of the howse of Saint Anthonye.
  *　　　*　　　*　　　*　　　*　　　*
  Lo here is a belle to hange upon your hogge,
  And save your cattell from the bytynge of a dogge."

The bell inscriptions, as alluded to by Fuller, in which
these mysterious powers are claimed for the bells, have been
cited in an earlier chapter ; one is here added, which is
noticeable among those of its kind from the lateness of its
date ; on a bell dated 1705 at Lois Weedon, Northamptonshire, is the legend, " Defunctos ploro : Cœlum reddoque
serenum."

But the voice of the bell was invoked to add solemnity
to a rite very different from the attempt to " restore a calm
heaven " to mankind, namely in the pronouncement of the
most dread form of the Church's excommunication, whereby,
until the sinner's penance have proved the depth and
sincerity of his contrition, he is cut off from all part and lot
in her offices, and is, as it were, already dead even while
he lives.　This rite, which is commonly spoken of as
" Cursing with bell, book, and candle," is seldom, or
never, used now in all its awful solemnity ; but there are
not wanting illustrations of its performance in the past.

In Shakespeare's " King John " (Act III., Sc. 3) Fal-
conbridge declares—

" Bell, book, and candle shall not drive me back,
  When gold and silver beck me to come on."

In another play founded on the same period of English
history, the " Kynge Johan " of Bishop Bale, Pandulph is
introduced pronouncing excommunication against the king,
in words which not only allude to, but partly explain,
the ceremony :—

> " For as moch as Kyng Johan doth Holy Church so handle,
> Here I do curse hym wyth crosse, boke, bell, and candle ;
> Like as this same roode turneth now from me his face,
> So God I requyre to sequester hym of his grace ;
> As this boke doth speare by my worke manuale,
> I wyll God to close uppe from hym his benefyttes all ;
> As his burnyng flame goeth from this candle in syght,
> I wyll God to put hym from his eternal light ;
> I take hym from Cryst, and after the sownd of this bell,
> Both body and sowle I geve hym to the devyll of hell."

Chaucer less fully refers to the same thing in the Manciple's Tale :—

> "   .   .   .   . Thus thei puttin us to pain,
> With candles queint (quenched), and belles clink,
> And Christis people proudly curse
> With brode boke, and braying bell."

The earliest trace of the ceremonial details of this rite is said to date about the year 900, when at the excommunication of some murderers at Rheims, the bishops flung down and extinguished the torches which they carried in their hands. In 1298 Archbishop Winchelsea ordered excommunication to be pronounced against those who infringed certain of his regulations, and he bids that the whole rite be "throughout explained in order in English, with bells tolling, and candles lighted," giving as a reason for these formalities, that "laymen have greater regard to this solemnity, than to the effect of such sentences."

General sentences of excommunication, directed not against particular offenders specified by name, but against all who were, or who might hereafter be, guilty of certain crimes, did not come into use until about the thirteenth century ; or were not, at any rate, pronounced with the full solemnity before that time. It became afterwards the rule to pronounce excommunication with all ceremonial accessories against every one who should defraud the Church of her dues; and in England this took place four times each year, namely on Advent Sunday, on the first Sunday in Lent, on Trinity Sunday, and the Sunday within the Octave of Our Lady (that is, no doubt, of the Assumption, not of the Annunciation).

In this denunciation of sinners the Bishop, vested in his albe, stood in the pulpit, or, more probably, at the altar steps, pulpits being by no means universally found in churches in the thirteenth and immediately following centuries. A cross was upheld beside him, the candles were lighted, and the book of offices was brought to him. He then proceeded to make solemn declaration "thorow authoritie of Lord God Almighty, and our Lady S. Mary, and all the saints of heaven, of angels and archangels, patriarches, and prophets, evangelists, apostles, martyrs, confessors, and virgins; also by the power of all holy Church." The offenders were cut off from all part in "the passion of our Lord Jesu Christ, in the sacraments that are in holy church, and in the prayers of Christian folk," and were declared liable to "dwell in the pain of hell for ever without end" except "they have grace of God for to amend them here in this life." After the solemnly repeated "fiat, fiat," which closes the denunciation, the order is given, "Doe to (close) the book; quench the candle; ring the bell; Amen. Amen." At this the great book is closed with a sudden thud, typifying the exclusion henceforth of these sinners from all share in the offices contained in it; a candle by the bishop's side is thrown down and trampled out, and the great bell tolls out as for a funeral knell. The "Encyclopaedia of Antiquities," however, says the bells were all jangled "with a hideous noise ;" it is possible also that the hand-bell used to draw attention to the most important parts of the mass, was also sounded here, just as a hand-bell was used (as we have seen) at funerals.

John Myrc, an Austin canon of Lilleshall, Shropshire, has an allusion to this periodical excommunication in his "Instructions for Parish Priests," a work translated, probably early in the fifteenth century, from some unknown Latin original. At least twice or thrice each year, so Myrc declares, this sentence upon sinners is to be publicly pronounced ; these are his words :—

> "Thou shalt pronounce without let,
> When the parish is together met ;
> Thou shalt pronounce this hideous thing,
> With cross, and candle, and bell-knelling."

After recounting the various classes of evil-doers who are to come under the ban, he proceeds :—

> "Then thou thy candle shalt cast to ground,
> And spit thereon the same stound (moment),
> And let also the bells knell,
> To make their hearts the more grylle."

An interesting record of this ceremony is preserved in a deed dated 1474, relating to the title of lands at Westhoughton. The deed, which is witnessed by the Vicar of Leigh ("Sir" Thurstan Percival), "Sir" James Culchett, a priest, and a number of the landed gentry of the district, sets forth that "On Sondey next after the feast of S. Andrew the apostell, in the yere of our Lord Jesu Christ, 1474," a certain

Nicholas de Ryland, or "Nicholas of the Rylond," came to the Parish Church of Leigh, and there in the presence of these witnesses made oath concerning the lands in question. He swore that he had made no grant of his rights in those lands to "Thomas Stanley Peris, of Legh, ne to Rogr. of Hulton, of Hulton Parke," nor to anyone else; also that he had made no assignment of lands to his son William, nor had he authorized him or any other persons to make certain grants, and draw up certain deeds in his name. The oath thus concluded, the document thus proceeds: "and then the say'd Nicholas kneiled down vnder the hand of the seid Viker, and there the seid Viker, by virtue of a Deynes (Dean's) letter to him direcket for to resaue (receive) a purgacon (purgation) of the seid Nicholas of all these p'ountts (points) . . . . . There the seid Viker cursed the seid Nicholas if eu' (ever) he was gilte in the p'ovntts before reherset wth bokke, bell, and Candle, and thereupon the Candel done out."*

Doubt has been cast in some quarters on the existence of any such ceremony as this "cursing with bell, book, and candle." It seems questionable whether it was ever widespread in its use, and local rituals probably employed varying forms of words; but that it was a ceremony not altogether infrequent in bygone England seems to be clear.

The General Excommunication above spoken of was abolished in 1534; of the awe-inspiring effect of it, John Bradford speaks in a sermon on Repentance, published (after his death) in 1574; "At the pope's curse with book,

---

* The whole of this curious deed, with notes and comments, appeared in the *Manchester Courier*, in 1878 and was afterwards published for private circulation.

bell, and candle, O! how trembled we which heard it but only, though the same was not directed unto us, but unto others!" A letter of the above date from Cranmer, then Archbishop of Canterbury, to the Archbishop of York (Edward Lee) refers to the suspension of this excommunication by the authority of convocation, pending the taking of other and more definite steps for its abrogation.

CHAPTER XIII.

𝕭𝖊𝖑𝖑𝖘 𝖆𝖘 𝕿𝖎𝖒𝖊-𝕸𝖆𝖗𝖐𝖊𝖗𝖘.

THE earliest use of the bell as an indicator of the flight of time was probably due to the Canonical Hours in the monasteries. Eight times a day the *Signum*, or tower-bell, rang out to summon the monks to prayer. At midnight Mattins was said, at three in the morning Lauds, at six Prime, at nine Terce; Sext followed at noon, Nones at three in the afternoon, Vespers at six, and the day was closed with Compline at nine. Thus every three hours throughout both day and night the abbey-bell was heard, not only in cell and cloister, but also in the streets of the town, or the scattered cottages of the hamlet, that lay around the sheltering walls of the religious house. The very early connection between bells and clocks is, however, clearly indicated by the word for a bell in German and in French. Alfred the Great, in translating into the Old English tongue a passage in which the Venerable Bede speaks of *campana*, renders that word with *cluggan*, or clock. It is probable, nevertheless, that the earliest clock-bells were not actually sounded mechanically by the horologe, but rung by hand at stated times. The exact date when clocks, in the modern sense, were invented is unknown; all kinds of devices were tried by the ancients for measuring time, and probably some of these slid, by almost imperceptible gradations, into the primitive dial with its one revolving hand. A curious clock, the admiration of all who saw it, was presented to Charlemagne by the Caliph Haroun al Raschid, and mention is made of one at Westminster in the year 1288.

Clocks, however, have no interest for us here unless they strike the hours upon a bell, and such pieces of mechanism were known in Italy at least as early as the end of the thirteenth century. Now practically all clocks are made to strike the hours, and most large ones ring the quarters also, a gong being usually employed in the smaller clocks, and a time-bell, or bells, in large public ones. Probably the most famous hour-bell in England is "Big Ben" of Westminster.

Some famous clocks have had a number of small bells or gongs which were struck by automaton figures.   Such is the great clock of Strasburg Cathedral; or rather the series of clocks, for there have been three. The first is said to have been completed in 1352; but the legend is that the artificer who made it destroyed it, in revenge for having had his eyes put out, lest he should make another equally wonderful for some other church.   The next was making from 1550 to 1574; the chief designer was Conrad Rauchfuss, assisted by David Volkenstein, an astronomer, the brothers Habrecht constructing the mechanism, and Tobias Stimmer doing the ornamental parts.   Michael Habrecht repaired the clock in 1669, and Jacques Straubhar again in 1732.   It ceased to act in 1789; and the present clock was commenced in 1838, by Schineque, and finished in 1842.   All three clocks were alike in the complexity of their works and the number of automata introduced.   In the present one a cherub strikes every quarter on a bell which it holds, and the stroke is repeated on each of the four dials by figures of Youth,

Childhood, Manhood, and Old Age; while the figure of
Death sounds the hours on a larger bell.

Such clocks were at one time not uncommon in England,
the automata being popularly known as "Jacks," or more
fully, "Jacks of the Clockhouse." Decker, in the "Gulls
Hornbook" (1609), thus refers to the clock and its bells in
Old S. Paul's:—"The great dial is your last monument,
where bestow some half of the three score minutes to
observe the sauciness of the Jacks that are above the Man
in the Moon there; the strangeness of their motion will quit
your labour." These Jacks of course perished with the
cathedral in the great fire of 1666; it was, however, at one
time in contemplation to replace them with others. A
paper entitled "The Affairs of the World," published in
1700, assures us that "Mr. Tompion, the famous watch-
maker in Fleet Street, is making a clock for S. Paul's
Cathedral, which it is said will go one hundred years
without winding up; will cost £3,000 or £4,000, and
be a far finer than the famous clock at Strasburg." For
some reason this scheme was never carried out, and S. Paul's
has had to be content without its Jacks. The boom of the
hour from the great bell now used must be infinitely more
impressive, than would have been possible had some imitation
of the Strasburg clock been the cathedral horologe. Mr. T.
Reid, writing on clocks, avers that on a still, clear day in
June, 1773, he heard S. Paul's bell toll noon at Windsor,
twenty-two miles off; and the story is well known of the
soldier, who was condemned to death for sleeping at his post
as sentry on Windsor terrace, but saved his life by declaring
that he had heard S. Paul's bell strike thirteen at midnight,
and producing evidence that it had actually done so.

The most famous Jacks in London were the Giants of S. Dunstan's; they and their clock were constructed in 1671 by Thomas Hany, and they continued the admiration of all country visitors to town until the old church was pulled down in 1830. Lord Hertford purchased the clock with all its appurtenances, and put it up at his villa in Regent's Park. The mechanism, which was rough, caused the two "giants" to strike two small bells hung beside them at each hour, and at each quarter. Two large figures, clad in armour, formed part of the clock of Holy Trinity, Bristol, until the year 1787; they struck a bell at the quarters with battle-axes. Jacks were put up in S. Martin's Church, Carfax, in 1624; one was to be found at Horsham until 1825; and at Blythburgh Church was a venerable Jack with a flowing beard. Norwich Cathedral and Southwold Church, Suffolk, still possess their Jacks, though they no longer perform their original duties. The Norwich figures, two in number, are Jacobean; they have ruffs and helmets, and wide breeches of blue and white. They struck two bells, suspended between them from the arms of a cross, with long hammers. They were sold, with the old clock, early in the present century, but were repurchased for the cathedral, and now stand in the south entrance. The Southwold Jack stood at one time on the church tower. It is a bold figure in full armour, armed with sword and battle-axe, with the latter of which he struck the bell. He now stands in the vestry window. The church of Nôtre Dame des Victoires, Brussels, has a clock, the hours on which are struck by a small automaton figure; and doubtless there are many other instances.

English literature has many allusions to these Jacks.

Thus Shakespeare (King Richard II., Act v. sc. 5,) says :—

> " My time
> Runs posting on in Bolingbroke's proud joy,
> While I stand fooling here, his Jack o' the clock."

and again (King Richard III., Act iv. sc. 2) :—

> ". . . like a Jack thou keep'st the stroke
> Betwixt thy begging and my meditation."

In an old comedy produced in 1615, "The Fleire," by Edward Sharpman, it is said of some gossips, "their tongues are like a Jack o' the clock, still in labour." Leigh in his "New Picture of London," Cowper in his "Table Talk," and Sir Walter Scott in the "Fortunes of Nigel," all refer to the giants of S. Dunstan's.

In addition to the use of bells as part of the mechanism of clocks, intentionally as markers of the flight of time, there are several usages by which they do so incidentally, the custom having been instituted for some other purpose. Prominent among such uses of the bells is the ringing of the Curfew.

The origin of the curfew, couvre-feu, or "cover-fire" bell is lost in obscurity. The old story, at one time universally accepted, was that William the Conqueror, fearful of plots and seditions amongst his newly vanquished subjects, invented and enforced the curfew as a check to such schemes ; and it has come, in consequence, to be often quoted as a badge of servitude, and an emblem of tyranny. It is quite evident, however, that the great Norman was not the originator of the idea ; and although he was probably the first to make it a general law in England, it is more

JACK OF SOUTHWOLD.

likely to have been a useful precaution against fire than an attempted preventive of rebellion.

On the first point we have evidence that a curfew bell was rung at Oxford in the days of King Alfred. Peshall's history of that city states that "the custom of ringing the bell at Carfax every night at eight o'clock was by order of King Alfred, the restorer of our university, who ordained that all the inhabitants of Oxford should, at the ringing of that bell, cover up their fires and go to bed, which custom is observed to this day, and the bell as constantly rings at eight, as Great Tom tolls at nine; it is also a custom added to the former, after the ringing and tolling this bell, to let the inhabitants know the day of the month by so many tolls." There is also "sufficient evidence," says Henry in his "History of Britain," that the use of the curfew prevailed in France, Spain, Italy, Scotland, and probably elsewhere in Europe. So late as the reign of James I. of Scotland (1424-1437), we find an act passed ordering the curfew to be rung in the boroughs of that country at nine o'clock, an hour which was afterwards changed to ten in the times of James VI. It is scarcely needful to point out that Scotland, never having been under the yoke of the Normans, could not in this be preserving a tradition of their rule. "Most of the monasteries and towns of the north of Europe," were, according to Brand, familiar with the curfew.

This bell, already known on the Continent, and in some places in England, William made obligatory on the whole country in the year 1068; but that his motive in so doing was of wider scope than the mere prevention of midnight plotting, will be evident if we consider that the law was of universal application. There is no suggestion but that it

15

was enforced just as strictly in the castle of the Norman
baron, as in the hall of the thane, or the hut of the serf. It
seems far more probable that it was a precaution against the
outbreak of fire, which the prevalence of wooden buildings
everywhere made only too probable at any time, and which
all history shows to have been, as a matter of fact, one of
the scourges of that period. Moreover it is well to note in
passing that the enforcement of the curfew laws in those
days was, if a hardship at all, a small one compared with
what it would be to-day. At a time when practically no
one but the clergy could read or write, when the amusements of all classes were chiefly out-door sports, and when
everyone began the labours of the day almost at sunrise,
there was little if any tyranny in a compulsory cessation of
work at eight, while in the nature of the case all recreation
ceased of itself at dark. The high probability is, in fact,
that the curfew-laws simply made compulsory on all the
bed-time which was at that date already commonly observed
by the great majority. The law enacted by the Conqueror
was repealed by Henry I. in the opening years of the
following century : many relics of the curfew bell still exist,
however, among us.

The original, and always the most usual, time for ringing
the curfew was eight o'clock ; and although the sound of the
bell soon ceased to be a signal for covering fires and retiring
for the night, it was still found in some places a convenient
mark of time in other ways. In 1291 it was ordered that
no wine was to be drawn after curfew, and down to the time
of Henry VII., although no restriction was made upon the
sale of liquors, it continued customary to close the public-
houses at that sound. The authorities at Tamworth made

GIANTS OLD ST. DUNSTAN'S CHURCH, LONDON.

a bye-law in 1390, forbidding anyone to go out after curfew, unless he carried a light with him. A relic of the yet earlier use of the bell meets us in the direction for the bellman of Loughborough in the sixteenth century, that "at viij of ye cloke at night in whinter and somer" he should ring the curfew, "and then go to bed." Even in the early part of this century it is said that the curfew was the accepted signal at Newcastle-on-Tyne for old people and children of the poorer class to retire for the night.

The hour for ringing the curfew is not now universally the same. In London and other large towns it is often rung at nine; the reason probably being that in these places it long marked the time for the closing of the shops; and thus, as the requirements of business called for a later hour than formerly for closing, the curfew was altered to meet the case. Bow Church rung the curfew for the city, but S. Bride's and S. Giles's were also authorities as to the hour for closing in their districts; as appears from a charge given to the Quest of Wardmote in each ward, in 1495, to the effect that "yf ther be anye paryshe clerke that ryngeth curfewe after the curfew be ronge at Bowe Chyrche, or Saint Brydes Chyrche, or Saint Gyles without Cripelgat, all suche to be presented." At some places in Lincolnshire, as at Bourn, Horncastle, Holbeach, and others, the curfew is rung at seven on Saturdays, and at Sleaford it is rung at the same hour, not only then, but on the eve of Christmas, Ascension, and other occasions when some special service is to be held. Middleton, Lancashire, supplies a probably unique instance of an evening bell, which is not a survival of a mediæval usage, but an introduction of recent times. The rector, early in this century, ordered a bell to be rung

nightly at ten minutes to ten o'clock, as a signal for closing
the shops, and a hint to all who were abroad to go home.
It is locally known as the "Nowster," a name which no one
seems able to explain, although the good folk of Middleton
say that it means "Now stir!" The curfew, which used to
be rung in the parish, has retired in favour of the "Nowster,"
whose summons used to be more strictly obeyed in its early
days than it is at present.

Shakespeare, who must, one would suppose, have been
familiar with the sound of the curfew tolling from Bow
Church and many another steeple, nevertheless refers to it
as indicative of the most unusual hours. In "Romeo and
Juliet" (Act iv., sc. 4), Lord Capulet says—

> "Come, stir, stir, stir, the second cock hath crow'd,
> The curfew bell hath rung, 'tis three o'clock."

and again, Prospero, in the "Tempest" (Act v., sc. 1) says:

> "You, whose pastime
> Is to make midnight mushrooms, that rejoice
> To hear the curfew."

In other cases in which the great dramatist alludes to this
bell the time is not indicated. In the old play, "The
Merry Devil of Edmonton" (1631), the sexton says, "Well,
'tis nine a clocke, 'tis time to ring curfew."

Several references to the ringing of this bell are to be found
in the parish accounts of past times. At Kingston-on-
Thames there is an entry under the year 1651, "For ringing
the curfew bell for one year, £1 10s."

It has been suggested that the survival of the curfew bell
in so many parishes is probably due in many cases to the
confusion of this bell with the evening Angelus, and this
seems to gain support from the fact that the former was

evidently regarded as in some sort a religious institution.
Thus in one of Bishop Hall's satires we find these lines :—

> " Who ever gives a paire of velvet shooes,
>   To th' Holy Rood, or liberally allowes
>   But a new rope to ring the couvre-feu bell,
>   But he desires that his great deed may dwell
>   Or graven in the chancel window glasse,
>   Or in his lasting tombe of plated brasse ? "

The connection between the two is yet more clearly seen
in an Indulgence issued to the diocese of Winchester by
Bishop John de Stratford, in 1324, wherein he says, "We
exhort you all that every day when you hear three short
interrupted peals of the bell at the beginning of the curfew
(or in places where you do not hear it, at vesper-time or
nightfall), you say with all possible devotion, kneeling where-
ever you may be, the Angelic Salutation three times at each
peal, so as to say it nine times in all."

There are also several instances where a bequest has been
made for the continued ringing of curfew ; to Mapander,
Dorset, land was left "to find a man to ring the morning
and curfeu bell throughout the year."

In bygone days when roads were neither so many nor so
good as they now are, and when large districts, now under
cultivation, were mere waste land, sometimes moor, sometimes the more treacherous fen, it was by no means
uncommon for the benighted wayfarer to lose his way.   In
such cases it happened repeatedly that the tolling of the
curfew from the tower of some church hard by, yet hidden
by the darkness, served to guide the wanderer to safety and
to shelter.   In grateful recognition of this several bequests
were made with a view to securing the same help to other
travellers in distress in future years.   A piece of land about

an acre and a half in extent, and known as the "Ding Dong Piece," at West Rasen, Lincolnshire, is said to have been left to the parish by some now unknown donor for the above purpose. "Bell-ringing Close," in South Luffenham, Rutland, commemorates a gift by a lady, grateful for the guidance of the curfew's sound; and land was bequeathed under similar circumstances to Chipping Warden, Northamptonshire. John Carey, once Mayor of Woodstock, left by will ten shillings per annum to that parish, that a bell might be rung at eight at night for the guidance of travellers. In several of these cases, and in others which might be given, the bequest only provides for the ringing of the bell during the winter months.

A reference was made above to the Angelus. This is a bell rung thrice a day, usually at six in the morning, at noon, and at six in the evening, at the sound of which everyone is supposed to say the "Angelus," a brief commemoration of the Incarnation, consisting of three appropriate passages of scripture, each followed by the "Ave Maria," and the whole closed with a collect. The custom is alleged to have been instituted by Urban II., Pope from 1088 to 1099, and the evening Angelus to date from the reign of John XXII., Pope from 1316 to 1334. In England, however, the evening Angelus seems to have come first into use; for, in 1399, Archbishop Arundel (acting, as he tells us, at the request of the King, Henry IV.) extended the practice by prescribing morning, in addition to the evening, devotion. His Constitution orders that, as up to that time the devotion of the faithful had been used to honour the Blessed Virgin at the ringing of the curfew by saying the Paternoster once and the Ave

five times, so also the bell should be rung early each
morning in all cathedral, monastic, collegiate, and parish
churches, and the same prayers be said.   In 1492, an
Indulgence promulgated by the two English archbishops,
with some of their suffragans, recognizes the Angelus as a
devotion to be said thrice daily ; and the " Hours of the
Blessed Virgin, according to the use of Sarum" (published
in Paris, in 1526), declares that Pope Sixtus ordained that
the times should be six in the morning and the evening,
and at noon.   Gregory IX., the celebrated Cardinal Hugo,
Pope from 1227 to 1241, directed the ringing of an evening
bell as a call to prayer on behalf of the Crusades.

Longfellow more than once refers to this bell in describing
the peaceful home of Evangeline in Acadie,—

> " Anon from the belfry,
> Softly the Angelus sounded ;"

and again—

> " Sweetly over the village the bell of the Angelus sounded."

Everyone is familiar with the beautiful picture of Millet's,
in which we see two Norman peasants, with bowed heads,
saying the Angelus, as they hear the village bell in the
distant steeple ringing out across the fields that are growing
dim in the coming twilight.   In Spain, if we may trust the
account of an American writer,* the ringing of the Angelus
is neither so soothing, nor so devotional.   "Once, as we
stood towards sunset in the high gallery where the bells
(of Seville Cathedral) are hung in rectangular or arched
apertures, we heard," so he tells us, " the *repique* sounding
the Angelus.   It was a furious explosion of metallic re-
sonance.   Twenty bells on swinging beams . . . such

* *Spanish Vistas*, in " Harper's Magazine," August, 1882.

is the battery at command.   They are not all used at once, however, for the Angelus.   The ringer and his two sons were satisfied with touching up Santa Catalina (of a tone peculiarly deep and acceptable), San José, and one or two others. . . .   One after another their tongues rolled forth a deafening roar, in a systematic disorder of thunderous tones, while the chief ringer went about unconcernedly with a smouldering cigarette in his lips."

Polydore Vergil, writing about 1550, tells us that "thrice every day at evening the bells are rung that every one may kneel and repeat the Angel's salutation to the Blessed Virgin."

The connection of this bell with the traditional ringing of the Curfew is further suggested by the inscription on a bell given to S. Alban's by Roger de Norton (died 1290), "to be struck every night at the time of Curfew."   It bears the legend,

"Missi de Celis Habeo Nomen Gabrielis;"

or, as we may translate it,

" To me was given
The Name of Gabriel, sent from Heaven."

This and similar inscriptions obtained for the Angelus bell in some places the name of the Gabriel bell, and "Old Gabriel" is still the acknowledged title of one in the Market Tower at Lewes ; in other cases portions of the *Ave*, used as a legend, gave the name Ave bell to examples used for a like purpose.

Since the Reformation the Angelus has not been rung as such in English churches, but the attempt to entirely suppress the ringing has not been altogether successful. Thomas Cromwell, acting as Vicar-General, forbade, in

1536, the "knolling of Aves." Hooper, in injunctions to the diocese of Gloucester in 1551, expressly orders "that from henceforth in no parish in the diocese shall the bells be rung to noon upon the Saturdays or other holy days even, nor at evening to curfaye (as it was called)"; yet many traditions of morning, noon, and evening ringings still survive in all parts of the country.

The morning bell is fast going out of use, but nevertheless is retained in many parishes, and has lapsed in others only in quite recent years. It rings at four o'clock still at Brixworth, Northamptonshire, at five at Towcester and other places in the same county; and at the same hour in the summer, but at six in the winter, at Gedney and Burgh in Lincolnshire. Six is the usual hour when the custom is yet maintained, and the sound of the bell has long since come to be considered the signal, or the tradition of a signal, for going to work. From this idea the early bell at Louth used, in years gone by, to be called the "Getting-up Bell." An interesting indenture dated in April, 1664, secures to the sexton of Wokingham, Berkshire, the sum of two pounds per annum, an endowment from Richard Palmer, for ringing daily, both morning and evening, from September 10th to March 11th. The reasons given for making this offering to the parish are, that all who heard the bell might be led to rise and go to bed in good time, that strangers might be aided by the sound of it, and also that the curfew might remind everyone of their own passing bell, and the morning ringing of the summons to the resurrection and the judgment.

The mid-day Angelus was never so universally used in in England as were those of morning and night; yet it obtained a footing in some places, and some few yet retain

a noontide bell, which may be a relic of it.   It is now
regarded merely as a sign to cease work for the mid-day
meal.   In three parishes near Doncaster, namely Fishlake,
Hatfield, and Thorne, the old hours are still kept, and the
bell rings out at six in the morning, at noon, and at six in
the evening; and the mid-day bell may still be heard in
several places in Leicestershire, Rutland, Lincolnshire, and
Northamptonshire.   According to the Constitutions of the
Monastery of Sion, Isleworth, an Angelus was to be rung
each day after the Lady Mass, and the method of ringing it
is given:—"At the end of our Lady Mass, after the benediction is said, the lay brother shall toll the Ave bell nine
strokes at three times, keeping the space of one Pater and
Ave between each three tollings; and after this he that kept
the Lady Mass shall quench the tapers there, and make up
the altar."

Probably the parish of King's Cliff stands quite alone in
the number of its daily ringings, as we have already seen
it is distinguished also in other bell usages.   The full tale
of the hours told out by the bell there was of old, in the
morning at four, seven, and eleven, and in the afternoon at
one, four, and eight.   The first morning bell is now dis-
continued, and the Curfew rings only in the winter; the
seven o'clock bell is said to be an early warning to the
school children of the district, and the others are regarded
as indicating the time to the various labourers of the place.

At Gateshead a bell used to ring at a quarter before noon,
and was commonly known as the "'tatie (potato) bell"; it
was supposed to be a warning to the housewives to get their
husbands' dinners ready against their return from work.

At S. Peter's, Nottingham, is a bell, the seventh of the

peal, which is rung each morning, except Sunday, to rouse the washerwomen of the town for their work. This bell was given for this purpose in 1544 by a washerwoman of the name of Margery Dubbleday, and bore the inscription "Ave Maria of you' Charitie for to Pray for the sole of Ma'gere Dubbyleay": it was recast later, and is now inscribed "I was given by Margery Dubbleday in 1544, and recast with other bells in 1771." The hour originally marked by its ringing was four; the modern "ladies of the laundry" are allowed to slumber undisturbed for two hours more.

The most anxious times in rural districts are naturally those connected with the various periods in the growing of the crops, and especially the commencement and the conclusion of that needful work, the seed-time and the harvest. If the weather be favourable, and still more if it be changeable and so favourable only at uncertain intervals, every available moment must be eagerly snatched and earnestly employed, to ensure the due ingathering of the food for the people. Thus it has come about that in some places special bells used to be rung, and in a few are so still, to call the labourers to work at an early hour during the spring and autumn.

Rushden, Northamptonshire, was formerly familiar with a Seed-sowing Bell, which rang at daybreak during seed-time; but the custom is now obsolete. The Harvest-bell appears to have been more general, and is not so entirely a thing of the past. At Driffield, in Yorkshire, the Harvest-bell sounds at five every morning during harvest-time, and again, as a signal for ceasing work, at seven in the evening. From an old book preserved in the parish chest at Barrow-on-

Humber, Lincolnshire, and containing the "Office and Duty of the Parish Clerk" about the year 1713, we learn that "he is to ring a Bell Every working day morning at Break of the day and Continue the ringing thereof until All Saints and also to ring a Bell Every Evening about the Sun-setting until harvest be fully ended; which bells are to begin to ring from the beginning of harvist." For this service the clerk received from every cottager two pecks of wheat at Easter. In several parishes the bell gives notice to the people when they may go a-gleaning. In some parts of South Warwickshire it rings at eight in the morning; in Leicestershire, as at Waltham-on-the-Wolds, in Northamptonshire, at Gretton, Staverton, and elsewhere, in Rutland, at Impingham and Orwell, and in other counties, this bell is known under the name of the Gleaning-bell. The clerk of Lyddington, Rutland, claims a penny from every adult gleaner for ringing the bell; and in West Deeping, Lincolnshire, the ringing only became obsolete when the people refused to pay the fee, which in this case was twopence.

A harvest-bell of a special kind used to be rung at Louth; where a piece of land, known as the "Gatherums," was tilled for the benefit of the poor, to whom the church bell announced when the "pescods" were ripe for their gathering. An entry in the Church Accounts for 1536 refers to this custom:—"Item, for knyllyng the bell in harvest for gatheringe of the pescods, iiijd." The gleaning-bell at Whittering, Northamptonshire, is a hand-bell rung through the village by a woman.

It was not only in the country, however, that it was found convenient to mark the time for commencing and ceasing the day's work by means of the church bell.   A Mr. Doune, mercer and citizen of London, bequeathed two tenements in Hosier Lane (afterwards called Bow Lane), that their rents might pay for the daily ringing of the tenor of Bow bells as a signal of this kind to the apprentices of London.   The bell was to ring at six in the morning and at eight at night; and the story goes that those jovial youths, "the London 'prentices," having occasion to complain of the clerk's carelessness in the performance of this duty, sent to him the following warning :—

> "Clerk of the Bow bell,
>   With thy yellow locks,
> For thy late ringing
>   Thy head shall have knocks."

The clerk, anxious doubtless to preserve inviolate the glory of the aforesaid "yellow locks," replied in the following conciliatory way :—

> "Children of Cheap,
>   Hold you all still,
> For you shall hear the Bow bell
>   Rung at your will."

One cannot help wondering whether the lads complained of the morning or of the evening bell being rung so late.

The introduction of these bell-signals for the labourers and mechanics, carries us back to a time when watches were seldom found in the pockets of poor men, and even clocks were not invariably seen in their cottages; the church clock and the church bell, often regulated by the ancient and not over trustworthy watch of the old parish clerk, then set the time for the parish, and performed a really needful work. The gradual dying out of these uses of the bells tells us of the diminishing need for such signals.   Where the need has ceased, and where no special endowment pays for the work, it is not very surprising that the clerk or sexton gets slack in ringing a bell at six, five, or even four, every morning, and at last abandons it altogether.

The flight of time at sea is marked by a number of strokes on a bell hung usually near the mizen mast, or in the forecastle. The whole day is divided into seven watches, five of four hours each, and two "dog watches" of two hours each. At the end of each half-hour a bell rings, telling by the number of its strokes how many of the half-hours constituting that particular watch have elapsed. Thus "three bells" does not of itself indicate the time of the day, but simply that three half-hours of the watch have passed.

CHAPTER XIV.

Secular Uses of Church and other Bells.

IN the manifold uses to which the church bells have
been put from time immemorial, there are several
which are secular rather than ecclesiastical, although it
would be wrong to infer that they are, for the most part,
therefore irreligious. The commemoration of national
deliverances, the rejoicing at certain happy events in the
national life, these things, although in themselves of a
secular character, are nevertheless such as the Church may
devoutly thank God for, and her bells may as appropriately
peal out their praises from the tower, as may her choristers
chant Te Deum in the choir. The almost universal
custom for the bells to take their share in every local or
national rejoicing, is in fact simply one striking illustration
of the intimate nature of the union between the Church and
the people. In spite of political and religious differences,
in spite too of attacks upon the Church often bitter, and
sometimes not over scrupulous, all classes of the community
would still feel that something was lacking if, amid the general
festivity of a parish, the voices of the bells did not peal out
with jubilant clangour from the old church steeple, as if to
give voice to the joy so evident around them.

In days gone by, before it became customary for the
thanksgiving of the parish for the blessing of the harvest to
be gathered up and presented to the "Lord of the Harvest"

in a special service at the church, it was usual in many
places to celebrate the conclusion of the ingathering with a
merry peal.   In Northamptonshire the last load was decked
with green boughs, and word having been sent to set the
church bells a-ringing, the harvesters accompanied the
waggon, groaning beneath its weight of golden grain, with
the following song—

> " Harvest home !   Harvest home !
>   The boughs they do shake, the bells they do ring,
>   So merrily we bring the harvest in,
>   The harvest in,
>   So merrily we bring the harvest in. "

Almost every parish festival is similarly greeted in the
belfry.   The local "feast" is honoured with a peal, the
completion of any public work of local importance, the
arrival or departure of a dignitary in Church or State, each
and all wake the sonorous voices of the bells.   A
manuscript quoted by Brand (Smith's Berkeley MSS.)
declares that "Antient ceremonies used throughout the
kingdome, continued from antiquity till the days of our
last fathers, that whensoever any nobleman or peer of the
realme passed through any parish, all the bells were
accustomed to be runge in honor of his person, and to
give notice of the passage of such eminency."   In the
churchwardens' accounts for Waltham Abbey in the year
1542 we find, "Item, paid for the ringing at the prince
his coming, a penny"; and in the accounts for Marlow
we read, in 1592, "Paid to John Black for mending the
bells when the queen came to Bisham, 1s. 6d."

The anniversary of the birth, accession, or coronation of
the Sovereign is constantly marked by pealing the bells.

Shakespeare twice alludes to such peals in "King Henry IV." (Part ii.). In the third act (scene 2) we hear Bull-calf say, "A cough, sir, which I caught with ringing in the King's affairs upon his Coronation day, sir;" and again in the following act (scene 4) are the words—

> " Bid the merry bells ring in thine ear
> That thou art crowned."

In the accounts of S. Mary-at-Hill, London, we find in 1509, "Paid to sevyn men that rong the bellis when the Kingis grace went to Westmyster to be crownyd—o. 1. o." The accounts of the parish of Wakefield allude to the coronation of King Charles I., "1624. Item. at the first ringinge for the Kinge, and other things at that tyme, o. 2. 2." It is not a little remarkable that the bells of Newbury, Berkshire, as proved by the parish accounts, rang for the anniversary of that ill-fated King's accession throughout all the time of the civil war, the last entry being only the year before his death ; and this despite the fact that Cromwellian forces occupied the town, and Presbyterian ministers the pulpit of the church. The execution of the King was also suitably commemorated, as we have seen, in the loyal town of Newcastle-on-Tyne ; and we may add an extract from the church books of Colne for 1710, " Paid for ringing on ye martyrdome of King Charles, oo. o1. oo."

The Restoration was greeted with unbounded enthusiasm throughout England, so much so that Oak-Apple Day, or Royal Oak Day (May 29th), is still observed in some places. Peals are rung at Swineshead, Benington, and at other places in Lincolnshire ; at Wroxeter, Middle, and elsewhere in Shropshire, and in some Yorkshire parishes. At Finedon, in Northamptonshire, they have the curious custom of

16

ringing on this day a half-muffled peal.   In the Wakefield accounts we have this entry:—" 1664.   Ringers for 29th May, o. 8. o. ;" at All Saints', Stamford, we meet with this item:—" 1712.   May 29, paid to the Ringers on King Charles' Restauration, oo. o5. oo."   Similar entries occur during the same century at S. Mary's, Stamford, and at S. Michael's, Bishop Stortford.

The ringing on S. Hugh's Day, which happened to be the accession day of Queen Elizabeth, has already been noticed. In several parishes, as at Bishop Stortford and at Kirton-in-Lindsey, we meet with notices of peals on S. Oswald's Day, August 5th; these were really in commemoration of the deliverance of King James I., while still ruler of Scotland only, from the Gowrie conspiracy.   A more common celebration of a similar kind was the thanksgiving for the nation's escape from Gunpowder Plot on November 5th, 1605.   Several bells have inscriptions alluding to their use on this day, as, for instance, the second at Owmby, in Lincolnshire, which bears the words : " Let vs Remember the 5 of November."   The earliest notice of the use of the bells in connection with this event is at S. Margaret's, West-minster, and, bearing date 1605, evidently refers to the rejoicing which followed immediately on the realization of the Parliament's escape ; it records that ten shillings were " paid the ringers at the time when the Parliament House should have been blown up."   At Stamford the custom of ringing on this day is noticed as early as 1608, and at Leverton, Lincolnshire, in 1610.   An item in the Wakefield accounts, for 1664, also alludes to it.   Half an acre of land, now called Pork-acre, was given to the church at Harlington, Middlesex, to secure the perpetual ringing on

November 5th, by providing a leg of pork for the ringers on
that day. Peals are still rung on this anniversary at many
places, though the custom is dying out; no doubt the
abolition, in 1859, of the special service formerly appointed
for "Gunpowder Plot" has had considerable influence in
reducing the prominence at one time given to the celebration.
At Halton-Holgate, Walcot, and elsewhere, the bells are
"fired," or clashed simultaneously, on this day; this method
of ringing is sometimes called "shooting" the bells, as at
Great Ponton and Rippingale, where, on this occasion, it is
described as "shooting old Guy."   At an archidiaconal
visitation held in Doncaster, on May 13th, 1691, it was
ordered "that the ringers shall have but 13s. 4d. for ringing
upon ye 29th of May and ye 5th of November."

Great victories by land or sea have frequently been celebrated by the church bells.   Admiral Vernon, having
captured Porto Bello from the Spaniards in 1739, was for a
time a popular hero in the country; this accounts for an
entry, dated 1740, in the accounts of Haslingden Church,
Lancashire:—"Nov. 22nd.   Pd the ringers at Admiral
Vernon's Birthday, o. 3. o."   In the same county, at Colne,
we find other entries of a similar character; thus, in 1706,
we read:—"It., Ring^g upon duke Marlbrough good success in Spaine, oo. o2. o6;" and again, in 1746:—"Ringing
on ye Duke's Birthday, o. 3. o."   This was the Duke of
Cumberland, the victor at Culloden in the previous year.
The ringers at Newport Pagnell, Buckinghamshire, evidently
took pride in being a band of public-spirited citizens.   The
Buckinghamshire Herald, for August 2nd, 1797, having
stated that a Mr. Botham had sent a handsome present
to the ringers that they might duly celebrate the fall of

Valenciennes, these gentlemen of the belfry sent a spirited denial of the statement to the next issue of the paper; they declare, moreover, that "on every occasion that does honour to our King and Country we come forward as Britons without any solicitation whatever, and the gentlemen of our own parish give us every Gratification we wish for."

Speaking of these loyal and patriotic peals, Southey says in his "Doctor":—"Doctor Daniel Dove had heard the bells of S. George's (Doncaster) ring for the Battles of Dettingen and Culloden, for Commodore Anson's return, and Admiral Hawke's victory, for the conquest of Quebec, for other victories (important in their day, though in the retrospect they may seem to have produced little effect), for more than one peace, for the going out of the Old Style and for the coming in of the New, for the accession, marriage, and coronation of George III., for the birth of George IV., and that of all his royal brethren and sisters." On the conclusion of peace in June, 1814, the Doncaster bells rang merrily, and were fired at intervals, with three times three, and six times six. Again, in January, 1819, they welcomed the 42nd Highlanders, who marched through the town on their way homewards from the Hundred Days' War and the occupation of Paris.

The commemoration of these loyal and patriotic rejoicings by means of the church bells did not command the admiration of at least one donor, who gave a bell to Witham-on-the-Hill, Lincolnshire, in 1831. It bears the following inscription :—

> " 'T was not to prosper pride or hate
> William Augustus Johnson gave me ;
> But peace and joy to celebrate,
> And call to prayer to heav'n to save ye :

Then keep the terms, and e'er remember
May 29th ye must not ring ;
Nor yet the 5th of each November,
Nor on the crowning of a king."

Two popular festivals in old England, now somewhat
overshadowed by modern Bank Holidays, were Plough
Monday (the Monday after Twelfth Day) and May Day
(May 1st). The former was formerly a great day for feasting
and jollity in agricultural districts. At Blakely, Northamptonshire, and probably in other country parishes, the bells
are still rung merrily, in memory for the most part of
departed joys The rural frolics of May Day were almost
without number ; May-poles, Morris-dances, hobby-horse
riding, the procession of Robin Hood and his merry men,
of the milk-maids with their garlanded pails, and Jack-in-the-
Green and his attendants,—these are but a few of the signs
of joy with which the people, in town as well as country,
hailed the promise of returning summer. Much of merri-
ment was suppressed by the Puritans, and never recovered
its place in popular esteem ; traces of the day's gladness,
however, still exist. At All Saints', Stamford, a charge of
five shillings was made in 1707 for the ringers on May Day;
and the rough usage of inexperienced hands is alleged to
have resulted in cracking the treble bell at Basham,
Cambridgeshire, on that day in 1774.

The bells were sometimes called upon to take part in
popular rejoicings of a more questionable kind. It is said
that in the days when cock-fighting was in all its glory, a
peal has been rung to celebrate the victory of a bird of local
fame. Certainly the triumphs of the race-course have
called forth a tribute from the bells in times past. The

churchwardens' accounts of S. Edmund's, Salisbury, have an entry for 1646, which illustrates this; "Ringing the Race day that the Earle of Pembroke his horse won the Cuppe, vs." Until comparatively recent years the Parish Church bells of Doncaster joined in the Yorkshire carnival of the September races held on the town moor there. In 1862 the bells of Thurnby were rung on the occasion of a meet of hounds in the village. In this case the vicar protested, and locked the belfry door; and subsequently won his case at law with the churchwardens, the clerk, and the ringers, for having broken into the belfry contrary to his orders.

Equally objectionable was the custom, once common enough, of ringing the church bells in token of a party victory at a Parliamentary election. In one case at least the passage of a bill through Parliament itself was hailed throughout the country with bell-ringing: this was when the first Reform Bill was read a third time in the House of Commons, in September, 1831. A tragic occurrence in connection with a political peal happened at Alphington, near Plymouth, on June 10th, 1826. The bells were ringing in honour of Mr. Kekewich's return to Parliament, when the tower was struck by lightning and damaged, and one of the ringers was killed.

The ancient method of summoning the local parliaments of the land, whether ward meetings, gild meetings, municipal, or vestry councils, was by the sound of a bell; and for the obvious reason that the parish church alone usually possessed bells large and loud enough to be heard at any distance, one of these was generally used. The practice dates at least as far back as the days of King Edward the Confessor, who enjoined the employment of this signal in cases of danger, or other emergency. This bell was known as the "Common-bell," and in many cases one special bell within the tower was devoted exclusively to this and kindred objects, under this name.

A large bell, hanging in the tower of the church (now the cathedral) of S. Nicholas, Newcastle-on-Tyne, was known centuries ago by this title; and Nottingham had its "Common-bell" so long since as 1315. The former example was cast, probably rather recast, in 1593-4, a process which it underwent again in 1615, 1622, and 1754; its weight at the final casting being thirty-six hundredweight. In the sixteenth century the churchwardens received an acknowledgment of five shillings per annum for having this bell rung on "Guild Day:" on this occasion it used to sound from nine in the morning until three in the afternoon almost continually, originally to call together the various guilds of the town to their respective halls, preparatory to the annual election of the mayor. It was popularly supposed to toll the knell of the expiring mayoralty. A bell, already alluded to under the name of the "Major," now summons the Freemen of the borough to their meetings at Christmas, Easter, and Michaelmas. The older bell, besides its name of Common-bell, is also called the Great, the Thief, and the Riever-bell. The first name refers obviously to its place as tenor in the peal; the other names allude to its ringing every night during the fairs, as a warning to all thieves to leave the town under pain of arrest.

The Common-bell of Stafford hung at S. Chad's, and was "accustomed to call the parishioners to geather to all things pertening to the towne of Stafford;" while the "grete belle of the parisshe of Seint Androwe" did a similar duty at

Worcester. Thetford, Norfolk, also had a bell assigned to this use in the parish church. An inventory of the church goods of Moulton, Northamptonshire, in 1552, illustrates the objects for which these bells were rung, and also shows that in some cases the Common-bell, although hung in the church steeple, was claimed as parochial, rather than as ecclesiastical, property. The entry runs as follows :—" Itm one other great bell hanging in one frame by it selfe, bought by Thomas Colls and Thomas Lucke, And by ye consent of ye hooll pyshe for theyse causes folowyng (yt is to say) to be ye clocke bell, And to have it ronge whan any casualtyes shall chaunce, And for ye gatheryng togyther ye Inhabitants of ye sayd towne for ye courte and other theyr necessaryes, And not gyven to ye sayd churche."

In the church of S. Mary, Stamford, hangs a bell anciently used for sundry municipal purposes, the ownership being vested in the town authorities. Its voice summoned the townsfolk to public meeting, it tolled when the Corporation was expected to attend the Mayor at an official appearance at church, and down to 1840 it announced at a quarter to eleven on the morning of each 13th November that the annual "bull-running" was on the point of commencing. Its chief civil duty now is to summon the jury and others interested to the Quarter Sessions. The old Common-bell was recast by Tobie Norris in 1626.

The seventh bell in the ring at Oakham is used to give notice of town meetings, and is known as the "Meeting-bell." At Lewes, the ancient bell, more than once already alluded to under the name of "Old Gabriel," serves as the Common-bell. It hangs, not in the church, however, but in the Market Tower.

The Guild Halls of mediæval days often had their bells, and in such cases it is reasonable to suppose that the duties of the Common-bell were largely discharged by these " Mote-bells." The Lincoln Guild Hall still possesses its ancient Mote-bell; it is in a wooden frame, on the roof of the Hall, and is complete with wheel and rope. It was cast in 1371, and used to ring at the opening and closing of the court; it now announces a meeting of the City Council. Many modern town-halls are now provided with a complete peal of bells.

In the *Gentleman's Magazine* for 1790, we read :—" At Kidderminster is a singular custom. On the election of a bailiff the inhabitants assemble in the principal streets to throw cabbage-stalks at each other. The town-house bell gives signal for the affray. This is called the lawless hour."

In many parishes, if not in most, notice of a vestry meeting is given by ringing one or more of the church bells. This custom, however, like many other belfry usages, is decaying, and probably the introduction of the new system of parish councils, by rendering almost all vestry meetings, except that of Easter, unnecessary, will lead to a still further decline in it. At Doncaster the sixth bell used of old to summon a meeting of the Corporation, the fifth the Highway Board, and the treble the Vestry.

Among local usages of a secular kind to which the church bells are put, the following may be mentioned :—

At Carlton-le-Moorland, Lincolnshire, a bell was rung once a year to assemble at the church gates such persons as desired to become tenants of a certain meadow, whose rental had been left to the poor of the parish. The letting of the grass on the sides of the lanes was similarly announced on May Day at Winterton, the bells being promiscuously jangled by way of notice. The collection of the Easter dues is notified at Horncastle by the sound of the second bell immediately after the morning service on Easter Monday and Tuesday. A similar custom also prevailed at Doncaster. In the accounts of Louth, Lincolnshire, for 1589, a payment is mentioned for "ringing at ye boundays." This refers to the "booning" or mending of the roads, towards which the occupiers of the land were formerly bound to contribute by lending horses and carts for the conveyance of the needful material. Notice of the days when this service was to be rendered was given in several places by the ringing of the church bell. The derivation and original meaning of the word "boon," used in the above sense in many parts of Lincolnshire, has given rise to much discussion.

A usage of a more general character was the ringing of a bell to notify the opening of a market or a fair. The Market-bell is very ancient. Strabo has a story which speaks of the commencement of the fish-market being thus made known. In England a hand-bell sometimes announced the hour for business to begin, and often the market-house, or the town-hall, bore a bell on its gable for this purpose. To secure that no one should have any undue advantage over his neighbours in the Corn Market at Stamford, it was ordered that no business should be done before the "Undernone" or "Undern" bell sounded. The terms of this bye-law were: "It is ordeyned that no person opyn ther sack or set ther corn to sale afore the hour of ten of the clock, or els the undernone bell be rongyn." This bell was apparently the property of the town, for in 1777 the

Corporation decided to give "the market-bell as an additional bell to the quarters in the church." Anciently the arrival of a cargo in the haven of Barton-upon-Humber was announced to the neighbourhood by the sound of a hand-bell, and for three days from that time the townsmen were protected in their exclusive right to purchase the goods, and that at wholesale rates. A somewhat similar privilege used to be given to the inhabitants of Sleaford in their butter-market; a small bell hanging in the church, and known as the Butter-bell, being rung when the market opened, and inhabitants having granted to them the opportunity of buying before others were served.

At Rotherham, and some other towns of Yorkshire, the custom still prevails of ringing a bell at a stated hour (usually about eleven o'clock) on Saturday nights, as a signal to close the market; and obedience to the summons is strictly enforced.

Like the Common-bells, Market-bells often though hung in the church were not counted as church property. The inventory of such property made in 1552 has this entry for Watford, in Hertfordshire, "Imprimis V Belles in the steple and one m'ket bell."

Market Peals were, and sometimes still are, rung with a different purpose from the bells which have just been considered. They were sounded out from the towers in villages around the market-towns to guide the farmers on their homeward way, especially during the dark months of winter. The Scotton bells ring out their welcome home from the Gainsborough market from seven to eight o'clock on Tuesday evenings. Kirton-in-Lindsey, being within the "sphere of influence" of more than one trade-centre, rings its bells during November and the two following months each Tuesday for the benefit of those coming from Gainsborough, Thursday for those from Brigg, and Saturday for Kirton. An attempt was made at one time to alter this "Winter Ringing," but fortunately without success.

Fairs are sometimes announced by the ringing of peals on their eves. This was once the custom at Louth, and is still so at Epworth.

One other secular use of bells which must be mentioned, is their employment to rouse the citizens in cases of danger, and especially to give notice of a fire. The accepted way of ringing in times of alarm was to "ring the bells backward." So were they anciently rung for a fire at Peterborough, and at Barrow-on-Soar, Leicestershire. The seventh bell at S. Ives speaks of the custom in its inscription,

> "When backwards rung we tell of fire.
> Think how the world shall thus expire."

In an old play, entitled "The City Match," we find an allusion to this :—

> "Then, Sir, in time
> You may be remembered at the quenching of
> Fir'd houses, when the bells ring backward, by
> Your name upon the buckets."

Sir Walter Scott, in his well-known and stirring ballad of "Bonnie Dundee," alludes to this fashion of ringing for the purpose of rousing the town,—

> "Dundee he is mounted, he rides up the street,
> The bells they ring backward, the drums they are beat."

So, too, in Percy's "Reliques," we read that when William of Cloudeslee attacked the citizens of Carlisle,—

> " There was many an outhorne in Carleil blowen,
> And the belles backward did ring."

In a similar spirit the fire-bell peal at Swaton, and at Stamford, Lincolnshire, formerly consisted in a wild jangling of the whole ring.*

Where only one or two bells are used to give warning of a fire, the shriller ones seem to be usually selected. At several places in Lincolnshire, as at Barkston, Hall Magna, and others, the treble bell is used, and at Caythorpe the first and second; while in some parishes the small priest's bell is now called the fire-bell, as at S. Peter-at-Arches, Lincoln, and at Higham Ferrers. At Horncastle, at S. John Baptist's, Peterborough, and at Sleaford, there are small bells specially used for the same purpose. A singular and striking effect must be produced by the fire-signal at Caistor, Louth, and some other places where the two extremes of the peal, the treble and the tenor, are employed. The inscriptions on several bells refer to their use as fire-alarms. Church bells are not now used for this purpose as frequently as was formerly the case, the methods of dealing with conflagrations being now more systematic, so that the rousing of the public generally is seldom necessary. Even where a bell is still called into requisition it is in modern days frequently a small shrill-voiced specimen on the fire-engine house, the police station, or some other public building of a secular character.

---

* In several books "ringing backwards" is defined as another term for a muffled peal. This must surely be a mistake, for nothing could be more absurd than to muffle bells by way of sounding an alarm. Moreover it is not easy to see why such a peal should be called " ringing *backwards*." Whatever meaning may attach to the phrase in a modern belfry, does it not seem probable that originally it implied ringing the bells in the order reverse to the usual one, that is from the tenor up to the treble? Such a peal would have a singularly startling effect, which is just what a fire-peal or an alarm-peal aims at.

It has been found advisable in several instances upon our coasts to supplement the strong light which shines from the lighthouse by the sonorous tones of a bell, so that even if thick fog muffle the first, the sound of the second may warn the mariner of impending danger. In the Eddystone light-house, which was completed in 1881, is a bell weighing two tons, which sounds two quick strokes every half-minute in foggy weather. The tradition of the bell hung on a buoy by the good Abbot of Aberbrothok, in order to warn seamen of the dangerous Inchcape Rock, opposite the mouth of the Tay, has been made familiar by Southey's ballad :—

> " On a buoy in the storm it floated and swung,
>   And over the waves its warning rung :
>   When the rock was hid by the surges' swell,
>   The mariners heard the warning bell ;
>   And then they knew the perilous rock,
>   And blessed the Abbot of Aberbrothok."

A more effectual warning is now given by a lighthouse erected in 1811, but the name of Bell Rock is still often given to the place, and the primitive use of the bell has not been abandoned. Two bells are rung by machinery during foggy weather, tolling regularly every half-minute.

A hospitable use of the bell was that of the Knights Hospitallers of S. John at Stainton Dale, near Scarborough. As the shadows of the evening fell one of their number, so the story goes, ascended a neighbouring eminence, still called Bell Hill, and there rang a bell, or blew his horn, as a guide for all wayfarers to the monastic house, where rest and refreshment for the night were offered. An equally hospitable motive evidently dictated the inscription carved beside the bell-rope which hung at one time near the door at Rosyth Castle, Fife,—

" In day time dray yis cord ye bel to clink,
     Queais mery voice warnis to meat and drink."

Part of the furniture of every sea-going vessel, and of most of our river steamers, is a bell, which is used, as was noticed in the last chapter, to mark the flight of time, but also for other purposes, such as announcing by its clangour the starting of the ship. An interesting example of these bells is now preserved in the library at "Lloyd's." This was originally on board "La Lutine," a French vessel captured by Admiral Duncan. In October, 1799, this ship sailed from Yarmouth Roads for the Elbe, carrying over a million pounds' worth of bullion and bar-silver; and was totally wrecked on a sand-bank at the entrance of the Zuyder Zee. Many attempts, more or less successful, have been made to recover the treasure carried by this frigate; and, in 1858, the bell was brought up by a diver. It now stands under a table made from the rudder-timbers of the ill-fated ship. It is inscribed with a cross and the date 1779.

As many church bells have at times been turned to secular uses, so there are not a few instances of the contrary having taken place; and among these are several instances in which ships' bells have been hung in the bell-turrets of country churches. This is especially true of Scotland, and more than one case is quoted in the work, already referred to, on the Bells of Kincardineshire.

CHAPTER XV.

𝕾𝖒𝖆𝖑𝖑 𝕭𝖊𝖑𝖑𝖘, 𝕾𝖊𝖈𝖚𝖑𝖆𝖗 𝖆𝖓𝖉 𝕾𝖆𝖈𝖗𝖊𝖉.

OCCASIONAL mention has already been made of such hand-bells as are used for purposes similar to those more generally served by bells of a larger size ; there are, however, sufficient usages in connection with small bells exclusively to warrant our devoting a few pages especially to them.

Some of the earliest bells on record were unquestionably very small, and probably of the kind one still sees on the baby's rattle, namely, a hollow metal sphere with a loose pellet within it. Such bells in all likelihood formed the musical fringe upon the robe of the Jewish High-priest, in which they were placed alternately with pomegranates, all being made of gold. The design of this addition to the vestments was probably intended to help the worshippers to follow mentally the steps of their hierarch as he passed into those sacred enclosures of the Tabernacle, which were concealed for ever from all eyes but his own. In mediæval days a similar method arose of adorning the vestments of the Christian priesthood. We have notices of several magnificent robes which were thus decorated. Conrad, Abbot of Canterbury, had a cope fringed with one hundred and forty little silver bells ; and fifty-one of silver gilt tinkled round a cope of Lanfranc's. Riculfus, Bishop of Soissons, in his will, dated 915, speaks of stoles adorned in a similar manner, and Peterborough Abbey had maniples of a like kind. The introduction of this curious sort of decoration may have been due to a wish to imitate the vestments of the older dispensation ; it may, however, have simply been the adoption by the Church of a fashion prevalent in the world. Ladies wore little bells jingling at their girdles, knights attached them to their armour, and the high curled shoes of the time frequently ended with a bell on the pointed toe. This usage was probably of Eastern origin, and has its place in the East to the present time. The Persian monarchs bedecked themselves with bells, and the women of Arabia and Persia wore them on their anklets. Isaiah seems to refer to a Jewish imitation of this custom when he describes (iii. 16) the "daughters of Zion " as "walking and mincing as they go, and making a tinkling with their feet ;" and further denounces a judgment upon them, and the destruction of all their finery and "the bravery of their tinkling ornaments." In the present century the ex-Queen of Oude paid a visit to this country, and was presented to the Queen, on which occasion the head-dress of the oriental lady was remarkable for its "tinkling ornaments." The wearing of bells became, however, at last one of the special badges of the professional jester, or "fool." It was about the fifteenth century that Society abandoned the use of bells as a matter of dress to the fools, and these latter attached them to their caps, their shoes, the elbows of their motley coats, the heads of their carved staves, and indeed promiscuously over their persons and their insignia. The princes of Tartary in the seven-teenth century were accompanied, whenever they went abroad, by a group of court fools, or *chaouls*, who wore

17

little bells at all points of their quaint costume. This jester's badge is so proverbial as scarcely to need illustration, yet we may quote Thornbury's "Songs of the Cavaliers," where we read that the jester, about to deliver himself of his "sermon,"

". . . Shook his hood and bells and leaped upon a chair;"

and Longfellow's "King Robert of Sicily," in which are the lines,

"Nay, not the King, but the King's jester, thou
Henceforth shall wear the bells and scalloped cape."

The last official jester at the English Court appears to have flourished as late as the reign of Charles II. ; and, if we may trust the gossip of Pepys, he had his cap and bells like his predecessors. Under date Feb. 13, 1667-8, in the immortal Diary, we read :—"Mr. Brisband tells me, in discourse, that Tom Killigrew hath a fee out of the Wardrobe for cap and bells ; under the title of the King's Foole or Jester, and may revile or jeere anybody, the greatest person, without offence, by the privilege of his place."

The Morris-dancers on May Day in the olden time were commonly bedecked with jingling bells, especially about the knees, so that their sound might keep time with the dancing. "Cobbe's Prophecies, his Signes and Tokens, his Madrigalls, Questions and Answers" (1614) thus allude to this custom :—

"It was my hap of late, by chance
To meet a country Morris-dance,
When, cheefest of them all, the Foole
Plaied with a ladle and a toole ;
When every younker shak't his bels."

In the churchwardens' accounts for S. Helen's, Abingdon, we have an entry under the date 1560, of "two dossin of

MORRIS DANCERS WITH SMALL BELLS, TEMP. JAMES I.

(From a Painting by Vickenb001).

Morres bells:" and in a similar record belonging to Kingston-upon-Thames we find, among other expenses connected with the "Mores dawnsars" in the reigns of Henry VII. and his successor, 12d. for "bellys."

Small bells anciently formed in several ways part of the equipment of war. The early Britons had bells fastened or suspended at the butt-ends of their spears, that they might make a rattling or jingling noise when the weapons were brandished. So Lingard, describing the accoutrement of the British warriors, says, "they possessed no other defensive armour than a narrow target; their weapons were a dirk, an unwieldy sword hanging from the waist by an iron chain, and a short lance, from one extremity of which was suspended a bell." The Goths also were accustomed to incite their forces to military ardour by clashing cymbals and bells in honour of their gods. In some similar way the Greeks waved their shields as they entered the battle, producing thereby a martial clangour from the sound of the innumerable little bells which were hung one within the hollow of each shield. Another use of bells in the Greek army was a more practical one, and was adopted by the Romans. This was the custom of providing a hand-bell to be rung by the sentries as they went their rounds upon the ramparts of a fortress; at each successive tower the guard turned out at the sound, and the bell was handed on to the sentry in charge of the next section of the wall. This was doubtless useful, in that it assured that all the guardians of the sleeping city were on the alert, but it had the disadvantage of informing the enemy of the moment when the sentry had passed any given spot. We are told by Thucydides that Brasidas, the Lacedaemonian commander

in the Peloponnesian War, nearly succeeded in capturing
the town of Potidaea in Macedonia, by planting his scaling
ladders and advancing to the assault, just when the sound
of the bell informed him that the sentry guarding the place
of the attack had gone by.

A curious and unique use of bells in warfare is recorded
by Plutarch in his life of Brutus. He tells us that Brutus
and Cassius drove the Lycians into Xanthus, and there
besieged them; "as a river ran close by the town," he
continues, "several attempted to escape by swimming and
diving, but they were prevented by nets let down for that
purpose, which had little bells at the top to give notice
when any one was taken."

The use of bells on the trappings of horses, and especially
of those trained to war, is very ancient. The prophet
Zechariah (xiv., 20), mentions "the bells of the horses;" and
several of the sculptures discovered at Nineveh represent
horses with bells hanging from their bridles, or (as is sometimes seen on a modern dray-horse), fixed on the tops of
their heads. Euripides, Æschylus, and Aristophanes, are
all witnesses on behalf of this usage in Greece. This form
of decoration for harness became very general, and is not
now entirely obsolete. One of the tokens, or "signs," used
by pilgrims who had visited the shrine of S. Thomas of
Canterbury, was a number of little bells inscribed
"Campana Thome," which they attached to their bridles.
No doubt the little bell-shaped flower has obtained its
name of Canterbury-bell from this ancient symbol of an
accomplished pilgrimage. The caparison of the horse, at
any rate on great occasions, being commonly thus adorned,
the man who played the part of the Hobby-horse in the

Morris-dance was not thought complete without similar treatment. In the old play of the "Vow-Breaker," by William Sampson (1636), Miles, the Miller, thus exclaims in high indignation when it is suggested that "Master Major shall play the Hobby-horse;" "Have I borrowed the fore horse-bells, his plumes, and braveries, nay, had his mane new shorne and frizl'd, and shall the Major put me besides the Hobby-horse? Let him hobby-horse at home, an he will!" Horse-bells are again mentioned in the description of a cruel game in vogue a century or more ago, and known as "Thrashing the fat hen:" a man carried a hen upon his back and had horse-bells fastened to him, by the sound of which his fellows, who were blindfolded, endeavoured to follow him, and to strike the hen with sticks. Children occasionally still play a kind of blindman's buff of a similar nature, all being blindfolded but one who carries and rings a bell, guided by the sound of which the others try to catch him. Edgar Allan Poe's reference to the use of bells on the harness of sleigh-horses is well known :—

> " Hear the sledges with the bells —
> Silver bells.
> What a world of merriment their melody foretells '
> How they tinkle, tinkle, tinkle,
> In the icy air of night !
> While the stars that oversprinkle
> All the heavens, seem to twinkle
> With a crystalline delight."

Russian horses frequently carry bells hung within the arch which surmounts the native horse-collar; in England the horses of tramway cars sometimes have a single bell suspended from the collar.

This usage, so far as it was not a mere matter of fancy, doubtless arose from the idea that the joyful clashing of the bells would stir the blood of the animals to greater exertion and higher courage. Andrew Marvel declares that "the pack-horse tires without his bells;" and for this reason the camels of an Eastern caravan carry their bells, as did the long lines of burdened horses, which with us preceded the introduction of the stage waggon. The sound of the bell is useful, also, in helping the owner to trace the animal that wears it; and thus it became common on the necks of cattle, and with flocks of sheep and goats. It was perhaps for this reason that the hawk and falcon, when trained for sporting purposes, wore two little bells round their legs. So says Touchstone, in "As You Like It" (Act iii., sc. 3):—
"As the ox hath his bow, sir, the horse his curb, and the falcon her bells, so man hath his desires;" and Master Stephen, in Jonson's "Every Man in His Humour," says:—
"I have bought me a hawk, and a hood, and bells and all."
In his edition of the "Boke of S. Albans," Gervase Markham thus describes these bells:—"The bells which your hawk shall wear, look in anywise that they be not too heavy, whereby they overload her, neither that one be heavier than another, but both of like weight: look also that they be well sounding and shrill, yet not both of one sound, but one at least a note under the other." To the present day it is usual, in many districts abroad, to hear the sound of sheep and cattle bells on the mountain sides, or on the broad plains, which form their pasturage. The same custom was at one time equally well known in England, and is referred to by Gray, in his "Elegy in a Country Churchyard":—

" Now fades the glimmering landscape on the sight,
 And all the air a solemn stillness holds,
 Save where the beetle wheels his droning flight,
 And drowsy tinklings lull the distant folds."

At the present day the enclosure of the land almost everywhere in this country has rendered the use of these bells
unnecessary, and thus they have for the most part disappeared; they may, however, occasionally still be heard,
where some wide moorland, or some unenclosed hillside, is
used as a sheep-walk. The term "bell-wether," sometimes
still employed in a slightly contemptuous sense to denote
the leader of a party or a faction, reminds us that the flock
was wont to follow in the footsteps of the sheep that wore
the bell, and thus the shepherd's task was lightened, in that
his charges were kept together, and their wanderings could
be easily traced by the tinkle of the bell.

Another proverbial phrase implying superiority is that
which speaks of "bearing away the bell." This arose from
an old custom of giving a bell as the prize for a horse-race.
It seems not impossible that this practice arose out of the
one just mentioned; it would be a simple transition of ideas,
when one was accustomed to see the sheep that led the flock
wearing a bell, to give a bell to the horse which "showed
the way home" to the rest of the competitors in a race.
Amongst the sports which anciently took place on the
Roodee, at Chester, on Easter Monday, was a horse-race,
the saddlers' company giving a silver bell as "a rewarde for
that horse which with speedy runninge should run before all
others." Another instance meets us at Dumfries, the magis-
trates of which town ordered the treasurer, on April 15th,
1662, to purchase a silver bell as a prize to be run for
annually by the "work-horses" of the burgh. This race

took place in May, one condition being that the same horse and rider must win it three consecutive years before the bell should "appertain unto the wooner theerof for evir." There were evidently shrewd men on the bench in Dumfries in those days, who were not prepared to risk too much in the purchase of silver bells. Whether anyone actually acquired the original bell or not, the present writer cannot say; the whole affair was suppressed in 1716, "severall irregularities and misdemeanours, to the scandal of the place and dishonour of God," having taken place; and the treasurer was ordered "to sell the muck-bell (as the race-prize was called) for the best advantage." In Camden's "Remains" is an epitaph commencing:—

> "Here lies the man whose horse did gaine
> The bell, in race on Salisbury plain."

The secular uses of hand-bells in both ancient and modern times are almost countless. The bellman, or town-cryer, was once a familiar character in every town; and in many of the smaller towns, and a few of the larger, he is still an "institution." Most of his glory has, however, departed. Of old he was a recognized public official, and often had his livery as such; but now he makes his proclamation of public auctions, of cattle "lost, stolen, or strayed," and other matters of interest, with nothing to add to such dignity as he can put into the clangour of his bell and the tone of his voice. A bellman in scarlet coat, and other insignia of ancient importance, may still be seen in Harrogate, and probably in a few other places. The watchmen of old carried bells, one so equipped being appointed for each ward of the city of London in the time of Queen Mary. As these went their rounds they were accustomed to sound their bells at intervals, and to proclaim the hour, to tell the state of the weather, and sometimes to pronounce a blessing on the town. Thus Milton speaks, in " Il Penseroso," of :—

> " The belman's drowsy charm
> To bless the door from nightly harm."

These proclamations were often thrown into rude verses, which suggested to Herrick the following lines entitled "The Belman," in his "Hesperides":—

> " From noise of scare-fires rest ye free,
> From murder's benedicite,
> From all mischances that may fright
> Your pleasing slumbers in the night ;
> Mercy secure ye all, and keep
> The goblin from ye, while ye sleep.
> Past one o'clock, and almost two,
> My masters all, Good day to you."

The bellman's verses survived in some instances almost to our own day.*

No more convenient method of attracting attention than the sound of the bell seems to have been devised by man. It announces to the waiting passengers the approach of the railway train, and in America it also serves the purpose fulfilled among us by the shrill engine whistle; it tells us when the steam-boat is about to start upon her journey, and its sharp tinkle announces the approach of the ubiquitous bicycle; it summons the scholars into school, and frequently is the accepted signal for silence and attention when they are there ; it is the president's call for order in several popular assemblies, as in the French Chamber; it marks the limit of time permitted to the various speakers in many congresses and conferences ; it announces the moment

---

* For some examples see the article " Arise, Mistress, Arise," in " England in the Days of Old " (Andrews and Co.).

when the curtain is about to rise for the commencement of
the opera or play; it calls the workmen to their labours in
many a factory and mill; and finally the vendor of small
wares in our streets, and even the prosaic but necessary
dustman, attracts public attention by the same means. Its
domestic use also is various and of long standing. A
Spartan announced his presence at his neighbour's door by
a shout; an Athenian or a Roman rapped with his
knuckles; the knocker was an improvement upon these
methods, but the door-bell was a further advance upon that.
House-bells are said to date from the days of Queen Anne,
and the electric variety is only of to-day. So far back as
the days of Shakespeare, however, the bell was evidently
known as a domestic signal, for we find Macbeth (Act ii.
scene 1) saying to his servant—

> " Go, bid thy mistress, when my drink is ready,
> She strike upon the bell."

Within the monasteries the inmates were assembled, not
only to worship, but for every other requisite purpose by the
sound of the bell; and in spite of the occasional introduction of other means of communication, such as gongs
(which are after all but a form of bell), telephones,
speaking-tubes, and what not, the clear tone of the bell is
still the usual call heard within our houses. It provides
what Byron called "the tocsin of the soul, the dinner-bell,"
it summons attendants when needed, and often rouses the
household to the duties of the day.

Small bells have been used in various ways in the public
worship of many of the religions of the world. The
Egyptians, who seem to have had no bells properly so
called, nevertheless made use of the *sistrum*, by them called

the *kemkem*, in their religious rites. It was a frame of bronze or brass, crossed by three or four bars of metal, at the ends of which were metal plates, which rattled when the instrument was struck with a metal rod. Cleopatra used kemkems, as we have seen other nations did bells, in war, a number of them being clashed by her forces at the battle of Actium in 31 B.C. The Buddhists, again, though they assemble their congregations by the sound of a horn, mark the most important parts of their services by the tinkling of little bells. The bells on the vestments of the Jewish priest need not be further described. In the Christian Church, in more than one of its branches, a small bell has long been used at the altar at the offering of the Eucharist ; it tells the people when the Cherubic hymn, " Sancte, Sancte, Sancte, Domine Deus Sabaoth," is to be sung ; it informs them when the Canon, or prayer of consecration, begins, and when the actual consecration of the elements takes place ; and it gives notice when the priest is ready to administer the Blessed Sacrament to the communicants. From the first of these usages the bell is generally called the Sanctus-bell ; though that name, sometimes varied to the Saunce-bell or Sacring-bell, in old English inventories commonly means a small bell hung in the steeple to be rung in a similar way. One of the larger church bells now usually echoes the ringing of the altar-bell at the consecration and elevation of the Sacrament, that the faithful who are prevented from being present may mingle their prayers at the supreme moment with those of the worshippers. John Myrc, whose " Instructions to Parish Priests " have already been quoted, thus refers to the Sacring bell :—

> " And when the Gospel is y-done
>   Teach them eft to kneel down soon ;
>   And when they hear the bell ring
>   To that holy sacring,
>   Teach them kneel down, both young and old,
>   And both their hands up to hold,
>   And say then in this manner,
>   ' Jesus, Lord, welcome Thou be
>   In form of bread as I Thee see.' "

In England in some cases a chime of little bells was hung upon a wheel on, or near, the rood-screen, and this was rung at the elevation. The will of John Baret, of Bury, dated 1463, mentions that "the berere of the paxbrede" should also " do the chymes goo at ye sacryng of the Messe." At Salhouse, and at Scarning, Norfolk, the old sanctus-bells are still in their place upon the rood-screen. As to the use of the external saunce-bell Myrc has also something to say :—

> " If thou may not come to church,
>   Wherever that thou do work,
>   When that thou hearest to Mass knell,
>   Pray to God with heart still
>   To give thee part of that service
>   That in the church y-done is."

Lyndwode, commenting upon the Constitutions of Archbishop Peckham (issued in 1281), which order the ringing of this bell, says that the bell which can be furthest heard ought to be used for the purpose.

Reference has already been made to several usages of hand-bells at funerals, a custom which is almost invariable in Italy, Sicily, and Malta, and of frequent occurrence in France and Spain. A bell is also rung before the Blessed Sacrament when it is carried to the sick, to notify all passers-by of its approach. A bell for this purpose is one of the articles of church furniture which, on the authority of

Archbishop Winchelsey, the parishioners are bound to provide at their own cost. The "Instructions for Parish Priests" gives directions also concerning this :—

> " When thou shalt to sick gone,
> A clean surplice cast thee on,
> Take thy stole with thee right,
> And pull thy hood over thy sight ;
> Bear thy Host anont thy breast
> In a box that is honest ;
> Make thy clerk before thee go
> To bear a light and bell ring."

In old days in England the Rogation-day processions for "beating the bounds" of the parish, were headed by the beadle with his bell.

Several of the reformers had a special dislike to these uses of the hand-bells, all of which have a practical utility, rather than any mystical meaning. Hooper, in his "Visitation Book," drawn up in 1551 and 1552, reckons "the ringing of the Sacring-bell" among forbidden rites ; in which he seems to be copying certain injunctions issued to the diocese of London by Ridley in 1550. Grindal, of course, was for extreme measures, absolutely revolutionary as he was on almost every ecclesiastical question. He orders "all hand-bells and Sacring-bells" not only to be disused, but destroyed, and forbids their employment at funerals or on "the days of rogations, commonly called Cross-week or Gang-days."

A curious usage formerly prevailed at Congleton, in Cheshire, on the Eve of Lammas Day, or S. Peter's Chains (August 1st). The chapel of the place—the parish church being at Astbury—was dedicated in the name of S. Peter *ad vincula*, and consequently the local wake took place on that

day; though (as is the case in so many instances) the
alteration in the calendar has never been accepted there so
far as this matter is concerned, so that Congleton wake now
takes place on the 12th of the month.   For a long time it
was customary for three acolytes to parade the town at
midnight on the vigil, girt about with leather belts to which
were hung a number of globular bells.   The ceremony was
known as "ringing S. Peter's chains," and ended with an
address at the Market-cross on the duties of the coming
festival.   The bells, or "chains," fell afterwards into lay
hands, and were used in a fashion more provocative of tipsy
jollity than of devotion; so that finally the town authorities
interposed, and took possession of the belts.   They are now
preserved at Congleton, among other relics of the past, by
the corporation.

The Burmese use a large number of small bells in the
external decoration of their pagodas; they are hung at the
angles of the many-gabled roofs, and produce a continuous
and not unpleasant tinkling as they sway in the breeze.

The Buddhists, of Japan, use in their temple-worship
gong-shaped bells of peculiar workmanship, and of a tone so
wonderfully sweet, that the American writer, "Mark Twain,"
says of them, "I don't believe I shall ever hear more
heavenly sounds until I reach the Golden City."   Buddhist
missionaries from Corea first introduced these *rin*, as they
are called, but the art-loving Japanese improved upon those
of foreign manufacture to an extraordinary degree.   They
are considered sacred objects, and consequently it was very
rarely that one could be purchased by a stranger, or that any
of them were met with outside the temples; until the
Japanese Government, some twenty years since, declared

RINGING THE CHAINS.

Shintooism the only state religion, since which time Buddhism has greatly declined in Japan.

The Turks alone of all nations seem to have an aversion to the use of bells ; the muezzin's voice "frequently," according to Lord Byron, "solemn and beautiful beyond all the bells of Christendom," calls them to prayers, and the clapping of the hands is the signal used by the wealthy for summoning their attendants ; yet the Turks look forward to hearing the soothing melodies of countless bells in the Paradise promised them by the Prophet. To this hope Moore twice alludes in "Lalla Rookh ;" thus he speaks, in the "Veiled Prophet," of

> ". . . Bells as musical
> As those that, on the golden-shafted trees
> Of Eden, shake in the Eternal Breeze."

And again (in "Paradise and the Peri")—

> " And she already hears the trees
> Of Eden, with their crystal bells
> Ringing in that ambrosial breeze
> That from the Throne of Alla swells."

CHAPTER XVI.

Carillons.

WE have spoken of chiming and of ringing bells in
the technical senses in which those words are
employed in the belfry; there is yet another method of
employing the bells which must be noticed; this is the
carillon, or the playing of tunes upon them by mechanical
or other means.

The word carillon is said to be derived from the Italian
quadriglio; and implied originally a simple and somewhat
monotonous dance-measure, which was popular throughout
Europe in the sixteenth century. From the fact that the
earliest attempts at bell-tunes consisted of adaptations of
the quadriglio, that term, or rather the French form of it,
carillon, came to be applied to all such settings of music.
The word is now used rather indefinitely; in France it
not only means the tune played, but also the set of bells
arranged for playing it; in England it usually denotes what
the French call *le carillon à clavier*, or a set of bells played
by means of a key-board, while one that is acted upon
mechanically is called a chime. In this latter sense the
carillon has only recently been introduced into this country,
and even the chimes are not very common, and seldom
attempt anything but a simple melody.

Belgium is emphatically the home of the carillon. There
we find belfries furnished with peals of bells varying from a

few pounds to as many tons, and forming three complete
octaves of notes, or even more, with their full complement
of semi-tones. Carillons of twenty or thirty bells are to be
found even in small towns ; and in the more considerable
cities, we find as many as forty (as at Louvain and Bruges),
forty-four (as at Mechlin), or sixty-five (as as Antwerp).
This last is the largest of them all ; Bruges claims to possess
the heaviest, but Mechlin is said to have the sweetest
carillon.

The mechanical contrivance for playing upon these peals
is similar in idea to that of a musical box, or of a barrel-
organ. A large drum, or barrel, set with pegs, is made to
revolve by machinery, usually as part of the mechanism of
the clock. These pegs, or studs, in turn raise levers, which
pull wires connected with hammers in the bell-chamber.
This is the means employed in the belfries of some of our
English parish churches, by which some simple hymn-tune
or popular melody is struck out upon the bells at regular
intervals throughout the day. All Saints', Derby, has such
a chiming apparatus, as also have several Lincolnshire
churches, Boston, Holbeach, Grantham, Haxey, and others;
and many other churches and town-halls in this country, as
well as in Scotland and Ireland.

The will of John Barnet (1463) left money to repair the
chimes of the parish church of Bury, and expressed the wish
that they should play " Requiem Eternam " in his memory
at stated times. We have already seen the precautions
taken in Grantham, in 1646, to protect the chime wires. In
1691, it was ordered, at an archidiaconal visitation at Doncaster, that " Christopher Shaw shall for the year ensuing
looke after the clock and chimes," in addition to other

18

duties. A set of chimes on hemispherical bells has been placed in S. James's Church, Bermondsey, in commemoration of the sixty years of Her Majesty's reign.

The Continental carillons are worked in a similar way, and chime out their melodies at frequent intervals; at Mechlin, for instance, a bar or two of music is played every ten minutes, giving way to a complete tune at the half-hour, while at the hour the tune is repeated several times. Few English belfries have more than one octave of bells, and that in one key only, and twelve bells we may call the maximum; thus the choice of tunes for the chime is with us very limited, and it has to be played in single notes. The Belgian peals of forty or more bells give a wide scope for the selection of the music, and moreover allow of the introduction of the full harmonies. But yet further latitude is provided in connection with the Belgian carillons from the fact that in almost every case a key-board is attached, by means of which any tune may be executed. The keys are arranged like those of an organ, though they are of course larger, and usually clumsier in make; and in the case of a large carillon like that at Mechlin there are two manuals, and a row of pedals. The manuals have to be struck smartly with the gloved hands, when the keys act the same part as the pegs on the drum; the pedals raise the hammers of the larger bells, and thus, as on an organ, sound the deepest notes.

The greatest carilloner that Belgium has seen was Matthias van den Gheyn, who died in 1785; and since that time it is said that the manual performances upon the bells have declined. How different, however, from anything that we are familiar with, is the capacity of a large carillon when under the hands of a skilled artist, the following passage forcibly illustrates. It is thus that the Rev. H. R. Haweis, an enthusiastic admirer of the Belgian bells, describes a recital given by "the greatest living carilloner," M. Denyn, of Mechlin ; and after reading his words one feels that if it is true that the modern players are much inferior to their predecessors, there must indeed have been "giants in those days." "I stood first at a remote corner of the Market-place . . . and after a short running prelude from the top bells weighing only a few pounds to the bottom ones of several tons, M. Denyn settled to his work in a brisk gallop, ably sustained at a good tearing pace without flagging for a single bar. Such an effort, in-volving the most violent muscular exercise, could not last long, as I quickly perceived when I entered the belfry and watched the player. He was bathed in sweat, and every muscle of his body seemed at full tension, as with feet he grappled with the huge pedal bells, and manipulated with gloved hands and incredible rapidity his two rows of key pegs. After a slight breathing pause, M. Denyn bade me mark the grand legato style most effective in such arias as Beethoven's 'Adelaide' and Bellini's 'Casta Diva,' which he played off accurately, melody and accompaniment, as from a pianoforte score. Then he gave me an astonishing specimen of bravura playing, putting down the great nine-ton and six-ton bells for the melody with his feet, and carrying on a rattling accompaniment of demi-semi-quavers on the treble bells, and finally, after a few sweeping arpeggio passages, he broke into a processional movement so stately that it reminded me of Chopin's 'Funeral March.' Just after this, when he was in the middle of a grand fantasia on the 'Dame Blanche,' the clock barrel began suddenly working at the hour with a pretty French tune :—

'Comme on aime à vingt ans.'

A lesser artist than Denyn would have been taken aback ; but . . . M. Denyn seized his opportunity, and waiting patiently until the barrel had done, plunged rapidly into an extempore continuation, which was so finely joined on to the mechanical tune that the people in the crowded market-place must have thought that the barrel had become suddenly inspired. Turning to me as he played, he bade me note the perfect control he had over the *pianos* and *fortes*, now lightly touching the bells, now giving them thundering strokes ; and as a personal compliment to his English guest, he wound up with 'God save the Queen,' beautifully harmonised. I must say that I never, on piano or violin, heard more admirable and expressive phrasing, whilst the vigour and fire of the virtuso reminded me of one of Rubinstein's finest performances."*

Within recent years key-boards have been introduced into several English belfries, as at the Manchester Town-hall, at Eaton Hall, and elsewhere. The Manchester peal numbers twenty-one bells, with a tenor of 6½ tons ; but we have as yet no instrument so complete as the Belgian carillons, and certainly no carilloner so accomplished as M. Denyn.

Messrs. Gillett and Bland, who have set up the best modern examples of carillon machinery in England, have greatly improved on the key-boards of past times, introducing

* Rev. H. R. Haweis, in "More about Bells" (*Magazine of Art*, Vol. v., p. 229. 1882).

a mechanism, whose delicacy of touch removes the severe strain formerly involved by a performance, and makes it possible even for a lady to use it.

The large and nicely graduated peals of hand-bells which one hears now and again in the hands of professional players, may be considered as holding the same relation to the carillon, as do other small bells to the ordinary peal. By distributing the whole set among four or five performers, a hundred or more bells are manipulated by practised artists, the most elaborate pieces of music being rendered with accuracy and effect. Many companies of church-bell ringers practise hand-bell ringing also, but generally on a less extended scale than this. The ringers at S. George's, Doncaster, had such a set at the beginning of this century, an order concerning the custody of "the set of sixteen hand-bells lately purchased" being issued in November, 1813. Such sets are sometimes used for practise in ordinary change-ringing; and a complete peal of Stedman Triples (5,040 changes) was rung in this way at the "Three Kings," Clerkenwell, in two hours, forty minutes, on December 19th, 1853, by members of the London Cumberland Society.

Frames containing a number of small bells were not unknown among the musical instruments of the Middle Ages; and the Turks, though hating bells in the ordinary way, have in their military bands a row of small bells suspended from a cross-bar, so that the bearer may clash them in time to the march. The cymbals and triangles, still retained in so many Western bands, are manifestly the survival of an equally barbaric idea of music.

CHAPTER XVII

Belfry Rhymes and Legends.

THAT the fancy of the people should weave about their bells many a quaint legend and homely proverb and curious rhyme is only what we should expect, when we realize the widespread usage of the bells. Just as the ancient oak has its huge limbs clothed with the clinging ivy, and the roughnesses of its sturdy form smoothed by moss and lichen ; or as the bells themselves gather, as the years roll on, a mellow tint from the dust of centuries, so do they gather also from the tide of time an incrustation of legendary lore, that makes their song the dearer to the children of a later age, even as their voices grow mellower.

One or two stories of the bells have been already told, such as the poetic legend of the Limerick bells, and several belfry proverbs have also been noticed in passing. Now as we are about to take our leave of the subject,—having in imagination seen the sweet-toned giants of the steeple moulded for their high duties, and having heard their voices ringing out in storm and shine for worship and for work, for life and death,—we turn, not unnaturally, to the quaint and curious folk-lore which their sounds suggest.

It has always been a common thing for the people to endeavour to hit off the peculiarities of their neighbours in homely rhymes ; cast in this form the words are easily remembered, and thus live on, in spite of the uncouthness of the lines, until they become proverbial in the district. There are several such sayings which contain allusions to bells.   One of the quaintest, and also one of the most severe upon the people satirized, refers to Kinkell, near Strathearn, and runs as follows :—

> " Was there e'er sic a parish, a parish, a parish,
> Was there e'er sic a parish as that o' Kinkell?
> They've hangit the minister, drowned the precentor,
> Dang down the steeple, and drucken the bell !"

The bell of this most unfortunate parish was sold, it is alleged, to Cockpen, near Edinburgh ; but one cannot help feeling some doubt as to the historic value of this account of Kinkell, when it is pointed out that the very same allegations are made against the parishioners of Dunkeld, save that these latter "sticket the minister" and "hanged the precentor."   We should be loth to suppose that Scotland could produce two such "fearful warnings" in the way of parishes.

The occasional sale of bells to raise money for church repairs has been spoken of in a former chapter.   It receives illustration from others of these ancient pieces of doggerel. Of Hatton, Lincolnshire, it is alleged

> " The poor Hatton people
> Sold the bells to build up the steeple ;"

and again of Owersby, in the same county :—

> " Owersby's parish, wicked people,
> Sold their bells to Kelsey to build a steeple ;"

and yet a third instance from the county meets us :—

> " Poor Scartho people
> Sold their bell to repair the steeple."

A longer rhyme of the same class is said to have been scrawled on the wall of Newington Church, when, in 1793, it was re-built without a tower :—

> " Pious parson, pious people,
>   Sold the bells to buy a steeple ;
>   A very fine trick for the Newington people,
>   To sell the bells to buy a steeple ;
>   Surely the devil will have the Newington people,
>   The rector and church without any steeple."

It is always, according to these sayings, for the specific purpose of erecting a steeple that the bells were disposed of. Probably the obvious rhyme of "people" and "steeple" was too great a temptation to the local "poet;" but the writer was no doubt also a bit of a wit, and he could not help hinting at the folly of people who sold their bells with a view to build a belfry to hang them in.

There are few things in his parish of which the rustic is commonly prouder than the church bells, and it is with him a point of honour to maintain their superiority over those of all other places within the neighbourhood. Thus arose such rhymes as the following, emanating obviously from an inhabitant of Stow S. Mary, in Lincolnshire :—

> " Marton's cracked pancheons,
>   And Torksey egg-shells,
>   Saxilby ding-dongs,
>   And Stow-Mary bells."

The parish of Whatton, Nottinghamshire, vaunts itself in another version of the same verse, Colston and Screveton being substituted for the other names in the first two lines, and the last two running :—

> " Bingham's two rollers,
>   Whatton's merry bells."

Some genius of Northern, in Cheshire, thus describes the
bells of his own parish, and disparages some others in the
district :—

> " Northern sweet music, and Didsbury pans,
>   Cheadle old kettles, and Stockport old cans."

The neighbours of Bowden, Northamptonshire, unkindly
describe it as :—

> " Little Bowden, poor people,
>   Leather bell, wooden steeple ; "

and yet more cuttingly is it said of Rockingham, Rutland-
shire :—

> " Rockingham, poor people,
>   Nasty town, castle down,
>   One bell, wooden steeple."

It was scarcely just for those who revelled in the possession
of a full peal and a stone church tower, to fling the want of
them in the face of Rockingham, since their absence was
due to her misfortunes.　Dugdale tells us that Cromwell
battered down the steeple.

The fancy that the bells ringing in monotonous rounds,
or the reiterated " ding-dong-bell " of the village church,
keeps repeating some phrase in words, is familiar to all.
The old story of Whittington and Bow bells turns on this,
and the long doggerel introducing many of the London city
churches, and beginning :—

> " You owe me three farthings,
>   Say the bells of S. Martin's,"

has been known to most of us from childhood ; while a
similar rigmarole exists concerning the Northamptonshire
bells.　The same idea has been quaintly applied to the
rivalry of the bells.　Thus the parishioner of Hawerby, as
he makes his way to his own parish church, hears in the

distance the three bells of North Thoresby, and an equal
number at Grainsby, chiming; and to him each set seems
to cry, "Who rings best? Who rings best?" But his
patriotic ear catches plainly the reply in the sound of the
two bells of his own church, "We do, we do!" A tradition
of the same verbal contest exists, locally, as to the churches
of Burton-on-Stather and Luddington on the opposite sides
of the Trent.

A few of these proverbial distichs aim at glorifying the
ringers rather than the bells. Thus the good folk of Bewdley
used to maintain that:—

> "For ringers, singers, and a crier,
> Bewdley excelled all Worcestershire."

Barrow-on-Humber combines rather incongruously its harmony and its ale in the proverb;—

> "Barrow for ringing,
> And Barrow for singing,
> And the 'Oak' for good stout ale."

It is remarkable what a number of legends there are of
what may be called "ghostly peals," stories of the ringing to
the present day of bells that were long since swept to
destruction in one way or another. About a mile outside
the town of Romford formerly stood an ancient church,
which was taken down in the fifteenth century; yet the
Romford folk used confidently to assert that at noon on
S. Andrew's Day in each year the bells of old S. Andrew's
could be distinctly heard ringing out to greet their patron
saint. Tradition asserts that many centuries since a village
near Raleigh was swallowed up, with its church and all
pertaining to it, by an earthquake; to this popular report
added that every Christmas the merry pealing of the

engulphed bells could be heard by any one who would place his ear to the ground near the spot. The coasts of Cornwall, with their vast cliffs and frowning rocks, their "dark, unfathomed caves," and countless hosts of screaming sea-birds, are full of weird and strange stories, among which is one of the kind that we have quoted. The people of Forrabury, near Tintagel, so goes the tale, longed to furnish their belfry with a fitting ring of bells, and at last were able to accomplish their wish. Over the sea the bells were brought, and arrived safely within sight of their destined home ; but as the vessel lay off the narrow harbour of Boscastle waiting for a favourable condition of tide to carry her in, the skipper broke into coarse and profane jests at seeing the pilot bend the knee to God in thanksgiving for their safe and speedy voyage. The vesper-bells rang clear from Tintagel's tower, but the skipper swore that he owed no thanks to any but himself, and scoffed at the thought of prayer and praise to the Almighty. Scarce were the words of scornful boasting uttered, when a huge Atlantic billow came rolling shorewards, towering high up towards the peaceful evening sky, and racing like wild horses. The little barque was seized, and whirled like a mere feather on the top of the seething waters ; then, overwhelmed by the sudden tumult of the sea, pent in by rocks and cliffs, she sank with crew and cargo to her doom. Only the pious pilot lived to tell the tale ; but ever after, when the long heaving of the sea, and the murky sky, and soughing wind, presage a coming storm, the listening ears of the fisher-folk hear deep down within the bay the muffled tolling of Forrabury bells. Sir Henry Spelman relates that Sir Hugh Paulet plundered the churches of Jersey of their bells, and

sold them into France ; in S. Malo Harbour, however, the
ship went down with the sacrilegious booty on board ; here
also the legend ran, that when a strong east wind was
blowing the islanders could hear again the pealing of their
bells.

A wild, weird story used to be told at Tunstall, near
Yarmouth. The tower of the church was damaged by fire,
and the parochial authorities took down the bells. A fierce
quarrel then began as to the ownership of these articles,
though whether the parson and wardens each claimed one
or more for himself, or whether it was a contest of the rights
of the church against private greed, we are not told. The
matter was brought to an abrupt conclusion by the
appearance of no less a being than the Devil, who grasped
the bells and made off with them. The priest started in
hot pursuit, and followed till the Prince of Darkness reached
a spot, since called Hell-hole, where he plunged into the
bowels of the earth and disappeared, leaving his clerical
pursuer panting and alone. Of the truth of all this there is
ample proof; you have but to go to Hell-hole, which is now
a pool with a boggy bed, and there you will frequently see
bubbles rising to the surface of the water; which shew
conclusively that the bells are still sinking, ever sinking,
down to the bottomless pit.

Another story comes from Inkberrow, to the effect that
the fairies took great offence at the pulling down of the
church at some remote date, and the re-building of it on a
new site. It would seem that the bells disturbed the
light sleep of the fays more than had formerly been the case,
and therefore they tried every means in their power to
prevent the completion of the work. Failing in this, they

took refuge, as ordinary mortals have been known to do in
the like circumstances, in abuse; and the villagers were
startled at night by hearing uncanny aërial voices that
seemed to sigh—

> " Neither sleep, neither lie,
> For Inkbro's ting-tangs hang so high."

Bells have not been left without their share of miraculous
stories. There is, for instance, the wonderful story of the
bell at Sens, in Burgundy. Clothaire II., King of France
in 615, having heard the sweet tones of this bell, was filled
with a covetous desire to possess it, and at last had it pulled
down and sent to Paris. But he was to gain no pleasure
from his sin, for the bell became absolutely dumb on the
journey, and was finally sent back to Sens. So joyous was
the unwilling exile to find itself on the way home again,
that four leagues from Sens it began to ring of itself so
lustily as to be heard even in the city.

A legend of another kind relates how it was revealed to
S. Catherine of Ledbury that she was to wander forth, and
not settle until invited by the spontaneous ringing of the
bells. Wordsworth thus tells us the story :—

> " When human touch (as monkish books attest)
> Nor was applied, nor could be, Ledbury bells
> Broke forth in concert, flung adown the dells
> And upward high as Malvern's cloudy crest
> Sweet tones, and caught by a noble lady blest
> To rapture ! Mabel listened at the side
> Of her loved mistress ; soon the music died,
> And Catherine said : ' Here set I up my rest.
> Warned by a dream, the wanderer long had sought
> A home, that by such miracle of sound
> Must be revealed ; she heard it now, and felt
> The deep, deep joy of a confiding though
> And there, a saintly anchoress, she dwelt,
> Till she exchanged for heaven that happy ground."

There are other legends of bells ringing spontaneously. Dumas, in his "Pictures of Travel in the South of France," tells how the people of Vienne were warned, in 1407, of the impending ruin of their ancient bridge over the Rhone. During the night of the 10th February, so they say, strange sounds were heard of horses galloping, of unearthly groans and cries, and of a bell ringing out untouched by human hand; and on the 11th the bridge crashed into the river. A tradition, which Cruikshank has illustrated, relates that a gang of robbers broke into a monastery; and that, for pure devilry, they began to ring the bells. In answer to the prayers of the terrified monks, however, the order of things was reversed; the bells rang of themselves, and that lustily, and the thieves, rendered unable to let go the ropes, were danced by them well-nigh to death.

A pretty story tells us how S. Odoceus of Llandaff, weary one day and thirsty with travel, asked a drink of water of some village maids who were washing butter; and on their replying they had no cup, he took butter from the hands of one of them and formed it into a bell, from which he drank, and which became a golden bell from that time forward, and endowed with healing powers. Sir John Sinclair relates, in his "Statistical Account of Scotland," that in 1778 the Chapel of S. Fillan, Perthshire, possessed a bell that was held to be efficacious for the cure of mental disorders. The sufferer was first bathed in the "Saint's Pool," and the bell, which had lain all night in the church bound with cords, was afterwards placed upon his head. Usually this bell had stood on a gravestone in the churchyard, and it was popularly supposed that, if it were stolen, it would return of itself; at the date given it was

ROBBER-RINGERS

(By George Cruikshank).

kept under lock and key. S. Mura's bell was alleged to
have come down from heaven, whither its clapper
immediately returned, leaving it for ever silent; this, also,
had miraculous gifts of healing.

A gruesome story in connection with bells is that told to
account for the undoubted use of human skin as a covering
for a door once used at Worcester Cathedral, and still
preserved there. It is said to be the token of a terrible
vengeance taken on a sacrilegious Dane, who during one of
the incursions of those wild sea-kings into the country,
stole the sanctus-bell from the church, and was caught
red-handed by the townspeople. A somewhat similar
account is given of the same strange covering of church
doors at Hadstock, Copford, and Castle Hedingham.*

Two passages of Continental history, each full of horrors,
are incidentally connected with the ringing of the bells.
The massacre of the French in Sicily on Easter Tuesday,
1282, commonly called the Sicilian Vespers, is said by
many to have been commenced on the ringing of the
vesper-bells, which had been agreed upon as a signal. It
is not certain, however, that such is the case; the massacre
took place unquestionably at vesper-time amid the Easter
festivities; but modern accounts represent it as less pre-
meditated than the traditional story would have us believe,
a quarrel between two individuals spreading among the
holiday crowds, and giving occasion to the pent-up rage and
hatred of the Sicilians. On the other hand, there is no
question that the tolling of the bell of S. Germain l'Aux-
errois for Mattins, or, as some say, of a bell in the Louvre,

* See an article on this curious subject in "The Church Treasury of History,
Custom, etc." (Andrews and Co.).

was the signal for the massacre of the Huguenots of Paris on S. Bartholomew's Day, 1572.

Let us turn to a pleasanter scene for our last story. In the belfry at Grosslaswitz in North Germany, hangs a bell engraved on which is a six-eared stalk of corn, and the date October 15th, 1729; "whereby hangs a tale." A century and a half since the villagers of Grosslaswitz were dissatisfied with their bell; it was small, and weak in tone, and only those who dwelt close about the church could hear its call to worship. But how to acquire a new bell was a question hard to answer; the village had no wealthy inhabitant or neighbour, and the sum total of all the peasants' "mites" came only to a small amount. But Gottfried Hayn, the schoolmaster, was a thoughtful man, who carried his eyes in his head, and knew that two and two make four, as a schoolmaster should. One Sunday, as he was coming back from church, where no doubt some of his neighbours had arrived late owing to the feeble summons of that pitiable bell, his eyes fell on a green shoot of corn springing up in the churchyard from a seed dropt, no doubt, by some passing bird. This was a common enough sight, and to most people would have suggested nothing at all. But our Gottfried could see beyond the end of his nose, and to folk endued with this unusual power things sometimes take strange shapes; and Gottfried saw that that single stalk could bear within its ripening head a large church bell! Carefully he watched it grow into a six-eared blade of corn, which in due time ripened into a strong golden stalk bearing its load of seeds. These seeds he gathered and planted in his own little plot of garden; and no farmer ever so rejoiced over the promise of his smiling acres as did our

Gottfried over his tiny harvest. Again and again he planted all that the good Lord sent him in the increase of the grain, until his garden was far too small to hold it all. Now, therefore, he imparted his little plan to the farmers of the village, and they devoted a portion of their land to the growing of the wonderful crop. And at last, after only eight years of patient waiting and watching, the fruit of the six-eared shoot of corn was valuable enough to purchase the bell. Whereby we learn many things, not the least among them being the usefulness of seeing at least a little beyond the end of one's nose.

How many a story of romance and poetry, how many a lesson of devotion and prayer, rings out from the belfries of the world ! Some of these we have endeavoured to touch upon, but the bells' deepest truths we must hear from their own sonorous throats. It is when the merry peal, the regular chime, the dreary toll, speak of joys, or duties, or of sorrows, that touch our own hearts and lives, it is then that we feel the kinship of the bells with all that goes to make up the checkered pathway of mankind. May we so harken to their constant chimes that for us their final tolling shall mean a fuller, if more solemn, gladness than ever did their merriest peal.

Indexes.

I.—Index of Subjects 291
II.—Index of Places 300

INDEX I.—SUBJECTS.

Abdication of Napoleon, 1, 88
Absence of bells in Egypt, 4
Accession of Elizabeth, 242
Accidents to bells, 122
Advent ringing, 170, 171
Aerschodt, Van, 21, 22
African bells, 121
Alarm bells, 252
Alexander of Gloucester, 15, 18
Alfred the Great, 225
"Alliance," 142
All Saints' Day, 181
All Souls' Day, 181
Alnewick, Bishop, 186
Alphabetical inscriptions, 93
Amboise, George d', 56
American bells, 120
Amusements of Shrove Tuesday, 176
Anable, Benjamin, 141
Ancient ringing customs, survival of, 166
Ancient Society of College Youths, 158
Anderson, Sir C. H. J., quoted, 180
Andrew's Day, S., 179
Angels, effigies of, 66
Angelus, 54, 90, 167, 228, 230-4
Annunciation, feast of, 180
Anthony, S., 164, 213
Apprentice peals, 186
Armada, defeat of, 181
Armorial devices, 67, 68

Arnold, Edward, 17
Ascension Day, 179
Ash Wednesday, 177
Associations of ringers, 157
Assumption, feast of, 180
Athelstan, statute of, 131
Aubrey, quoted, 178
Automata on clocks, 222-4
Ave bell, 167, 232

Backwards, ringing, 252-3
Bacon, quoted, 212
Bale, Bishop, quoted, 213-5
Ball of clapper, 33
Bands, bells in military, 217
Banns peals, 187
Baptism peals, 185 ; of bells, 58
Barclay, David, 23
Bartholomew's Day, S., 288
Bartlet, Thomas, 66
Baudricks or bawdrills, 33
Bayeux tapestry, 205
Bayley, Henry, 18
Beadle or bellman, 205-6, 227, 264-5
" Bearing the bell," 263
Beating the bounds, 269
Beaumont and Fletcher, quoted, 194, 201
Beckwith peal, York, 16, 108
Bede, the Venerable, quoted, 6
Belgian Carillons, 272
Bell, book, and candle, 214-19
Belleyetere, Thomas, 14

Belfry, 131-6 ; rules for, 145-53 ;
    proverbs of, 145 197, 263 ;
    bequests, 158, 229, 230, 233,
    242
Bell, derivation of the word, 5 ;
    metal, 24-8 ; frames, 96 ; tones,
    38 ; wether, 263 ; cotes, 133
Bell-founder's window, 20
Bell, Harry, 53, 108
Bellman. (See Beadle)
Bell-ringing, 136, 137-43 ; ringers,
    143-58
Bells made from guns, 27 ; on
    vestments, 256-7 ; prize for
    races, 263
Benedict Biscop, S., 6
Bentinck's victory at Genoa, 27
Big Ben, 113, 114
Bilbie, 24, 116
Birdcage belfries, 133
Bishop's visitation, 185
Black Tom of Sothill, 56
Blaickie & Sons, 23, 56
Blessed Sacrament, bell carried
    before, 268
Blessed Virgin, dedications to,
    56, 57
Blessing bells, Russian rite, 39 ;
    Roman rite, 59 ; English rite,
    61 ; bell-metal, 34
Bleys, Bp. Constitutions of, 198
Boastful Inscriptions, 76
Bob Major, 142
Bolshoi, 56, 99
" Boke of S. Albans," 262
Book of Ceremonies, 198
Borgia, S. Francis, 162
" Boundaries," 250
Bowler, Richard, 73
Bow Church, 158, 227 ; bells, 114,
    237, 281
Bradford, quoted, 218
Brass bells, 24
Brasses, 42
Brassey, Lady, quoted, 101
Brazier, 19
Briant, John, 17
Brins, 30
Briscoe, Mr. J. P., 153
British war-bells, 259

Brittany, storm in, 213
Bronze bells, 24
Buddhist bells, 267, 270
Buffeting the bells, 201, 202
Bullinger, quoted, 211
Bull-running, 248
Bunyan, John, 143
Burgerhuys, 22
Burmese bells, 270
Butter bell, 251
Byron, quoted, 266, 271

Cadilhac, Mme., quoted, 178
Camdem, quoted, 264
Campana, 4, 5, 161
Campania, 4, 5
Campanologia, 200
Campaniles, 132-3
Campbell, quoted, 8
Candlemas, 174
Canons, Ecclesiastical, 195
Canons of bells, 32
Canonical hours, 220
" Canterbury Bells," 260
Capture of S. Sebastian, 50
Cardaillac, of Toulouse, 103
Care needed in using bells, 123-4
Carillons, 52, 272
Carilloners, 274-6
Carolus, of Antwerp, 56, 120
Carthusian rule, 137
Catechism at S. Sulpice, 162
Catherine, S., 285
Cators, 142
Cealcythe, the council of, 161
Celebrated bells, 97-121
Central towers, 133
Change-ringing, 77-8, 129, 135
    140-1
Chapman, William, 16, 107
Charlemagne, 58, 137, 161
Charles V., Emperor, 56, 120
Charles I., 205, 241
Chaucer, quoted, 206, 215
Chauncy, quoted, 58
Childbirth, ringing at, 184-5
Childermas peals, 173
Children's services, 162, 167
Chiming, 42
Chimes, 177, 272, 273

Chinese bells, 2, 28 ; music, 101
Christian Year, bells of, 170
Christmas peals, 172
Churches, repaired by sale of bells, 129, 279, 280 ; ships' bells used for, 255
Church-going bell, 84, 159-169
Chyche, Thomas, 18
Circumcision, Feast of the, 173
City Hall bell, New York, 120
Clacks for Holy Week, 177, 178
Clapper, 33, 37 ; of wood 177
Classic names for bells, 4 ; allusions to bells, 3, 259, 260
Clay, Henry, 121
Clerical ringers, 137, 162
Clocks, early, 220 ; at Strasbourg, 221 ; bells of, 25
Clocke, 5
Closing the Market, 251
Clothes decked with bells, 257
Cock-fighting, 245
Coleridge, quoted, 10
College Youths, Ancient Society of, 121, 139
Colonial bells, 121
Commemoration peals, 204
Common Bell, 247
Commonwealth, bells during, 50, 174, 180, 203
Company Bell, 200, 206
Confirmation, Ringing at, 185
Construction of Carillons, 273
Cope, 32, Cope-case, 32
Corbet, Richard, 109
Core, 31
Cornish bells, 126, 283
Coronation peals, 241
Corr, William and Robert, 18, 66
Corvehill, Wm., 19
Cost of bells, 104, 107, 114, 116
Council of Cealcythe, 161 ; of Trent, 167
Court Fools, 257
Covey, Tobias, 23
Cowper, quoted, 10
Cranmer, 182
Criminals, Roman, 205
Cromwell, Thos., 126, 232
Crook, 31

Crosses on bells, 64
Crotulum, 5
" Curiosities of the Belfry," 153
Cureton, Wm., 14
Curfew, 8, 9, 224, 232

Dalton, Geo. and Robt., 15
Danckwart, Adam, 22
Dates of bells, 45-52, 73
Dead bell, 196
Death in the belfry, 156, 246
Decker, quoted, 222
Declaration of American Independence, 120
Decoration of bells, 63-96
Dedication of bells, 58 ; to the Holy Trinity, 71 ; the Holy Spirit, 71 ; the Holy Name, 70 ; the Blessed Virgin, 69
Denison, Sir E. B. (Lord Grimthorpe), 113
Denyn, M., 275
Destruction, wilful, of bells, 124-5
Devil's Knell, 172 ; frightened of bells, 210
Devon bells, 126
Diamond Jubilee of Queen Victoria, 88, 155 274
Dickson, J., 23, 30
Diocesan Associations of ringers, 157
Distinguished ringers, 157-8
Dodona, Oracle at, 4
Doggerel verses on bells, 9
Domestic bells, 266
Donors of bells, 71-3
Door bells, 266
Doubles, 142
Drake, Admiral, 116
Draper, John, 65, 95
Dunbar, Thos. of, 52
Dunstan, S., 13, 173; bell so called, 106-8; Church of, 223
Durandus, quoted, 192

Easter 179; notice of dues at, 250
Eayres, Thos., 17
Edmund the founder, 14
Edward the confessor, S., 206

Eeles, F. C., quoted, 166
Effigies of Saints and Angels, 66, 67
Egbert, Excerptions of, 7, 161
Egelric, 13
Egypt, absence of bells in, 4
Ehem, Andreas, 22
Elections, peals at, 246
Elizabeth, accession of, 181
England, blessing bells in; 61; reception of new bells in, 41; oldest bell, 45
English bells, 103-116; Carillons, 273, 276; inscriptions, 72, 73; Saints, 70
Epiphany, 174
Epitaphs of ringers, 154
Ethelwold, S., 13
Europe, oldest bell in, 45; large bells of, 102-120
Evangelists, symbols of, 67
Evans, Wm., 113
Excerptions of Egbert, 7, 161
Excommunication, 214-219
Executions, bells at, in Rome, 205; England, 207-209
Exportation of bells forbidden, 125-6

Fabyan, 203
Fair bells, 247 250, 252
Fairfax, Lord, at York, 48
Fairies and bells, 284
Famous bells, 97-121; peals, 142, 143; ringers, 157, 158
Fashion of wearing bells, 257
Fees for ringing, 188, 193, 199
Female ringers, 156
Fire-bells, 84, 252; destruction by fire, 54, 116, 129
Firing bells, 243
Flemish bells, 84
Flight of clapper, 33
Flint, Wm. of, 65
Fog-bells, 254
Folk rhymes, 280
Foreign founders, 21, 22; bells in England, 21, 22
Founder, Daniel, 18; Wm., 19, 66
Founding of bells, 24-37

Founders, 13-24; marks of, 65; rhymes of, 75
Foundries in churchyards, 20; in churches, 21
Fox, George, quoted, 144
Fremy, Claudius, 22
French bells, 24-103; inscriptions, 72
Fritter bell, 176
Fuller, quoted, 212
Funeral bells, 82, 202; hand-bells at, 268; of S. Edward, 206
Furnace for bell-castings, 36
Fylfot, 64

Gabriel bells, 53, 54, 232
Gall, S., 12
Games with bells, 261
Ganzaga, Guido, 29
Gate-bell, Strasbourg, 120
"Gatherums," 236
Gay, quoted, 189
Gely, Albert, 23
Genoa, guns taken at, 27
George's day, S., 180
George III., illness of, 88
"Getting-up" bell, 85, 233
Gheyn, Van den, 21, 274
Ghostly peals, 282
Gilds of ringers, 17, 138
Gillett and Bland, Messrs., 17, 276
Glass bells, 24
Gleaning bell, 236
"Golden Legend," Longfellow's, 81
Goodening, 172
Good Friday, 179
Googe, Barnabe, quoted, 204, 211
Gothic war-bells, 259
Gowrie conspiracy, 242
Grandison, Bp., 200; bell at Exeter, 112, 113
Grandsire, Bob, 141; triple, 141
Gray, Thos., quoted, 9, 262
Graye, Miles, 18, 20
"Great Paul," 34, 36, 63, 103-105; Peter (Exeter), 112; (Gloucester), 113; Tom (Lincoln),

21, 26, 56, 111, 179; "Great Bell" of S. Paul's, 106, 199
Greek sentry's bell, 259; substitutes for bells, 161
Gregory, S., sacramentary of, 58
Grimthorpe, Lord, 113
Grindal, injunctions of, 182, 192, 269
Grose, quoted, 210
Gudgeons, 42
Guild Hall bells, 249
Gunpowder Plot, 89, 242
Gurney, Robert, 73
Guns made from bells, 27
Guthlac, S., 13, 53
Gwynne, Nell, 158

Hagiosideron, 160
Hall, Bp., quoted, 194, 229
Hallowmas, 181
Hampden, John, 116
Hand-bells, 161, 162, 205, 250, 264, 277
Harness, bells on, 260
Harrington and Lathom, Messrs., 31
"Harry" (bell), 108
Harvest bell, 235; harvest home peals, 240
Haweis, Rev. H. R., quoted, 275
Hawks' bells, 262
Hazfelde, Simon de, 17
Heathcote, R., 64, 65
Heber, Bp., quoted, 199
Hedderley, Daniel, 18; Thomas, 76
Hemony, 92
Henry VIII., 55, 124, 182
Hentzner, quoted, 138
Hering, Dr., quoted, 213
Herrick, quoted, 265
Hilda, S., death of, 7, 192
Hobby-horses, 260, 261
Hodges, Thomas, 23
Hodson, Christopher, 16, 110
Hog, Robert, 52
Holy-week, 177
Hooper, Injunctions of, 165, 192, 233, 269
Horns, Jewish use of, 91, 159, 174; at Rouen, 178; at

Thorney and Willoughton, 178
Horner, Gerhard, 22
"Horida," 56
Horse-bells, 260-262; racing, 245, 263
Horst, H. Ter., 22
Hoton, John, 14, 49
Hounds, meet of, 246
"Hours," the, 229
House-bells, 266
Huc, quoted, 159
Hugh's Day, S., 181, 242
"Hum," note, 38

Illness of George III., 88
Induction bell, 168
Ingulphus, quoted, 7
Initial crosses on bells, 64
Injunctions of Edward VI., 163
Inscriptions on bells, 45-47, 50, 56, 57, 64, 68-96, 104, 188, 214, 232, 242, 244, 252
Invention of bells, 1-7
Invitation peal, 200
Invocations of Saints, 69, 70
Irish bells, 23, 116, 132
Iron bells, 12, 24
Isaiah, allusion by, to wearing bells, 257
Italian bells, 103; campaniles, 132, 133; bell-custom, 178
Itinerant founders, 17, 18
Ivan Kiliki, 98
Iveagh, Lord, 119

Jacks of the Clock-house, 222-224
"Jacqueline," 56, 103
James' Day, S., 181
Jansen, Peter, 22
Japanese bells, 101, 270; music, 2
Jester's bells, 257
"Jesus" bells, 55
Jewish use of trumpets, 91, 159, 174; rise of bells on vestments, 256
Jonson, Ben, quoted, 189
John the Founder, 14; of Gloucester, 15; of Stafford, 24; of York, 14, 16

Jubilee of Queen Victoria, 88, 155, 274
Jugs, ringers', 144

Keene, Richard, 78, 110
Kettle and Jarvis, Messrs., 89
Kemkem, 267
Kilgour, Patrick, 23
Killigrew, Tom, 258
Kincardineshire bells, 51, 166, 255
Knells, 195
" Knocks for the dead," 197
Knight, Ellis, 65 ; Henry, 18
Koster, Gerhard, 22
Kodon, 4
Krotalum, 5

Lady bells, Lincoln, 112, 180
Lady Day, 180
" La Lutine," bell of, 255
Lamps, bells converted into, 128
Lanfranc, constitutions of, 161
Lateran, the, 58
Latimer, Bp., 163, 185
Latin inscriptions, 72, 73, 77, 79
Lawson, Andrew, 23
" Leaving-off bell," 167
Lebetes, 4
Legends, 282, 289 ; of Limerick bells, 116 ; of Breslau, 35
Leicestershire bells, 122, 163
Lent, 175
Lester, T., 48
Lester and Pack, Messrs., 16, 107
Liberty bell, 120
Light-house bells, 254
Lincolnshire bells, 46, 64, 122, 129, 163
Local meetings, 246 ; history in bell inscriptions, 89
Lomax, Mr., quoted, 27
London Cumberland Society, 277 ; Scholars, 139
Long inscription, 92
Longfellow, quoted, 8, 81, 85, 231, 258
Loss of old bells, 122-130
Loyal emblems, 67 ; inscriptions, 86 ; peals, 240

Lukis, Rev. W. C., quoted, 122 153

Magdalen College, Oxford, 207
" Magna Britannia," quoted, 26
Major, A., 142 ; of Newcastle, 247
Mallet used for bell, 161
Manifold uses of small bells, 265
Marks of founders, 65
Market ringings, 250, 251
" Mark Twain," quoted, 270
Martyrdom of Charles I., 241
Marvel, Andrew, quoted, 262
Mary, S., Dedications to, 69
Massacre of S. Bartholomew, 288
May Day, 245
Mayers, Samuel, 155
Maximus, 142
Maxwell, Bp., 68
Mears, Thos., 112 ; Messrs., 15, 16, 36, 108, 114, 116 ; and Stainbank, 16
Mediæval bells, shape of, 28
Meeting bell, 248
Merston, Robt., 17, 65
Method of summoning the faithful in the early church, 160 ; of ringing the Angelus, 234
Meyer, Gert., 22
Mexican custom, 177
Midday Angelus, 231
" Mighty Tom " of Oxford, 56, 57, 109, 110
Millet's " Angelus," 231
Military uses of small bells, 25 277
Milton, quoted, 8, 265
Minor, 142
Minimus, 142
Miraculous bells, 285
" Mittags " of Strasbourg, 81, 120
Mohammedans, 128, 168, 271
Monastic bells, 161 ; rhymes, 79
Month's mind peals, 203
Moore, quoted, 9, 271
Morning bell, 233
Morris Dancers, 258
Mot, Wm., 15
Mote bells, 249
Mowat, John, 23

Muck bell, 264
Mulzzin, the, 168, 271
Muffled peals, 179, 201, 202
Multiplication of modern bells, 79
Mumpsing, 172
Mura, S., bell of, 12, 287
Murphy, John, 23
Mutilation of bells, 128
Myrc, John, quoted, 217, 267-269

Names of bells, 53-57
Napoleon I., abdication of, 88
Neale, Dr., quoted, 161
Nelson, Lord, death of, 199; John, quoted, 195
Newcombe, 17, 64, 75, 111
Newgate, 208
New Year's Day, 173, 174
Netherlands, bells of the, 21
Nimroud, bells at, 3
Nola, 4
Norfolk bells, 125
Norris, Tobie and Isaac, 24, 120, 248
North, Thomas, 46, 69, 167
Northamptonshire, bells of, 122
Northern Youths, Society of, 154
Noteworthy bells, 97-121
"Nowster," 228

Oak-apple Day, 241
Obits, 204
Odoceus, S., 286
Old bells, 125; rarity of, 122; loss of, 122-130; Scottish, 52
Old Gabriel, 232, 248; Kate, 56; Lawrie, 56; S. Paul's, 55, 129, 222; Year, knell of, 173, 174
Oldest English bell, 45; European, 45
Oldfield, Wm., 18, 64, 111
Ostens, Peter, 22, 63
Ouderogge, 22
Overall, Bp., quoted, 199
Oxfordshire Custom, 178

Pack and Chapman, Messrs., 16
Painting of ringers, 156
Panburn bell, 176
Pancake bell 166, 175, 176

"Paradise, bells of," 271
Paris, Henry, 79
Partridge, Sir Miles, 124
Passing bell, 191
Patrick, S., bell of, 12
Patrick, composer of peals, 142
Paulinus of Nola, 6
Paul's, S., Cathedral, 51, 104-106, 133, 199, 212; bells of, 61
Peals at funerals, 195, 202; on hand-bells, 277
Peckham, Archbp., constitution of, 268
Pennant, quoted, 190, 195
Pennington, 113
"Penny Magazine," quoted, 28, 37
Pepys, quoted, 258
Percy, quoted, 252
Peruvian bells, 3
Pestilence, bells during, 213
Petasus, 4
"Peter" of York, 108; the Great, 27
Peter's chains, S., 269
Phelps, Richard, 16, 48, 106
Pilkington, Bp., 212
Plain Bob, 142
Pleasant, Henry, 76
Plough Monday, 245
Poe, E. A., quoted, 10, 261
Poets and the bells, 7
Polydore Vergil, 232
"Poor Robin's Almanack," 176
"Poor Sinner's Bell," 35
Pope, quoted, 115
Popular English dedications, 70
Potter, 19
Prayer Book, rubrics of, on bells, 162
Prayer for the dead, 198
Pre-reformation bells, 49
Priest's bell, 164
Priestly, bell-founder, 19
Primitive bells, 12: music, 1, 2. method of summoning the laity, 160
Prize for races, a bell, 263
Proportions of bell-metal, 25; of bells, 30

Prout, quoted, 118
Proverbs on bells, 145, 197, 263
Public events commemorated on bells, 88
Pudding bell, 167
Punning inscriptions, 76
Purdue, Thos., 64, 112
Puritan era and the bells, 50, 174, 180, 203

Quadriglio, 272

Rainold's, John, 194
Rarity of old bells, 122
Rattles substituted for bells, 162, 177
Reception of bells in Russia, 39 ; in England, 41
Reformation, Scottish, 51
Reform Bill, passage of, 246
Reformers and hand-bells, 269
Religious uses of small bells, 266
Restoration of Charles II., 241
Repair of churches by the sale of the bells, 129, 279, 280
Repeal of the Curfew Law, 226
Repute of ringers, 143
Reve, Roger, 18
Rhymes of the founders, 75
Riever bell, 247
Rin, 270
Ringers, 86, 136-158 ; jugs for, 144
Ringing, 42 ; backwards, 252, 253
Roman rite of blessing bells, 59
Rood-screens with bells, 268
Ropeforde, 18
Rounds, 141
Royal heads on bells, 67 ; Oak Day, 241; Cumberland youths, 139
Royais, 142
Rubric on bells in the Prayer-book, 162
Rudhall, 15, 51, 74, 76, 94
Rules for belfries, 145-153
Russian bells, 98-100, 102 ; sleigh-bells, 261 ; rite for blessing, 39 ; bell-custom, 200
Rutland, bells of, 163

" Runners " in the early church, 160

Sabinianus, Pope, 6
Sacramentary of S. Gregory, 58
Sacrament bell, 165
Saints, effigies of, 66, 67 ; invocation of, 69, 70
Sales of bells, 125-7, 129, 279, 280
Sanctus bell, 136, 165, 267
Sandre of Gloucester, 15, 18, 65
Satiric verses, 279
Saunce bell, 267
" Sayings " of bells, 281
Scarlet, the Sexton, 193
Schiller's " Lay of the Bell,' 10
Schimmel, Gerrit, 22
Scott, Sir W., quoted, 252
Scottish bells, 21, 22, 51, 52, 116, 127, 132, 166 ; curfew, 225 ; founders, 52 ; towers, 133 ; ringing customs, 166
Scriptural allusions to bells, 3, 257, 260 ; passages on bells, 90
Sea, time at, 238
Sebastian, S., capture of, 50
Secular ownership of church bells, 134
Seed-sowing bell, 235
Seller, Edward, 14
Semantia, 161
Sentry's bell, Greek, 259
Sepulchre's, S., bell, 208
Sermon bell, 84, 163
Ser, Jacob, 22
Shakespeare, quoted, 9, 175, 194, 199, 201, 214, 224, 228, 241, 262, 266
Shape of bells, 28-31
Sheep-bells, 262
Sheridan, 23
Sherwood Youths, 154
Ships' bells, 238, 255
Shooting the bells, 243
Shrove Tuesday, 175, 176
Sicilian Vespers, 287
Signum, 5, 161
Silence of bells in Holy Week, 177
Silver in bells, 26

Sinclair, Sir J., quoted, 206, 286
Singles, 142
Sino, 5
Sistrum, 266
Skeleton bells, 29
Slide, 42
Small bells, various uses of, 265; religious uses of, 266
Societies of ringers, 139; of northern youths, 154
Soul bell, 191, 194
South African bells, 121
Southey, quoted, 34, 58, 244, 254
Sovereigns' effigies on bells, 99, 100; names, 86
Spanish bells, 128; Angelus, 231; campaniles, 133; custom, 184
Spelling of inscriptions, 95
Spelman, Sir H., quoted, 125
Spencer, quoted, 188
"Sponsors" for bells, 59
"Spurrings," 187
Squilla, 5
Strabo, 250
Stafford, John of, 49
Stays, 42
Stedman, 139, 140
Steel bells, 24
Stops in inscriptions, 64
Storm-bell, Strasbourg, 120
Storms, bells rung during, 211
Strutt, quoted, 196
Sullivan, A. M., quoted, 118, 119
Superscription of the cross, 71
Survival of the Curfew, 166; of old ringing customs, 166
Sweep, 31
Symbols of the Evangelists, 67

"'Tandrew" Bell, 179
"'Tanthony" Bell, 164
"'Tatie" Bell, 234
Taylor, the Water Poet, quoted, 176
Taylor & Son, Messrs., 16, 17, 95, 103, 119, 198
Tellers, 197, 202
Tennyson, quoted, 11, 174
Tertullian, quoted, 160
"Thrashing the fat hen," 261

Thickness, 32
Thief bell, 247
Thomas's Day, S., 172
Thomas, S., of Canterbury, 260
"Thomasing," 172
Thornbury, quoted, 258
Time of curfew, 226, 227; at sea, 238
Tintinabulum, 4, 5
"Tintinalogia," 139, 140
Tolling on Good Friday, 179
Tomb of a founder, 19
Tones of bells, 38
Touch, 141
Towers, 131-136
Town Hall bells, 114
Trafalgar, victory of, 199
Treble Bob, 142
Trees, bells hung on, 132
Trent, Council of, 167
Trinity Sunday, 179
Triumph, Roman, 205
Triples, 142
Trumpets, use of, by Jews, 91, 159, 174; in English Churches, 160; in Thibet, 160
Tsar Ivan, 158
Tsar Kolokol, 56, 98, 102
Tubular bells, 30
Tuning bells, 37
Tunnoc, Richard, 20
Turketul, Abbot, 13
Turkish bells, 277
Turrets, 131, 133, 136
Tyndale, Wm., 168

"Undernone," 250
Union Scholars, 139
Uses of small bells, various, 265

Verses, Bellemen's, 265
Vestments, bells on, 256, 257
Vestry meetings, 249
Vickers, 24
Victories, celebration of, 199, 243
Vincent de Paul, S., 162
Virgin Beal, 37
Visitation, Bishop's, 185

Waghevens, 22

Wallis, John, 73
Warner & Son, Messrs., 16, 113
Washerwomen's bell, 235
Watchmen, 264, 265
Watches at sea, 238
Waynflete, Wm. of, 207
Wedding peals, 83, 188
Wells, James, 18; Robt., 75
Welsh bells, 116
Wheatley, quoted, 194
Wheels, 42
White, Gilbert, quoted, 41
Whitgift, Archbishop, 165, 168
Whitsun Day, 179
Wiburn, quoted, 182
Wightman, P., 106
Wilful destruction of bells, 124, 125
William I and the curfew, 224
William of Flint, 65
Wiltshire bells, 122; ringers, 153
Wimbish, Richard de, 18, 48
Winchelsey, Archbishop, 215, 269

Winding bell, 200
Window, bell-founder's, 20
Winter ringing, 252
Wolsey, Cardinal, 115
Women ringers, 156
Wood, bells of, 25, 177; belfry, 132, 135; used in place of bells, 160
Wood, Anthony, quoted, 158
Wordsworth, Wm., quoted, 10, 285

Xavier, S. Francis, 162; quoted, 177

Year's mind peals, 203
York, John of, 49, 64, 65
Young, quoted, 8
Youths, a term for ringers, 155

Zachariah, invention of bells by, 3, 260

INDEX II.—PLACES.

Note.—In the following Index the names of places beginning with *Saint*, as S. Alban's, are placed under the letter S.: names having a distinguishing adjective, as *All Cannings* and *South Lopham*, are ranged under the initial of the first word in each case.

Abdie, 133
Aberdeen, 23, 52, 56, 116, 132, 133
Aberdovey, 116
Abingdon, 13, 258
Addington, 82
Addlethorpe, 82
Aisthorpe, 179
Albourne, 18, 72, 155
Aldburgh, 93
Alderford, 72
Aldgate, 48
All Cannings, 96
Almely, 202
Alphington, 246
Amsterdam, 116
Antwerp, 21, 56, 120, 273
Apethorpe, 128
Arbuthnott, 68
Ashby-de-la-Zouch, 17

Ashover, 55
Asbury, 266
Asterby, 187
Aston Rowant, 70
Aveley, 70

Badgworth, 76
Bakewell, 71, 77, 78, 82, 83
Baldock, 18, 58
Banbury, 84, 87
Banchory Ternan, 63
Bapchild, 66
Barston, 253
Barrow-on-Humber, 124, 193, 199, 235, 251, 282
Barrow-on-Soar, 252
Barwell, 189
Basham, 245
Baslow, 65

Bath, 74
Battle Abbey, 161
Bawtry, 18, 76
Beauchief Abbey 111
Beesby, 46, 47
Belfast, 12
Belgrave, 176
Bell Rock, 254
Belton, 138
Bemerton, 93
Bemonia, 43
Benefield, 202
Benington, 241
Benniworth, 73
Bentley, 74, 79, 83
Berechurch, 48
Berwick-on-Tweed, 135
Beverley, 133
Bewdley, 282
Billesden, 69
Bingham, 280
Binstead, 74
Bisham, 240
Bishop Stortford, 181, 242
Bitterley, 72
Blakesley, 171, 245
Bletchley, 93
Bloxham, 136
Blyth, 41
Blythburgh, 223
Bochum, 24
Bologna, 133
Bolton-in-Craven, 72
Bonsall, 64
Borrowdale, 24
Borrowstowness, 206
Boston (Lincolnshire), 83, 136, 193, 273
Botolphs, 74
Bottesford, 87
Bourn, 227
Bowden, 281
Bowden Magna, 73
Bozeat, 179
Brattleby, 56
Bremhill, 83
Breslau, 35
Bridgewater, 25
Brigg, 252
Brington, 77

Bristol, 69, 204, 223
Brixworth, 233
Brize-Norton, 136
Broadchalk, 76, 77
Bromeswell, 22
Bromham, 87
Bronellys, 132
Bruges, 85, 103, 273
Brussels, 223
Bugbrooke, 75, 86
Bulwick, 187
Burgh, 233
Burham, 48
Burley-on-the-Hill, 202
Burscough, 49
Burton-on-Stather, 282
Bury, 273
Bury (Sussex), 70
Buxted, 75

Cadney, 129
Caistor, 179, 253
Calne, 175
Cambridge, 18, 21, 67, 70, 73, 94, 95, 139, 140
Candlesby, 82
Cannings Bishops, 85
Canterbury, 13, 16, 20, 53, 106, 161, 260
Capetown, 121
Carlton-le-Moorland, 249
Castle Hedingham, 287
Caythorpe, 253
Chapel-en-le-Frith, 146
Charwelton, 93
Cheadle, 281
Chepstow, 113
Chester, 207, 263
Chewstoke, 24
Chichester, 73, 91, 132, 193
Chilton, 86
Chilton Foliat, 83
Chippenham, 86
Chipping Warden, 230
Churston Ferrers, 70
Clapham, 96
Clare, 144
Claughton, 45
Claxby, 171
Clee, 152

Cleethorpes, 82
Clerkenwell, 277
Clyst Honiton, 204
Clyst S. George, 71, 95
Cockpen, 279
Cold Ashby, 46, 65
Collingtree, 198
Colne, 69, 82, 241, 243
Cologne, 28, 102, 138, 280
Compostella, 128
Conington, 69
Congleton, 269
Coombe, 136
Corby, 90
Cordova, 128
Corsragnel, 133
Copford, 287
Cossington, 67
Cotes Magna, 187
Cotterstock, 83
Cottingham, 88
Coventry, 83, 85, 132, 137
Cradley, 202
Crail, 21
Cremona, 133
Croft, 82
Crofton, 90
Croydon, 17
Croyland, or Crowland, 7, 13, 53,
    129, 131
Culmington, 147
Cults, 56
Culsalmond, 21
Culworth, 167, 171
Cumnor, 90

Daghestan, 27
Dalby-on-the Wolds, 74
Damerham, 88
Darley Dale, 80
Daventry, 176
Derby, 91, 144, 176, 273
Desborough, 136
Deventer, 22
Devizes, 86, 127
Dewsbury, 56, 172
Didsbury, 281
Dodworth, 171
Doncaster, 18, 156, 244, 246, 249,
    273, 277

Dorchester, 115
Downton, 69
Driffield, 235
Drumlithe, 30, 166
Dublin, 79, 119
Dumfries, 263
Dunbar, 127
Dundee, 128, 133
Dunkeld, 279
Dunmer, 145, 146
Dunsforth, 96
Dunton, 71
Durham, 163
Dyce, 133
Dyrham, 71

East Dean, 77
East Dereham, 132
East Farandon, 86
Eaton Hall, 276
Ecton, 156
Eddystone, 254
Edinburgh, 52, 116
Edington, 83
Elford, 93
Elgin, 52
Elsham, 187
Elstow, 143
Ely, 15
Empingham, 20
Epworth, 171, 252
Erfurt, 29, 102
Exeter, 18, 54, 112, 137, 164
Eydon, 75
Eye, 88

Farringdon Gurney, 56
Fawsley, 57
Ferring, 20
Fett, 154
Fettercairn, 30
Filey, 14
Findon, 73
Finedon, 241
Fishlake, 234
Florence, 103, 132
Floore, 91
Fontenville, 45
Forfar, 133
Forrabury, 283

Fosdyke, 129
Fotherby, 82
Fotheringhay, 23, 73
Foulden, 83, 87
Fowey, 149
Freiborg, 45
Frindsbury, 22
Frolesworth, 71
Frome, 84
Fulbeck, 185
Fulletby, 129

Gainsborough, 251, 252
Garvoc, 133
Gateshead, 234
Gedney, 233
Gedney Hill, 167
Geneva, 80
Gion Chiosiu, 101
Glasgow, 92, 132
Glastonbury, 13
Glencairn, 52
Gloucester, 14, 15, 113
Goring, 48
Goxhill, 86
Grahamstown, 121
Grainsby, 282
Grantham, 77, 149, 177, 273
Great Cheverell, 70
Great Hampden, 115
Great Ponton, 243
Gretton, 236
Grittleton, 72
Grosslaswitz, 288
Guernsey, 77
Gunby S. Nicholas, 72
Gunby S Peter, 46, 47

Haddenham, 21
Hadleigh, 144
Hadstock, 287
Halifax, 51, 114
Hallaton. 179
Hall Magna, 253
Halton-Holgate, 243
Hambleton, 95
Hammeringham, 46, 47
Hanbury, 123
Hanley Castle, 87
Hannington, 90

Harleigh, 158
Harlington, 242
Harloxton, 204
Harrogate, 264
Haslingden, 243
Hastings, 24
Hatfield, 234
Hatherleigh, 202
Hathersage, 146
Hatton, 279
Hawerby, 281
Haxey, 273
Headington, 68
Heddington, 83
Heighington, 49
Helidon, 202
Hemel Hempsted, 86, 91
Hempsted, 202
Hertford, 17
Heybridge, 181
Heytesbury, 68
Higham Ferrers, 253
Hilmarton, 115
Hinderclay, 144
Hoby, 93
Hogsthorpe, 83, 190
Holbeach, 227, 273
Holcombe, 56
Holt, 70
Holton-le-Clay, 96
Holywell, 195
Horbury, 172
Horncastle, 227, 250, 253
Horsham, 223
Howell, 129
Hunstanton, 125

Impingham, 67, 236
Inchcape Rock, 254
Ingoldsby, 187
Inkberrow, 287
Inverarity, 21
Isham, 136
Isleworth, 234

Jersey, 125
Johnshaven, 166

Kelsey, 279
Kempsey, 69

Kenton, 87
Kendal, 188
Kettering, 17
Kidderminster, 249
Killingholm, 54
Kimpton, 73
King's Cliffe, 194, 200, 234
King's Sutton, 202
Kingsthorpe, 84
Kingston-upon-Thames, 228, 259
Kinkell, 279
Kinneff, 63, 65, 133
Kirby Malzeard, 21
Kirkwall, 52
Kirton-in-Holland, 77, 88
Kirton-in-Lindsey, 174, 180, 242, 251, 252
Knaresborough, 77, 86
Kynspindie, 128

Landulph, 148
Laneast, 79
Lanlivery, 149
Launceston, 89, 90
Lavenham, 26, 38
Lavenheath, 22
Lawrence Kirk, 24
Ledbury, 285
Leeds, 85, 114
Leeds (Kent), 142
Leicester, 24, 111, 183, 204
Leigh, 51, 217
Leighton Bromswold, 71, 93
Lenton, 25, 177
Leominster, 75
Leverton, 181, 197, 242
Lewes, 232, 248
Lilleshall, 217
Limerick, 116
Lincoln, 21, 55, 56, 71, 111, 112, 156, 179, 180, 249, 253
Little Snoring, 132
Liversedge, 27
Llanbadarn, 116
Lois Weedon, 214
London, 13, 14, 15, 18, 50, 61, 103-106, 114, 139, 158, 204, 205, 208, 222, 223, 227, 237, 241, 264, 281
Louth, 167, 233, 236, 250, 252, 253

Long Compton, 16, 17, 119, 174, 188, 227
Louvain, 21, 22, 273
Lower Beeding, 22
Low Toynton, 129
Luddington, 70, 282
Ludlow, 137
Lutterworth, 165
Lyddington, 236
Lyff, 128
Lynn, 13, 53, 204
Lyons, 103

Maidstone, 176
Maldon, 182
Malmesbury, 212
Manchester, 114, 276
Mantua, 29
Mapander, 229
Marbury, 195
Marlow, 240
Markby, 111
Market Stainton, 57, 69
Marsham, 197
Marston-on-Dove, 91
Marston S. Lawrence, 57
Meaux Abbey, 21
Mechlin, 21, 273, 274, 275
Melksham, 87
Melton Mowbray, 163, 194
Middelburg, 22
Middle, 241
Middleton, 135, 227
Milan, 167
Milton Clevedon, 69
Milton Lislebourne, 75
Mingoon, 97
Mitford, 28
Montreal, 36, 120
Montrose, 23, 133
Moreton, 200
Moreton Pinkney, 171
Morton-by-Gainsborough, 196
Moscow, 29, 56, 98, 158
Moulton, 248
Mumby, 190

Nankin, 101
Newbury, 18, 33, 50, 241
Newington, 280

Newcastle-on-Tyne, 49 55, 203, 205, 227, 241, 247
Newport Pagnell, 243
New York, 120
Nineveh, 24
Normanton-on-Soar, 90
Northampton, 75, 76, 86, 88, 89
Northborough, 57
North Burlingham, 93
North Cockerington, 187
Northern, 281
Northfield, 79, 89, 94
North Kelsey, 187
North Newton, 68
North Thoresby, 282
North Walsham, 53
Norton, 87
Norton Bavant, 70
Nottingham, 14, 81, 111, 154, 234
Norwich, 21, 53, 128, 139, 223
Novgorod, 100

Oakham, 248
Ogbourne S. George, 71
Olmutz, 102
Orkney, 67, 68, 116
Orlingbury, 91
Ormskirk, 49, 68
Orwell, 236
Oseney, 54, 109
Oxford, 16, 17, 56, 57, 64, 66, 71, 87, 90, 91, 94, 109-111, 139, 143, 158, 207, 223, 225
Owersby, 279
Owmby, 88, 242
Owston, 187

Padua, 133
Painswick, 155
Paris, 56, 137, 162, 205, 212, 285, 287
Peebles, 133
Pekin, 101
Peterborough. 85, 87, 91, 111, 193, 203, 204, 252, 253, 257
Petrovsk, 27
Philadelphia. 120
Picton, 95
Piddington, 87
Pisa, 54, 133

Plymouth, 116, 148
Pontefract, 203
Poole, 87, 89
Portlemouth, 77
Pottersbury, 171
Preston, 114
Preston (Suffolk), 125
Prestwold, 17
Priddy, 69

Quedgeley, 83
Quorndon, 17

Raleigh, 282
Ramsbury, 86
Ravenna, 133
Ravenstondale, 168
Reading, 18, 65, 89, 90, 123, 127
Rheims, 215
Ricardean, 172
Ripon, 25, 177
Rippingale, 243
Rochester, 66
Rockingham, 281
Rome, 58, 205
Romford, 282
Ross, 173
Rosyth Castle, 254
Rothley, 17
Rothwell, 136
Rotterdam, 22, 251
Rouen, 27, 56, 103 178
Rowde, 83
Rushton, 190, 235
Rye, 21

S. Albans, 21, 89, 232
Salerno, 167
Salhouse, 268
Salisbury, 67, 73, 92, 95, 246
Salworthy, 173
Sandwich, 212
Saxelby, 202, 280
Scalford, 20
Scarning, 268
Scartho, 279
Schaffhausen, 80
Scothorne, 154
Scotter, 145, 147, 190
Scotton, 251

Screveton, 280
S. Cyrus, 52
Searby, 185, 187
Sedbergh, 69
Selborne, 41
Sens, 285
Seville, 231
S. Fillan, 286
Shandon, 118, 119
Sherborne, 84
Shipton, 67, 70, 73
Siena, 133
Sidmouth, 70, 127
S. Ives, 84, 85, 252
Skegness, 129
Skene, 63
Skidbrooke, 127
Skirbeck, 197
Slapton, 48, 96
Sleaford, 251, 253, 277
Slobodsky, 40
Snaith, 18
S. Neots, 17
Socotra, 162, 177
Soissons, 256
Somerby, 46, 47
Somerleyton, 69
Somersby, 46, 47
Southampton, 89
Southill, 149, 163
South Lopham, 128
South Luffenham, 230
South Reston, 129
South Somercotes, 46, 47, 57
South Witham, 76
Southwold, 223
Spalding, 132, 156, 207, 212
S. Petersburgh, 100
Springthorpe, 156
Sproxton, 14
Stafford, 247
Stanion, 66
Stainton Dale, 254
Stamford, 24, 165, 242, 245, 248, 250, 253
Stapleton, 74, 88
Staverton, 171, 236
Steeple Ashton, 68
Stirling, 52, 133
Stockholm, 22

Stockport, 281
Stockton-on-Tees, 113
Stoke-Dry, 138
Stonehaven, 51, 166
Stowe, 69
Stow S. Mary, 151, 152, 280
Strachan, 52
Stratton, 199
Strasburg, 81, 119, 120, 221
Stroxton, 189
Strubby, 129
Sturton Magna, 129
Sudeley Castle, 70, 74
Sutton (Northants), 187
Swalcliffe, 136
Swaton, 253
Swineshead, 174, 197, 241
Swyncombe, 69

Taddington, 67
Tamworth, 226
Teignmouth, 70
Thame, 78
Theddlethorpe S. Helen, 69
Thetford, 65, 248
Thibet, 160
Thorne, 234
Thorney, 160, 178
Thornton Curtis, 73
Thorp, S. Peter, 84
Thurcaston, 66
Thurnby, 246
Ticehurst, 77
Tong, 147
Tonge, 50
Torksey, 280
Torrington, 132
Towcester, 76, 93, 233
Toynton S. Peter, 46, 47
Trent, 71
Tunstall, 284

Upminster, 70
Upottery, 88
Uppingham, 86, 165
Upton Lovell, 95

Valdaï, 100
Venice, 132
Vienna, 102

Vienne, 286
Volkinsk, 40, 98

Waddington, 186
Wadingham, 82
Wainfleet, 154
Wainfleet S. Mary, 84
Wakefield, 242
Wakerley, 73
Walcot, 243
Waltham Abbey, 240
Waltham-on-the-Wolds, 236
Wappenham, 87
Warburton, 50
Ware, 164
Watford, 251
Wearmouth, 6
Weasenham S. Peter, 69
Week, 70
Welham, 66
Wellesbourne, 172
Wendron, 149
Wenlock, 19
Westborough, 76, 187
West Deeping, 236
Westerleigh, 74
Westhoughton, 217
West Lynn, 207
Westminster, 47, 51, 106, 113, 114, 124, 138, 199, 206, 221, 242
West Rasen, 230
Whatton, 280

Whetstone, 71
Whissendine, 82
Whitby, 7
Whitechapel, 16, 108, 114, 195
Whittering, 236
Willington, 57
Willoughton, 160, 178
Wilsford, 80
Wilton, 133
Winchester, 13, 72
Winkfield, 70
Winterbourne Dantsey, 72
Winterton, 18, 250
Winthorpe, 71
Witham-on-the-Hill, 244
Woburn, 132
Wokingham, 233
Wolchurch, 193
Woodstock, 110, 230
Worcester, 13, 51, 132, 193, 207, 248, 287
Wragby, 172
Wrexham, 15, 116
Wroxeter, 241
Wynington, 67

Yarmouth, 16, 198, 207
York, 14, 15, 16, 19, 21, 33, 48, 108, 109

Zanzibar, 121